NATIONAL ACADEMIES Sciences
                    Engineering
                    Medicine

NATIONAL
ACADEMIES
PRESS
Washington, DC

An Updated Measure of Poverty

(Re)Drawing the Line

James P. Ziliak, Christopher Mackie, and
Constance F. Citro, *Editors*

Panel on Evaluation and Improvements to the
Supplemental Poverty Measure

Committee on National Statistics

Division of Behavioral and Social Sciences and Education

Consensus Study Report

NATIONAL ACADEMIES PRESS 500 Fifth Street, NW Washington, DC 20001

This activity was supported by a contract between the National Academies of Sciences, Engineering, and Medicine and the National Science Foundation under grant number 1822391. Support of the work of the Committee on National Statistics is provided by a consortium of federal agencies through a grant from the National Science Foundation (award number SES-1560294) and several individual contracts. Any opinions, findings, conclusions, or recommendations expressed in this publication do not necessarily reflect the views of any organization or agency that provided support for the project.

International Standard Book Number-13: 978-0-309-69739-2
International Standard Book Number-10: 0-309-69739-5
Digital Object Identifier: https://doi.org/10.17226/26825
Library of Congress Control Number: 2023938927

This publication is available from the National Academies Press, 500 Fifth Street, NW, Keck 360, Washington, DC 20001; (800) 624-6242 or (202) 334-3313; http://www.nap.edu.

Copyright 2023 by the National Academy of Sciences. National Academies of Sciences, Engineering, and Medicine and National Academies Press and the graphical logos for each are all trademarks of the National Academy of Sciences. All rights reserved.

Printed in the United States of America.

Suggested citation: National Academies of Sciences, Engineering, and Medicine. 2023. *An Updated Measure of Poverty: (Re)Drawing the Line*. Washington, DC: The National Academies Press. https://doi.org/10.17226/26825.

The **National Academy of Sciences** was established in 1863 by an Act of Congress, signed by President Lincoln, as a private, nongovernmental institution to advise the nation on issues related to science and technology. Members are elected by their peers for outstanding contributions to research. Dr. Marcia McNutt is president.

The **National Academy of Engineering** was established in 1964 under the charter of the National Academy of Sciences to bring the practices of engineering to advising the nation. Members are elected by their peers for extraordinary contributions to engineering. Dr. John L. Anderson is president.

The **National Academy of Medicine** (formerly the Institute of Medicine) was established in 1970 under the charter of the National Academy of Sciences to advise the nation on medical and health issues. Members are elected by their peers for distinguished contributions to medicine and health. Dr. Victor J. Dzau is president.

The three Academies work together as the **National Academies of Sciences, Engineering, and Medicine** to provide independent, objective analysis and advice to the nation and conduct other activities to solve complex problems and inform public policy decisions. The National Academies also encourage education and research, recognize outstanding contributions to knowledge, and increase public understanding in matters of science, engineering, and medicine.

Learn more about the National Academies of Sciences, Engineering, and Medicine at **www.nationalacademies.org**.

Consensus Study Reports published by the National Academies of Sciences, Engineering, and Medicine document the evidence-based consensus on the study's statement of task by an authoring committee of experts. Reports typically include findings, conclusions, and recommendations based on information gathered by the committee and the committee's deliberations. Each report has been subjected to a rigorous and independent peer-review process and it represents the position of the National Academies on the statement of task.

Proceedings published by the National Academies of Sciences, Engineering, and Medicine chronicle the presentations and discussions at a workshop, symposium, or other event convened by the National Academies. The statements and opinions contained in proceedings are those of the participants and are not endorsed by other participants, the planning committee, or the National Academies.

Rapid Expert Consultations published by the National Academies of Sciences, Engineering, and Medicine are authored by subject-matter experts on narrowly focused topics that can be supported by a body of evidence. The discussions contained in rapid expert consultations are considered those of the authors and do not contain policy recommendations. Rapid expert consultations are reviewed by the institution before release.

For information about other products and activities of the National Academies, please visit www.nationalacademies.org/about/whatwedo.

PANEL ON EVALUATION AND IMPROVEMENTS TO THE SUPPLEMENTAL POVERTY MEASURE

JAMES P. ZILIAK, Department of Economics, University of Kentucky, *Chair*
RANDALL K.Q. AKEE, Department of Public Policy and Department of American Indian Studies,
　　University of California, Los Angeles
SARAH E. BOHN, Public Policy Institute of California
INDIVAR DUTTA-GUPTA, Center for Law and Social Policy
INGRID GOULD ELLEN, Wagner Graduate School of Public Service, New York University
BRADLEY L. HARDY, McCourt School of Public Policy, Georgetown University
DAVID S. JOHNSON, Institute for Social Research, University of Michigan
SANDERS KORENMAN, Austin W. Marxe School of Public and International Affairs,
　　City University of New York
HELEN G. LEVY, Gerald R. Ford School of Public Policy, University of Michigan
JORDAN D. MATSUDAIRA, Teachers College, Columbia University
JOSÉ D. PACAS, Kids First Chicago
MICHELE VER PLOEG, Economic Research Service, U.S. Department of Agriculture
JANE WALDFOGEL, School of Social Work, Columbia University
BARBARA L. WOLFE, Institute for Research on Policy, University of Wisconsin–Madison

CHRISTOPHER D. MACKIE, *Study Director*
CONSTANCE F. CITRO, *Senior Scholar*
ANTHONY S. MANN, *Program Associate*

COMMITTEE ON NATIONAL STATISTICS

ROBERT M. GROVES, Georgetown University, *Chair*
LAWRENCE D. BOBO, Harvard University
ANNE C. CASE, Princeton University, *Emerita*
MICK P. COUPER, University of Michigan
DIANA FARRELL, JPMorgan Chase Institute, Washington, DC
ROBERT M. GOERGE, The University of Chicago
ERICA L. GROSHEN, Cornell University
DANIEL E. HO, Stanford University
HILARY HOYNES, University of California, Berkeley
DANIEL KIFER, The Pennsylvania State University
SHARON LOHR, Arizona State University, *Emerita*
JEROME P. REITER, Duke University
NELA RICHARDSON, ADP Research Institute, New York
JUDITH A. SELTZER, University of California, Los Angeles, *Emerita*
C. MATTHEW SNIPP, Stanford University
ELIZABETH A. STUART, Johns Hopkins University

MELISSA CHIU, *Director*
BRIAN HARRIS-KOJETIN, *Senior Scholar*

Dedication

This report is dedicated to the memory of our friend and inspiration, Rebecca Blank, who passed away on February 17, 2023. Becky was President-Elect of Northwestern University and immediate past Chancellor of the University of Wisconsin–Madison. She previously served as Dean of the Ford School of Public Policy at the University of Michigan and co-director of the National Poverty Center, and Professor of Economics at Northwestern University where she was director of the Joint Center for Poverty Research. Becky served the nation during three presidential administrations, including as Deputy Secretary of the U.S. Department of Commerce under President Obama and as a member of President Clinton's Council of Economic Advisers. Becky was one of the nation's most influential scholars on poverty and inequality, who made numerous contributions to both research and policy. She also had an uncanny ability to synthesize huge volumes of research that simultaneously provided a coherent discussion of the current state of knowledge, and also prodded scholars and policy makers to delve more deeply to examine what we need to know to improve the wellbeing of our most vulnerable citizens. Becky was a member of the groundbreaking 1995 National Research Council panel on measuring poverty, led the efforts at the Department of Commerce to implement the Supplemental Poverty Measure, and served as the review coordinator of this report until her untimely passing. We will miss her infectious energy, keen insights, and friendship.

Acknowledgments

Nearly three decades have passed since the seminal National Academies of Sciences, Engineering, and Medicine's report *Measuring Poverty: A New Approach* set in motion a research agenda on how income poverty is conceived of and measured in the United States. Standing on the shoulders of Mollie Orshansky, a giant of poverty measurement, the 1995 panel recommended changes to the original Orshansky approach—both in how the poverty line is drawn and in how resources available to families to meet basic budgetary needs are measured. In the ensuing decades, great conceptual and data-collection progress has been made to produce annual estimates of what is now known as the Supplemental Poverty Measure (SPM). This progress has been spearheaded by the tremendous efforts of staff at the Census Bureau and the Bureau of Labor Statistics (BLS)—notably Trudi Renwick, Thesia Garner, Kathy Short, and Liana Fox.

In 2020, the Census Bureau commissioned the National Academies to convene a new panel of poverty experts, to assess the strengths and shortcomings of the current SPM and, if needed, to recommend changes. This report is the culmination of that panel's work over the past 2 years. It would have been impossible without the time and commitment of many individuals. I wish to express my deep gratitude to the members of the panel who dedicated many hours to meetings, emails, chapter writing, and editing. All members made important contributions to the report; however, I do wish to convey a special thanks to Sarah Bohn, Ingrid Gould Ellen, Sanders Korenman, David Johnson, Jane Waldfogel, and Barbara Wolfe—each of whom provided strategic guidance and writing on key aspects of the panel's report and recommendations.

I am extremely grateful for the leadership and numerous insightful contributions of the study director, Christopher Mackie, and senior scholar, Connie Citro, from the Committee on National Statistics in crafting and writing the report. I also thank Anthony Mann of the National Academies for facilitating the panel's online meetings. Additionally, Brian Harris-Kojetin, director of the Committee on National Statistics, provided institutional leadership and overarching guidance about the study process; Kirsten Sampson-Snyder, Division of Behavioral and Social Sciences and Education, coordinated the review process expertly; and Susan Debad provided thorough final editing that improved the readability of the report.

The panel benefited greatly from many outside scholars, who contributed their time and expertise in their formal presentations to the panel, particularly on the challenging topics of medical care, housing, childcare, and the data infrastructure. We especially thank Trudi Renwick and Liana Fox of the Census Bureau, and Thesia Garner of BLS for spelling out in great detail how the current SPM is estimated, and for responding to our numerous clarifying questions along the way. In the treatment of medical care in the SPM we benefited from the insights of

John Creamer of the Census Bureau, Janet Currie of Princeton University, Mustafa Hussein of the University of Wisconsin–Milwaukee, Jeff Larrimore of the Federal Reserve Board of Governors, and Dahlia Remler of Baruch College. In the area of housing, we appreciate the insights of Rebecca Diamond of Stanford University, Chris Herbert of Harvard University, Stephen Malpezzi of the University of Wisconsin–Madison, Stuart Rosenthal of Syracuse University, and Jenny Schuetz of the Brookings Institution. On the topic of childcare, we thank Caroline Danielson of the Public Policy Institute of California and Mary Beth Mattingly of the Federal Reserve Bank of Boston. In the area of data infrastructure, and in particular the treatment of missing and un(der)-reported income, we are grateful for the insights of Chris Bollinger of the University of Kentucky, Linda Gianarrelli of the Urban Institute, Jonathan Rothbaum of the Census Bureau, and Laura Wheaton of the Urban Institute. Although the panel ultimately decided to not pursue explicit recommendations on all topics presented, we do wish to thank Robert Joyce of the Institute for Fiscal Studies for his presentation on the recommendations of the UK poverty panel regarding the treatment of assets and debts in high-frequency poverty measurement, and Michael Burrows of the Census Bureau and Alexandra Murphy of the University of Michigan for their presentations on the transportation challenges facing low-income households. The panel also benefited from public comments on our deliberations, and we extend our gratitude to members of the policy, research, and advocacy communities for their commitment to improving the measure of poverty in America.

James P. Ziliak, University of Kentucky
Chair, Panel on Evaluation and Improvements to the Supplemental Poverty Measure

Reviewers

This Consensus Study Report was reviewed in draft form by individuals chosen for their diverse perspectives and technical expertise. The purpose of this independent review is to provide candid and critical comments that will assist the National Academies in making each published report as sound as possible and ensuring that it meets the institutional standards for quality, objectivity, evidence, and responsiveness to the study charge. The review comments and draft manuscript remain confidential to protect the integrity of the deliberative process.

The panel thanks the following individuals for their review of this report: Marianne P. Bitler, Department of Economics, University of California, Davis; Janet Currie, Princeton School of Public and International Affairs, Princeton University; Caroline Danielson, Public Policy Institute of California; Jonathan D. Fisher, Washington Center for Equitable Growth; Timothy M. Smeeding, Robert M. LaFollette School of Public Affairs, University of Wisconsin–Madison; Laura Wheaton, Urban Institute; and Scott Winship, American Enterprise Institute.

Although the reviewers listed above provided many constructive comments and suggestions that significantly improved the quality of this report, they were not asked to endorse the conclusions or recommendations, nor did they see the final draft of the report before its release. The review of the report was overseen by Robert A. Moffitt, Department of Economics, Johns Hopkins University. He was responsible for making certain that an independent examination of this report was carried out in accordance with the standards of the National Academies and that all review comments were carefully considered. Responsibility for the final content rests entirely with the authoring panel and the National Academies.

Contents

Summary   **1**

1   **Introduction**   **11**

    1.1. Policy and Research Purposes of Poverty Measurement, 12
    1.2. Specifying an Economic Poverty Measure, 13
    1.3. Motivation for the Study and Charge to the Panel, 13
    1.4. Organization of the Report, 15

2   **Conceptual Basis of the Supplemental Poverty Measure**   **17**

    2.1. Current Supplemental Poverty Measure Specifications, 17
    2.2. Guiding Principles: Desirable Characteristics of a Poverty Measure, 21
    2.3. Proposal for a New "Principal Poverty Measure," 27
    2.4. Modernizing Poverty Thresholds, 28
    2.5. Alternative Concepts of Resources, 36
    2.6. Unit of Analysis, 38
    Appendix 2A: Algebraic Representations of the Supplemental
           Poverty Measure and the Principal Poverty Measure, 40

3   **Challenging Categories: Medical Care**   **43**

    3.1. Background/Motivation, 43
    3.2. Treatment of Health/Medical Care in the Supplemental
         Poverty Measure: Strengths and Limitations, 45
    3.3. Incorporating Health into the Principal Poverty Measure, 48
    Appendix 3A: Alternative Approaches to Accounting for
           Medical Care in a Poverty Measure, 53
    Appendix 3B: Examples of PPM versus SPM Treatment of
           Health Insurance and Medical Care, 56

| 4 | **Challenging Categories: Childcare** | **59** |

    4.1. Background and Motivation, 59
    4.2. Current Supplemental Poverty Measure Treatment—
        Strengths and Weaknesses, 59
    4.3. An Improved Approach, 61

| 5 | **Challenging Categories: Housing/Shelter** | **67** |

    5.1. Conceptual Measurement Goal, 67
    5.2. Defining and Estimating Housing/Shelter Needs, 69
    5.3. Adjusting Shelter and Utility Thresholds, 72
    5.4. Valuing Resources, 75

| 6 | **Data and Statistical Issues** | **81** |

    6.1. The Need for and Benefits of Improving the Data Infrastructure, 81
    6.2. Data Needs Created by the Proposed Principal Poverty Measure, 83
    6.3. The Current Survey-Based Data Infrastructure, 86
    6.4. Administrative Data for Improving Income Estimates, 93
    6.5. Data Recommendations for the Principal Poverty Measure, 97
    6.6. Opportunities for Improving Estimation of Thresholds, 97
    Appendix 6A: SPM/PPM Threshold Components—Availability in the
        CE Interview Survey/Taken from Other Sources, 100
    Appendix 6B: SPM/PPM Resource Components—Availability in the
        CPS-ASEC and ACS, 102

References   **105**

Appendix A Background and Specifications of the OPM and the SPM   **113**

Appendix B Summary of Public Comments   **123**

Appendix C Biographical Sketches of Panel Members   **131**

Summary

Poverty statistics are essential for determining the size and composition of the population whose basic needs are going unmet and for tracking how conditions facing this group are changing over time. Poverty statistics help society target resources to alleviate hardships experienced by disadvantaged populations and allow assessment of the effectiveness of programs designed to improve the wellbeing of these populations. The statistical construct serving the widest range of these research and policy purposes in the United States is the Supplemental Poverty Measure (SPM). The SPM was first published in accordance with a 2011 report by the Interagency Technical Working Group on Developing a Supplemental Poverty Measure. That report was based on a National Academies of Sciences, Engineering, and Medicine report, *Measuring Poverty: A New Approach* (NRC, 1995), and over a decade of research by the Census Bureau and the Bureau of Labor Statistics (BLS) to evaluate the methods recommended in the National Academies' 1995 report.

In 2022, the Census Bureau reported both an increase and a decrease in poverty for families between 2019 and 2021. The poverty rate under the Official Poverty Measure (OPM), developed in the 1960s and methodologically unchanged since then, grew from an estimated 10.5 to 11.6 percent of the population. In contrast, the rate under the SPM declined from 11.8 to 7.8 percent. These poverty rates moved in sharply opposing directions primarily because the SPM counts income support received through the tax system which, during this period, included COVID-19 stimulus payments, while the OPM does not. In other words, the SPM reflected that the stimulus payments—along with regular in-kind government support programs such as the Supplemental Nutrition Assistance Program (SNAP) and tax benefits such as the Earned Income Tax Credit and Child Tax Credit—helped reduce poverty during the pandemic.

This study, requested by the Census Bureau, assesses the strengths and weaknesses of the SPM and provides recommendations for updating the methodology to more accurately reflect the basic needs of, and resources available to, households. The Census Bureau recognizes the need to periodically revisit SPM construction to account for changes in the population's consumption patterns, social and economic norms, perceptions of wellbeing, and the goods and services needed to participate fully in the economy. In addition, public policies evolve over time, as do the data sources available for their evaluation.

The guidance provided in this report builds on recent changes to the SPM by the Census Bureau and BLS in defining basic needs categories and setting thresholds (the minimum level of resources required to cover basic needs), adjusting thresholds for geographic differences in living costs, estimating household resources, and imputing income and in-kind benefit levels. During the panel's deliberations, which took place from spring 2020 through fall 2022, much of the focus was on improving measurement of SPM categories—most notably, medical care, childcare, and housing—for which conceptual and data questions have proven most difficult to resolve.

STATISTICAL ROLE OF THE SPM

Because its role in economic statistics extends well beyond a "supplemental" one, this report will refer to the next iteration of the SPM as the Principal Poverty Measure (PPM).

> **RECOMMENDATION 2.1[1]: Due to its vital role in tracking the effects of public policies and programs on the size and composition of the population living in or near poverty, and its resulting status as the preferred measure of many researchers and policy makers, the Supplemental Poverty Measure should be elevated to the nation's headline poverty statistic and renamed accordingly (e.g., to the Principal Poverty Measure).**

In the panel's judgment, given the essential statistical functions that it serves, the more comprehensive PPM (as opposed to the OPM) should feature most prominently in Census Bureau publications and announcements—a direction that the agency has already begun taking in its recent reports.

MODERNIZING THE SPECIFICATION OF BASIC NEEDS AND ECONOMIC RESOURCES

The measurement of economic poverty involves estimating two components: (1) a basic needs level—a budget or threshold; and (2) the economic resources available to families, individuals, or households. The SPM estimates the income and other resources (including government cash and in-kind assistance, subsidies, and tax credits) available to households to meet a threshold based on a well-defined concept of basic needs; if the resource estimate falls below the threshold, a household is considered to be living in poverty. The threshold is determined by the cost of acquiring a specific bundle of basic goods, as represented by the level of spending on the items. Because the threshold is set based in part on the distribution of people's expenditures on the set of included budget items, the SPM was referred to as a "quasi-relative poverty measure" in the National Academies' 1995 report.

In the SPM, a "multiplier" is added to the budget to allow for the inclusion of other necessities not explicitly included in the bundle such as nonwork-related transportation, personal care products, and household supplies. In the calculation of resources, some types of expenditures (e.g., taxes or work expenses) are subtracted to reflect that not all incoming funds to an SPM resource unit (which, for readability, will be referred to as a household) are available to spend on the basic needs specified in the threshold.

Since its inception, the basic bundle spending categories in the SPM have been food, clothing, shelter, and utilities (FCSU); the multiplier has been set at 20 percent. Additional adjustments are applied to threshold levels to capture differences in needs related to the size, composition, housing tenure (renting, owning with mortgage, and owning without a mortgage), and geographic location of households.

SPM methodology, including specification of the threshold, requires periodic reexamination to reflect changing circumstances. One aspect of this reexamination involves consideration of how both the basic needs bundle and the resources available to households can be categorized intuitively and transparently. The Census Bureau clearly views the SPM as an evolving measure. For example, beginning in 2021, internet service was added as an explicit basic bundle category and telephone service was extracted from utilities to become a separate item, thus reformulating the threshold as food, clothing, shelter, utilities, telephone, and internet (FCSUti). The revised SPM can benefit from further refinement along these lines.

> **RECOMMENDATION 2.2: For the Principal Poverty Measure, the set of threshold categories should be expanded beyond the current food, clothing, shelter, utilities, telephone, and internet (FCSUti) to explicitly recognize that minimum basic needs—as well as policies designed to help households meet those needs—have evolved since the establishment of the Supplemental Poverty Measure.**

---

[1] The numbering of recommendations reflects their locations in the body of the report—e.g., Recommendation 2.1 is the first recommendation in Chapter 2. This Summary includes only a selection of the recommendations included in the full report.

Compelling cases can be made for establishing explicit categories in the basic needs bundle for medical care and, with further research, possibly childcare; and for updating the treatment of shelter. While medical care and childcare are by no means ignored in the current SPM methodology, they are incorporated indirectly as expenditure subtractions from household resource estimates.

Methodological research and development of data sources may, in the future, allow other basic needs categories to be considered for inclusion in the threshold bundle, as opposed to being part of the multiplier or handled exclusively on the resource-estimate side of the PPM. Transportation (both commuting and nonwork-related) is an obvious candidate, given its prominence in household budgets. Shifting such elements from the resource side to the threshold side of the calculation will likely raise threshold levels in the PPM. However, by accounting for health insurance benefits and childcare subsidies in the resource estimates, measured poverty rates will not necessarily be affected (at least for the population that receives those benefits and subsidies).

Given the recommendations to respecify the PPM threshold, the 20-percent multiplier would also need to be updated to account for changes in the basic bundle.

RECOMMENDATION 2.5: The Census Bureau and Bureau of Labor Statistics should conduct a review of the basis for the 20-percent multiplier. This review should include:

- **Assessing whether a multiplier set at a different level better matches current spending patterns on the basket of goods currently included in the Supplemental Poverty Measure threshold;**
- **Evaluating the spending categories included in the threshold multiplier;**
- **Recalculating the multiplier based on the new basic needs bundle; and**
- **Developing a plan for updating the multiplier for future changes in spending patterns.**

Alternatives to Exclusively Expenditure-Based Thresholds

The current method of estimating SPM thresholds is based on household spending as reported in the Consumer Expenditure Survey (CE). Even so, setting threshold levels requires an element of expert judgment—for example, in determining the appropriate subset of CE respondents on which to base spending estimates, or in establishing the point in the expenditure distribution to represent the base need level. Modifying the PPM approach to medical care and housing—and, at some point, childcare—as recommended in this report shifts the methodology further toward a hybrid model, wherein a mix of survey-reported spending levels and nonsurvey programmatic data are used to set basic needs thresholds. In is also worth noting that, by introducing medical care, and possibly childcare, into the threshold as elements that are not directly based on the distribution of the population's actual reported expenditures, the hybrid methodology of the PPM could be interpreted to be a less "quasi-relative" measure than the current SPM.

The panel weighed tradeoffs among desirable statistical properties—accuracy, consistency, transparency, and feasibility—and concluded that this hybrid approach could be productively utilized on a case-by-case basis to improve the PPM. In terms of research foundations and data requirements, medical care has most clearly met the necessary criteria to warrant the shift away from expenditure-based estimates of basic need. Additionally, new methods are now available to address flaws in the current SPM approach. Specifically, due to both data and conceptual shortcomings, subtracting household medical out-of-pocket (MOOP) spending from resources, as is done currently, does not accurately reflect the true medical care needs of households.

Medical Care

Per capita expenditure on medical care exceeded $12,000 in 2020. Additionally, the federal government spends more than $1.2 trillion annually on medical care, nearly all of it on insurance, accounting for more than 15 percent of federal outlays and dwarfing the next-largest in-kind transfer program (the Supplemental Nutrition Assistance Program). The high level and rapid growth of spending on medical care and health insurance underscores the importance of explicitly and accurately incorporating this basic need into the measurement of poverty.

Despite the central role of medical care in people's wellbeing, the SPM does not currently itemize medical care and health insurance as basic needs in the threshold calculation; nor are the values of government- or employer-provided health insurance benefits counted toward household resources. Instead, MOOP expenses—including insurance premiums, copayments, deductibles, and other payments—are treated as nondiscretionary (like taxes or work-related expenses) and subtracted from each household's resources. Because medical care is not included as a need category in the SPM threshold, this measure does not capture the unmet medical care need of persons who are uninsured or underinsured. Additionally, because the deduction of MOOP expenses from available resources is not capped, the SPM estimate implicitly assumes that a family's medical care need is equal to the amount spent out of pocket on insurance and medical care, which is often not the case. Most medical care is paid for by insurance benefits, not out of pocket, and the uninsured may need more care than they can purchase out of pocket. For these and other reasons, the proposed PPM can improve upon the SPM through implementation of a new approach that explicitly adds a need for health insurance to the PPM threshold, while counting subsidies for health insurance (including those from the government and employers) as resources received by the household.

RECOMMENDATION 3.1: For the Principal Poverty Measure, the current approach to medical spending in the Supplemental Poverty Measure should be replaced with one that includes health insurance in the estimates of both the needs threshold and resources.

The research on and development of a medical-care-inclusive poverty measure is sufficiently advanced that the Census Bureau could immediately begin implementation of this recommendation. Indeed, the Census Bureau has already begun investigating the practical implications (e.g., data needs) of moving toward a health-inclusive poverty measure.

For nondisabled individuals younger than 65, the Affordable Care Act (ACA) benchmark plan provides a practical and conceptually valid answer to the question of how much cash income an uninsured person would need to obtain a basic health insurance policy.

RECOMMENDATION 3.2: For individuals under age 65 (excluding those who have Medicare due to disability), the Affordable Care Act (ACA) benchmark health insurance plan should be used to represent the basic health insurance need for a typical American household (or the designated resource-sharing unit for poverty measurement). The ACA defines a benchmark plan as the second-lowest-cost Silver plan available in the health insurance Marketplace in an individual's geographic area. The Silver plan for those age 65 and over who are not covered by Medicare is also the basic health insurance need.

Just as the ACA represents a benchmark health insurance plan that provides financial protection and affordable coverage for an essential package of medical care, so too does the Medicare coverage for populations that are over 65 or disabled.

RECOMMENDATION 3.3: For the population age 65 and older covered by Medicare, as well as those under 65 who qualify for Medicare based on disability, the basic need level should be set based on the full cost of a Medicare Advantage plan that provides prescription drug coverage. The cost of this plan should be calculated as per-recipient federal spending on Medicare parts A, B, and D, *plus* the lowest-cost out-of-pocket premium for the Medicare Advantage plan that includes a prescription drug plan.

Introduction of a basic medical care need in the PPM threshold means that medical-related benefits received by households must be accounted for in the calculation of available resources.

RECOMMENDATION 3.4: The definition of resources in the Principal Poverty Measure should include a value for any health insurance benefits or subsidies received from an employer or from the government but must also reflect the fact that such transfers cannot be used to pay for nonhealth needs. This is achieved by capping the value of the transfer that is added to resources at an amount that is less than or equal to the health insurance need that is added to the threshold.

Finally, medical out-of-pocket payments for nonpremium expenses should also be deducted from resources, subject to a cap, operationalized using the out-of-pocket limits specified in Marketplace plans or other information about actual health insurance status and household characteristics.

RECOMMENDATION 3.5: Medical out-of-pocket spending should be subtracted from resources in the Principal Poverty Measure. For individuals who are not covered by Medicare, this subtraction should be capped at the out-of-pocket maximum for Affordable Care Act Marketplace plans or lower, depending on health insurance status and other household characteristics. Medical out-of-pocket spending by Medicare recipients can also be capped starting in 2025 due to changes enacted under the Inflation Reduction Act, and the panel recommends doing so.

This approach allows variation in actual medical care spending needs associated with differences in health status to be captured without implicitly deeming an unlimited amount of MOOP spending to be necessary for basic care.

Childcare

Inclusion of medical care in the PPM thresholds suggests that the method might be fruitfully applied to other threshold needs categories. Prime among these are childcare and housing. As with medical care, childcare represents a large and rapidly growing component of families' out-of-pocket spending. Among families who pay for it, childcare accounts for approximately 16 percent of direct expenditures, making it the third largest budget component after housing (29%) and transportation (18%) for such families. Childcare costs are even higher, and represent a larger share of household budgets, for families with preschool-aged children, and these costs vary greatly across the country. A complete and transparent accounting of childcare needs is therefore essential for understanding families' economic wellbeing.

In the current SPM, paid childcare costs, like commuting costs, are deducted from a family's resources as a work expense—and thus apply only to working parents. In the proposed PPM, assuming adequate data are available, childcare, like medical care and shelter, would be included as an explicit element of the basic needs bundle; the estimated threshold amount (adjusted for number and age of children and geographic location) would apply to *all* households with children. Subsidies for childcare, whether paid to families or directly to childcare centers, would be added to a household's resources. Since unpaid childcare also has value, it too would ideally be accounted for in the resource estimation—however, an appropriate methodology for valuing unpaid care has yet to be determined.

As a first step, the Census Bureau could consider expanding the population of households credited with a childcare expense (and, hence, a deduction from available resources) in the SPM, beyond those who are employed, to include parents using paid care who are engaged in education or training, or who are disabled.

RECOMMENDATION 4.1: In households with children under the age of 13 (or, in line with current childcare subsidy rules, up to age 18 if disabled), parents who are in education or training should be treated like parents who are employed, and a parent who is not working and is disabled should not be assumed to be available to provide childcare while the other parent is working or in education/training.

This correction would be consistent with childcare subsidy rules that consider educational activities equivalent to work for the purpose of subsidy eligibility and would more accurately reflect families' childcare needs.

The next step toward the conceptual ideal would be to create an explicit childcare category in the PPM threshold for those households utilizing paid childcare.

RECOMMENDATION 4.2: For households with children under the age of 13 (or up to age 18 if disabled) and that are using paid childcare (paid out of pocket and/or subsidized), a basic childcare need should be included in the threshold. In the near future, the Census Bureau should conduct research to develop and implement a methodology for defining the amount of this basic childcare need, varying by age and number of children, geographic location, and hours of paid care used.

Placing childcare needs in the threshold alongside other elements of the basic bundle creates transparency by making explicit a more complete range of families' basic needs. Childcare market rate surveys, conducted by each state as part of Child Care and Development Fund programs, provide a promising information source for setting the basic need amount, as does the National Database of Childcare Prices, an official (Department of Labor) data source that provides county-level price information by type of provider and age of children.

If childcare needs are incorporated into the PPM threshold, childcare assistance from programs funded by federal and state governments would need to be added to household resources.

RECOMMENDATION 4.3: To accurately assess a household's ability to meet its needs, for households that have children and that use paid childcare, in the near future, the Census Bureau should research, develop, and implement a methodology for valuing assistance received by the household for childcare, so that it can enter into the calculation of the household's available resources.

Even with the proposed expansions, a poverty measure may still be incomplete given that all young children require care—including school-aged children outside of school hours—even if childcare is not obtained through the market. In a very real sense, *all* households with children expend resources on childcare, regardless of whether they use paid services. Such an acknowledgment would impart consistency with other parts of the PPM, for example, the assumption that all households have the same basic housing need, independent of how they obtain it. Estimating resources using this inclusive approach would require further research into the value of nonmarket childcare—specifically parent care, family (e.g., grandparent) care, and informal collective care.

Housing

Housing is often the largest component of a household's spending. In 2020, about 30 percent of U.S. households paid more than 30 percent of their incomes for housing. The figures for renters and households with lower incomes are even higher. Given their magnitude, the methodological and data choices used in estimating housing costs have major implications for the performance of economic statistics like the SPM.

An accurate poverty measure will reflect whether households have adequate resources to obtain a basic level of shelter while still being able to afford other necessities such as food, clothing, childcare, transportation, and medical care. A straightforward way of representing this basic need is to establish the cost, based on geographic location and family size, to rent an "acceptable quality" house or apartment. For low-income households, rental housing is typically more attainable than is homeownership. Unsurprisingly, renting is the dominant tenure mode—ahead of owning a home with a mortgage or owning without a mortgage—for families with low incomes. In this sense, renting represents the baseline housing need.

RECOMMENDATION 5.1: The Principal Poverty Measure housing thresholds should be set based on shelter costs for renters only. Rental levels should be based on the Department of Housing and Urban Development's annual Fair Market Rent estimates for various shelter unit sizes, which are anchored to the 40th percentile of gross rent for a recently available "standard quality" two-bedroom unit in a given local area (metropolitan area or nonmetropolitan county).

Conceptual clarity is an important advantage of this approach. The Department of Housing and Urban Development's (HUD's) Fair Market Rents (FMRs) are, in principle, the baseline cost that any household must be able to afford to obtain basic shelter. Statistical transparency is enhanced by eliminating the tenure-adjustment feature of the current SPM thresholds, which is complicated as it conflates the asset value of home ownership with the flow of services derived. The FMR approach is also feasible in terms of PPM publication timelines, because it is based on American Community Survey (ACS) data for every county, which are available on an annual basis from HUD. The proposed approach also lends consistency, in that it introduces a threshold already used by HUD to estimate local rents for those who receive housing assistance. Finally, the FMR approach echoes the proposed approach for medical care, in that it uses a preexisting standard of basic need currently in use by government programs.

The SPM currently specifies separate sets of poverty thresholds based on tenure status. However, consistent with Recommendation 5.1, it will no longer be necessary to distinguish between renters and homeowners on the threshold side of the PPM.

RECOMMENDATION 5.3: The Principal Poverty Measure should discontinue the practice of maintaining separate thresholds for homeowners with a mortgage, homeowners without a mortgage, and renters. While owners without mortgages face lower monthly housing costs, these differences can be accounted for on the resource side.

The rationale for such a methodological switch again rests on simplicity and transparency. There is little difference found in monthly costs between owners with mortgages and renters and, conceptually, the basic shelter need is the same regardless of renter/owner status.

While the panel views cost variation associated with housing tenure as somewhat independent from the question of basic shelter need, adjusting PPM thresholds for rental cost differences across geographic areas remains sensible. The conceptual goal of geographic adjustments is to ensure that all families can purchase comparable basic bundles of necessities, regardless of geographic location. Housing is the most impactful component of cross-area variation in the cost of living. Geographic adjustment of housing thresholds needs to be consistent with the broader methodology proposed for using FMRs to represent the basic housing need.

RECOMMENDATION 5.5: Principal Poverty Measure thresholds should continue to reflect geographic differences in housing costs. Geographic adjustments should apply to owners and renters based on official Fair Market Rents, which are set at the individual metropolitan area or nonmetropolitan county level.

Using FMRs to make geographic adjustments in costs of living offers two advantages over the current method. First, FMRs incorporate price variation across metropolitan areas and rural counties, eliminating the need for the Census Bureau to perform geographic adjustments. Second, FMRs offer more refined, sub-state-level geographic estimates, particularly for rural areas.

The proposed approach of determining housing needs requires that resource estimation also be modified. For renters, housing assistance should continue to be accounted for in PPM resource estimates. Subsidies are typically set at the difference between market rent and expected tenant payment (i.e., the greater of 10% of household gross income and 30% of household net income). This structure mirrors the approach that the Census Bureau currently uses to calculate housing subsidies.

For homeowners, implicit rental income earned should factor into PPM resource estimates. Homeowners receive a benefit from "renting to themselves" or, perhaps more accurately, from not having to pay monthly rent, which frees up resources to cover other needs.

RECOMMENDATION 5.6: For estimating Principal Poverty Measure unit resources, implicit rental income should be included for households that own homes. In the short run, this implicit rental income could be the local Fair Market Rent (FMR) value for the particular family size, minus user costs—implying that implicit rental income will automatically be capped at the housing cost threshold. The Census Bureau should also analyze how the estimated implicit rent would differ under the FMR approach compared with alternative approaches of estimating rental equivalence based on self-reported home value or average American Community Survey rents for units of the same structure type in the local market. For these alternatives, the panel recommends that implicit rent be capped at the FMR value for the relevant consumer unit size, but the Census Bureau should research the alternative of capping net implicit rent at the FMR value.

In addition to benefits, homeowners incur real costs that factor into their monthly budgets, which should also be reflected in the estimate of resources.

RECOMMENDATION 5.7: Homeowners' user costs in the local area—including mortgage interest payments, property taxes, insurance, and other maintenance expenses—should be netted out of the implicit

rental income when estimating Principal Poverty Measure (PPM) unit resources. **The PPM should continue estimating user costs separately for homeowners with and without mortgages as is currently done for the SPM. For consistency with FMRs, user costs could be estimated as the average of the 37th–43rd percentiles of costs for homeowners with and without mortgages. Also, if the Census Bureau accounts for within-market differences in the size and quality of homes in its estimates of rental equivalence, then it should similarly allow user costs to vary with home size and value. User costs should be capped at the value of the rental equivalence, so net implicit rental income cannot be negative.**

The choice to include (or exclude) mortgage principal payments as part of user costs hinges on whether housing is viewed as a good for immediate consumption or as an asset with a projected future return on investment. The Census Bureau should conduct further research into this aspect of the treatment of housing.

DATA AND STATISTICAL ISSUES

As the methodology underlying the SPM/PPM is updated to keep pace with changing economic conditions, social norms, and policy environment—perhaps once a decade as recommended in *Measuring Poverty: A New Approach* (NRC, 1995)—the data infrastructure must likewise be modified to respond to challenges and opportunities. Investing in the PPM data infrastructure creates benefits that extend well beyond improving the usefulness of the measure; these include more accurate measurement of income and expenditures, improved resources to assess the effectiveness of antipoverty assistance programs and other policies (e.g., increases in the minimum wage), and better economic statistics to analyze income distribution/inequality at the household level.

For surveys that contribute to the PPM, impaired data quality arising from growing problems of nonresponse, coverage error, and reporting error must be further addressed. For example, underreporting is significant and imputation rates are high for many sources of income. These defects skew poverty rates and other economic measures. To increase the accuracy of income and benefit estimates, programs integrating survey and administrative data sources should continue to be expanded. For many applications, a mixed-data approach, combining tax reports with survey reports, is preferable to either source alone. Specifically, the Census Bureau would benefit from an aggressive exploration into using federal and state administrative records to improve models for imputation in cases of item nonresponse, including for nonreporting of receipt as well as amounts.

RECOMMENDATION 6.2: The Census Bureau should expand the use of administrative data (income and program benefits) to improve estimates of resources in the Principal Poverty Measure (PPM). Methods should be developed to incorporate state-level administrative data to improve survey-based PPM estimates, and to extrapolate from currently available state data to other states. In particular, the Census Bureau should aggressively explore the strategy of using federal and state administrative records to improve models for imputation for item nonresponse, including nonreporting of receipt as well as amounts.

The expanded use of administrative data, the depth of geographic adjustments for housing, and the common need for geographic and race/ethnicity detail make it challenging to produce a public-use microdata file for researchers to use in evaluating the PPM. Currently, the Census Bureau releases all the variables necessary to replicate SPM calculations on the Current Population Survey Annual Social and Economic Supplement (CPS-ASEC). It is vitally important that the Census Bureau continue to release high-quality public-use data sets for the CPS-ASEC and the ACS, including all the variables necessary to replicate PPM calculations on the two data sets. While some detailed information may need to be accessed within secure research data centers, the Census Bureau should continue to assess the appropriate tradeoffs between new disclosure-avoidance methods and the usefulness of PPM data for researchers and other users.

Among improvements to the surveys contributing data to the PPM, it would be desirable to increase the sample sizes of the CPS-ASEC and CE to improve estimates of subnational geographic areas. One simple modification to effectively increase the CE sample would be to include in PPM estimation all CE units (households) that may be experiencing a period of low income. To use the broadest and most representative group of respondents, single persons, couples, and all other CE unit types could be included in the PPM sample for threshold calculation.

RECOMMENDATION 6.5: For calculating Principal Poverty Measure thresholds, the Census Bureau and Bureau of Labor Statistics should use all consumer units captured in the Consumer Expenditure Survey (CE; not just those with children) to determine the median values for basic needs categories (e.g., food, clothing, internet). Equivalence scales should then be used to adjust each CE unit to the two-adult, two-child reference (as is done currently for consumer units with children).

Since the basic bundle proposed for the PPM only includes food, clothing, telephone, and internet (FCti), the economies of scale experienced by families of various sizes will differ. The PPM will likely necessitate the creation of separate equivalence scales for food and clothing, which is important because greater economies of scale are expected for housing. Given the recommendations to respecify the PPM threshold, the 20-percent multiplier would also need to be updated to account for changes in the basic bundle.

1

Introduction

In fall 2021, the U.S. Census Bureau (2021a, p. 1; Creamer et al., 2021) reported both an increase and a decrease in poverty for families between 2019 and 2020. The poverty rate under the Official Poverty Measure (OPM), developed in the 1960s and methodologically unchanged since then, grew from an estimated 10.5 to 11.4 percent of the population (and then to 11.6% in 2021). In contrast, the rate under the Supplemental Poverty Measure (SPM), introduced in 2011 (U.S. Census Bureau, 2011), declined from 11.8 to 9.1 percent (then to 7.8% in 2021). The primary reason for the opposing directions of the two measures was that the SPM counts income support received through the tax system which, during this period, included COVID-19 stimulus payments, while the OPM does not. The media chose to highlight the SPM findings, which more accurately portrayed the efforts of the government to bolster families' economic wellbeing during the pandemic.[1]

The SPM, which is published annually by the U.S. Census Bureau working closely with the U.S. Bureau of Labor Statistics (BLS), is largely based on a congressionally mandated National Academies of Sciences, Engineering, and Medicine consensus report from almost 30 years ago. That 1995 report, *Measuring Poverty: A New Approach*, recommended that the OPM be replaced with a new measure (NRC, 1995). The Interagency Technical Working Group (ITWG) on Developing a Supplemental Poverty Measure, which set the SPM in motion (Short, 2011), suggested a "supplemental" measure because of the previously established status of the OPM.[2]

The National Academies' 1995 report and the ITWG document both urged that the SPM be revisited at least every 10 years and appropriate changes made to keep it up to date. Accordingly, the Census Bureau approached the National Academies to examine needed improvements to the SPM. This report is the result of that examination. The charge to the study panel and the organization of this report are presented following a brief discussion of the importance of poverty measurement, the key elements of an economic poverty measure, and the motivation for the current study.

---

[1] For example, see Casselman and Smialek (2021).

[2] In May 1965, the Office of Economic Opportunity, part of the Johnson administration's War on Poverty, adopted the OPM as its working definition of poverty. In 1969, the Bureau of the Budget (now the Office of Management and Budget) adopted the OPM as the federal government's official statistical definition of poverty in Statistical Policy Directive No. 14 (Fisher, 1992).

1.1. POLICY AND RESEARCH PURPOSES OF POVERTY MEASUREMENT

Poverty statistics are essential for determining the size and composition of the population whose basic needs are unmet, and for tracking changes in conditions for this group over time. Poverty reflects economic inequalities that exclude a portion of the population from the social mainstream to the extent that their experienced deprivation pushes them below what is viewed as a basic standard of living (Sen, 1997). While not all countries publish an "official" poverty measure, it is standard practice for national statistical offices to estimate the extent of poverty, to collect data to assess the wellbeing of the nation's people along a range of dimensions, and to examine factors that affect wellbeing at both national and subnational levels.[3]

Poverty statistics also inform society's response in terms of targeting resources to alleviate hardships experienced by disadvantaged populations and assessing the effectiveness of programs designed to improve the wellbeing of those populations. Individual-level data are often needed for program applications performed by federal, state, and local government agencies, for purposes including determining assistance eligibility against a standard of need. Poverty measures are also important for evaluating the role and effectiveness of safety net programs and for prioritizing funding options. Additionally, these measures are essential for identifying populations—whether defined by geography, age, gender, race, or ethnicity—that are at particular risk.

While few would disagree that data and statistics serving these purposes are central to a comprehensive economic statistics program, the way poverty is defined and measured elicits extensive debate. Clearly, no single metric can serve all purposes. For example, a suitable metric used by an international agency such as the World Bank to compare global poverty across countries, or one that researchers use to study intergenerational poverty, will differ from the metric used to establish program eligibility of households in a particular country. Organizations also differ based on methods used to measure household resources for meeting household needs. International statistics groups, such as those within the World Bank and United Nations, often use consumption (or expenditures) per capita as an indicator of welfare rather than income as used in the United States or they use a deprivation index focused on lack of access to certain goods and services considered necessary for functioning in society (Townsend, 1979). Some poverty measures are absolute (their need standard is fixed and adjusted simply for price inflation, as in the OPM), but a long-argued shortcoming of absolute poverty measures is that they "do not take account of the concerns people face about relative deprivation, shame, and social exclusion" (Ravallion, 2015, p. 231). Many countries have relative poverty measures in which the need standard is a percentage of median income or expenditures, thereby relative to changes in the standard of living.[4] Yet, such relative measures have their own drawbacks (e.g., depending on the recency of the data utilized, the needs standard may decline in economic downturns and thereby counterintuitively reduce measured poverty as hardship rises). The computation of the SPM includes aspects of both relative and absolute poverty measures (see Chapter 2). A key point is that, due to their differing conceptual bases, the quasi-relative SPM[5] and the absolute OPM poverty levels are not comparable with one another.

The SPM is the statistical construct serving the greatest range of research and policy purposes in the United States. The goal of the SPM is to provide information on economic needs for the population as a whole, and for particular subpopulations, to inform public understanding of economic conditions and trends affecting people with low incomes. It is also used to assess the effectiveness of various antipoverty social safety net programs not captured by the OPM. Indeed, several states and municipalities (e.g., California, Wisconsin, New York City) have implemented variations on the SPM to assess the effectiveness of specific policies adopted at the state and local levels. The Census Bureau's budget justification states: "The Supplemental Poverty Measure uses new data and

---

[3] For an overview of alternative approaches to measuring poverty in various countries, see Atkinson (2019).

[4] European Union countries (and the Organisation for Economic Co-operation and Development) most often rely on relative poverty measures (e.g., set at 50–60% of national median incomes). International agencies (e.g., the World Bank) have used absolute poverty measures (e.g., set at $1.90 per person per day, in 2011 purchasing power parity dollars) for cross comparisons of lower-income countries.

[5] The 1995 National Academies' report (NRC, 1995, p. 23) used the term "quasi-relative" based on the following explanation: "Under our threshold concept, we propose that the values for food, shelter, and clothing—the basic bundle—and for a small amount of other needed spending—the multiplier—be developed by direct reference to spending patterns of American families below the median expenditure level. More important, we propose that real changes in spending on food, clothing, and shelter be used to update the poverty thresholds each year. By so doing, the thresholds will maintain a relationship to real changes in living standards, but only to the extent that these changes affect consumption of basic goods and services that pertain to a concept of poverty, not all goods and services. In this sense, our concept is quasi-relative in nature."

methodologies to obtain an improved understanding of the economic wellbeing of American families and of how Federal policies affect those living in poverty [in a way that] complements, and is released alongside, the official poverty measure" (United States Census Bureau, 2021b, p. 80). Given its leading role as the poverty measure of choice for most research and policy purposes, and its greater precision compared with the OPM, use of the term "supplemental" is a misnomer in the name "SPM."

1.2. SPECIFYING AN ECONOMIC POVERTY MEASURE

The measurement of economic poverty involves estimating two components: (1) a basic needs level—a budget or threshold—below which people are considered poor; and (2) the resources available to families, individuals, or households, to determine whether they have met the threshold. As discussed in greater detail in Chapter 2, the major advances of the SPM over the OPM are that it uses a more encompassing bundle of goods reflecting contemporary budgetary needs and it measures resources to include both cash income and in-kind government benefits such as food assistance and housing subsidies, as well as income provided through the tax system (e.g., the Earned Income Tax Credit). The SPM resource concept also considers nondiscretionary expenditures (taxes, work expenses, child support payments, and medical out-of-pocket expenses) as reductions in resources available to meet basic needs.[6]

Methodological differences between measures significantly affect estimates of poverty and rates of change over time. For example, the rates of poverty among children and their families tend to be lower under the SPM than the OPM, due to the SPM's inclusion of food assistance through the Supplemental Nutrition Assistance Program (Wimer et al., 2016; Pac et al., 2017); whereas rates of SPM poverty among the elderly tend to be higher than the OPM because the SPM accounts for out-of-pocket medical expenditures.

This report reflects the panel's focus on specific statistical objectives of the SPM.[7] The SPM was not conceived for the purpose of directly informing decisions regarding qualification or payment amounts for specific safety net programs. As articulated by Blank (2011), "a number of programs have eligibility formulas that use the relationship between household income and the official poverty line as one of the criteria for eligibility" (p. 12).[8] In contrast, the SPM is meant as a statistical monitoring tool that provides accurate, granular estimates of poverty in a way that is critical to inform evidence-based policy decision making. Nonetheless, as discussed in Chapter 2, a variant of the SPM *thresholds* could be developed to serve additional functions, such as those that currently default to the OPM or to other statistics. Regardless, in the panel's judgment, specification of official statistics should be driven by the information needs of policy makers and researchers. For the SPM, these needs include identifying population groups experiencing the greatest economic deprivation, tracking changes in these populations over time, and assessing the effectiveness of public policies and safety net programs designed to alleviate poverty.

1.3. MOTIVATION FOR THE STUDY AND CHARGE TO THE PANEL

The objective of this study is to assess the strengths and weaknesses of the SPM in the context of the information priorities, objectives, and goals of the measure. This assessment takes into account the historical development of poverty measurement, focusing on the period since the implementation of the SPM in 2011, and harking back to the National Academies' 1995 report recommending a new measure (NRC, 1995). Building on recent or planned changes to the SPM by the Census Bureau and BLS, the guidance provided in this report involves reviewing and updating the basic needs categories, the approach to setting and adjusting thresholds, and the way household

---

[6] Appendix A summarizes how this methodological framework creates meaningful conceptual differences between the SPM and OPM. Table A-1 details specifications for the OPM, notes criticisms of the measure, and documents changes (virtually none) since the measure was officially adopted in 1969. Table A-2 provides specifications for the SPM, notes differences from the OPM and from the recommendations in the National Academies' 1995 report, and indicates changes that the Census Bureau, working with BLS, has made to the SPM to date.

[7] The literature contains many detailed comparisons of the OPM, the SPM, and other poverty and wellbeing statistics—including resource versus consumption-based concepts—some of which require very different data sources to construct. See, for example, National Academies of Sciences, Engineering, and Medicine (2019, Appendix D) and Fox and Burns (2021b).

[8] Key differences between the OPM "poverty thresholds" and the "poverty guidelines" are described here: www.aspe.hhs.gov/topics/poverty-economic-mobility/poverty-guidelines/frequently-asked-questions-related-poverty-guidelines-poverty#differences.

> **BOX 1-1**
> **Statement of Task for the Study**
>
> The National Academies of Sciences, Engineering, and Medicine will convene an expert consensus panel to evaluate the Supplemental Poverty Measure (SPM) and recommend improvements to the measure. The intent of the panel is to assist the Census Bureau and the Bureau of Labor Statistics to ensure that the SPM is fulfilling its mandate to provide information on aggregate levels of economic need that informs public understanding of economic conditions and trends affecting people with lower incomes. After reviewing the strengths and weaknesses of the SPM in its current form, the panel will consider modifications that would increase its value to policy makers and researchers for the uses to which it is, or potentially could be, applied.
>
> The panel will focus its attention on factors affecting economic wellbeing for which conceptual and measurement questions have proven most difficult to resolve. Factors that the panel may review in this regard include, but are not limited to, medical care, child and other dependent care, housing/shelter, taxes, nonhealth and nonhousing in-kind transfers, and assets/debts. Such factors present challenges in establishing what constitutes people's "basic needs" and in determining the resources on hand to meet those needs. The panel will also review methods for adjusting poverty thresholds (e.g., for family size, price changes, or geographic variation in cost of living), survey quality issues, and the potential role of alternative data sources for poverty measurement purposes.
>
> The panel will note instances where its recommendations for improving the SPM are consistent with or, if such cases arise, diverge from guidance proposed by other expert groups. The panel may also evaluate the process whereby the SPM is periodically updated to incorporate methodological advances or improvements in source data.
>
> At the conclusion of the 24-month study, the panel will issue a consensus report with conclusions and recommendations. The focus of the report will be on changes that may be considered for revision cycles beyond 2021, after recommendations issued by the SPM Interagency Technical Working Group are expected to have been implemented (although the panel may comment on those changes in terms of their usefulness going forward).

resources (including income and in-kind benefits) are estimated.[9] A key element of this report's recommendations involves a broadening of explicit basic needs categories—particularly for high-expenditure budget items such as medical care and childcare—in the conceptualization of the SPM.

This report is intended to serve as the basis for proposed reforms and adjustments, at least until the next major review of the SPM in another decade or so. As suggested by Ruggles (1990) and by the initial Interagency Technical Working Group developing the SPM (ITWG, 2010), the poverty measure would benefit from periodic updating. Unlike Ruggles,[10] this report does not specifically discuss drawing the poverty line, but the panel does view this report as a reconceptualization of the poverty line. To provide guidance for improving the SPM in light of social and economic changes since its inception, the panel concentrated its efforts on the measurement of resource and threshold elements for which conceptual and data questions have proven most difficult to resolve and, consequently, led to inaccuracies in measuring poverty. In so doing, the report focuses on medical care, childcare, and housing expenditure categories as encouraged by the study sponsors outlined in the Statement of Task (Box 1-1). The recent ITWG also focused on the inclusion of medical care and housing in a poverty measure and the importance of using administrative data (BLS, 2020). Prioritization of these three areas is further motivated by their prominent

---

[9]Throughout this report, "household" is used as shorthand for the SPM resource unit, which is not quite the same as a household (the OPM resource unit differs even more from a household—see Table 2.1). Chapter 2 reviews revisions to the SPM specifications that took effect in 2021 or are still being considered; these changes are also listed in Appendix A, Table A-2.

[10]The title of Ruggles' book is *Drawing the line: Alternative poverty measures and their implications for public policy.*

presence in family budgets, where expenditures on these basic needs have tended to grow faster than lower- and middle-income family resources available to pay for them.

To identify underlying data deficiencies for poverty measurement, the panel considered promising alternative data sources, both survey and nonsurvey. The panel also identified measurement gaps—such as the lack of adequate data to measure poverty status longitudinally—and considered ways to address those gaps.

Prior to assembling the panel of experts to conduct this study, the National Academies' Committee on National Statistics, in collaboration with the Census Bureau and BLS, developed the study scope. The Statement of Task was further refined by the panel during its initial meetings.

While there are many alternative approaches to measuring poverty—including relative incomes, consumption, wealth, and material hardships—during its deliberations, the panel adhered to the guidelines outlined in the Statement of Task—focusing on the strengths and shortcomings of the SPM and possible improvements that could be made. Notwithstanding their value, this report does not discuss or make recommendations on alternative approaches vis-à-vis the SPM.

1.4. ORGANIZATION OF THE REPORT

This report is intended to clarify measurement objectives of the SPM, to provide guidance for improving several traditionally difficult-to-measure resource and needs categories, and to explore strategies for advancing the data infrastructure from which the SPM is estimated. To this end, Chapter 2 covers the conceptual basis of the SPM, articulating the guiding measurement principles of the process. Chapters 3, 4, and 5 describe the current treatment of three prominent (large budget share) expenditure categories—medical care, childcare, and housing—and provide recommendations for changes. These chapters address advantages and drawbacks of approaches currently used in the SPM and propose alternative approaches for the estimation of households' basic needs thresholds and their resources available to meet those thresholds. Chapter 6 addresses data and statistical issues, assessing the strengths and shortcomings of the current (largely survey-based) data infrastructure, alongside opportunities for improving measures of resources that feed into the SPM. The report concludes with a set of appendixes providing background and specifications of the OPM and SPM; description of data input sources for poverty measurement—specifically, the Current Population Survey/Annual Social and Economic Supplement and the American Community Survey; a summary of public comments on this study; and biographical information on panel members and staff.

2

Conceptual Basis of the Supplemental Poverty Measure

This chapter outlines the key conceptual elements of the Supplemental Poverty Measure (SPM) and proposes options for improving and updating their measurement. First, the SPM, as currently specified, is reviewed. Next, the core measurement principles that guided the panel's deliberations on potential changes to the SPM are identified, and arguments for maintaining multiple statistical poverty measures are considered. The chapter then addresses conceptual and practical issues in setting (and adjusting) need thresholds and in estimating household resources. To a large extent, the panel's recommendations involve suggestions for a more intuitive and consistent characterization of both households' basic needs and the resources available to them. The chapter concludes by considering alternative units of analysis, focusing on the relative strengths and weakness of the household and the current SPM resource unit.[1]

2.1. CURRENT SUPPLEMENTAL POVERTY MEASURE SPECIFICATIONS

2.1.1. Thresholds

The Official Poverty Measure (OPM) threshold is defined as three times the cost of a minimum food diet in 1963. The SPM threshold, in contrast, relies on a broader concept of material wellbeing. Since its inception, the basic categories in the SPM have been food, clothing, shelter, and utilities (FCSU, referred to throughout this chapter as the basic bundle), plus "a little more." "A little more" has been set at 20 percent of the basic bundle since the introduction of the SPM. The use of a 0.2 multiplier represents the cost of other necessities, such as nonwork-related transportation, personal care, and household supplies.[2] Beginning in 2021, internet service was added to the basic bundle and telephone service was pulled out of utilities and made a separate item. This updated categorization was renamed FCSUti.

The SPM threshold amount was originally estimated as the 33rd percentile of spending for families (or, more accurately, SPM resource units) with two children sampled in the Consumer Expenditure Survey (CE). In this sense, because the threshold is set based on the distribution of people's expenditures on the set of included budget

---

[1] The SPM "resource unit" is defined slightly differently than "household." While the latter term is often used in this report to lend intuition and for ease of exposition, the strengths and limitations of various resource units are addressed in the final section of this chapter.

[2] Details of the SPM specification are presented in Appendix A and can be found in Census Bureau documentation (www.census.gov/content/dam/Census/library/publications/2021/demo/p60-275.pdf). The basis of this threshold concept is described the National Academies' 1995 report (NRC, 1995), Chapter 2.

items, the SPM is a quasi-relative poverty measure (NRC, 1995). The five most recent years (20 quarters) of CE data were used for the estimation, with dollar amounts for each quarter adjusted for inflation to the threshold year using the all-items Consumer Price Index for All Urban Consumers (CPI-U). So, for example, thresholds for 2021 were based on data collected in the CE interview from 2017 (Q2) through 2022 (Q1).

As of the September 2021 SPM release, estimation of the threshold base changed from using the 33rd percentile—as represented by CE units sampled from within the 30th–36th FCSU expenditure percentile range—to using estimates based on 83 percent of the averages of the 47th–53rd percentile range of the FCSUti distribution among households with children. This shift, recommended by the previous National Academies of Sciences, Engineering, and Medicine panel (NRC, 1995), is a sensible one given that median-based measures are better at preventing distortions at the lower end of the distribution.[3] For example, using a median-based measure "lessens the impact of imputing in-kind benefits into the threshold, as fewer consumer units receive in-kind benefits at the median than at the 33rd percentile" (Fox and Garner, 2018, p. 16). In addition, the new estimation sampling procedure used in the SPM includes all consumer units with children, as opposed to only those with exactly two children, yielding a larger CE sample size. As of 2020, CE data used in the threshold base are lagged by one year, in this case using the 5 years (20 quarters) of CE data preceding the threshold year. With the new methodology, 2021 thresholds were based on data from 2016 (Q2) through 2021 (Q1) with each quarter of data adjusted using an annual average FCSUti price index.[4] Once the SPM threshold is set, adjustments are made to reflect the impact of a range of factors—including family size and composition, geographic location and, currently, housing mode (renting versus owning)—on the level of resources needed to obtain a basic material standard of living.

Family Size

The thresholds in the SPM are adjusted to reflect that households' needs typically increase with size. Equivalence scales adjust the basic two-adult, two-child family size to reflect that larger households require more income than smaller households to attain a similar standard of living. However, the equivalence scales are not linear; they build on the fact that economies of scale can be achieved as household size increases and that needs differ between children and adults—specifically, children are assumed to require less resources than adults. For example, to reach the poverty threshold, a two-parent, one-child family is assumed to require about 88 percent of the level of resources required by a two-parent, two-child family. Equivalence scales also attempt to reflect that the functional relationship between the number of household members and costs differs for specific basic needs. For example, economies of scale may be quite limited for food, while they are often substantial for shelter. Scale factors for numbers of SPM household members are currently set in the range recommended by the 1995 National Academies panel (NRC, 1995).[5]

Geographic Variation in Cost of Living

National-level SPM thresholds are adjusted to reflect differences in rental prices across areas; the geographic adjustment is only applied to the housing component (shelter plus utilities) of the threshold. The inter-area price adjustment is based on a median rent index estimated from the American Community Survey (ACS) (Garner and Munoz, 2021). Differences in housing costs are identified for 342 metropolitan and nonmetropolitan areas in the

---

[3] The National Academies' 1995 report (NRC, 1995) recommended that the starting threshold for a new measure be around the 33rd percentile, which would be turned into a percentage of the FCSUti median (around 80% at the time) and used to update the measure.

[4] See www.bls.gov/pir/spm/spm_2019re_changes.htm for a description of SPM methodological changes that became effective in 2021. This site also shows comparisons between revised versions of the 2019 thresholds and 2019 published thresholds.

[5] Census Bureau documentation (Fox, 2020) includes the full specification of the "three-parameter" equivalence scale—to account for units with one and two adults, with single parents, and for all other families. For example, the one- and two-adults scale = $(adults)^{0.5}$; the single parent scale = $adults + 0.8 * \text{first child} + 0.5 * \text{additional children})^{0.7}$. The scale for all other families = $(adults + 0.5 * children)^{0.7}$. As currently specified in the SPM, once geographic and housing tenure adjustments are factored in, there are, in effect, 46,170 thresholds—342 areas * 3 housing tenures * 45 equivalence scale categories. A detailed explanation of how equivalence scales are used in the SPM, and more generally in poverty measurement, can be found in National Academies of Sciences, Engineering, and Medicine (2019, Appendix D.2-4).

United States. For SPM resource units in metropolitan areas, the geographic adjustment is based on the characteristics of the metropolitan area; for those in nonmetropolitan areas, the adjustment considers the characteristics of all nonmetropolitan counties within the state. In both instances, the adjustment is based on the median gross rent (rent plus utilities) of a two-bedroom unit (Renwick, 2018). As detailed in Chapter 5, although likely interrelated with other factors (e.g., access to amenities, school quality, length of commutes), the justification for limiting the geographic adjustment to housing expenditures is that it is the most likely threshold category to differ substantially in terms of costs by area and, thus, to affect the level of resources needed to live in an area. The best way to estimate commuting and other transportation costs and factor them into geographic adjustments is an important issue for future research.

Stakeholders have long stressed the need for finer geographic detail to capture spatial variation of poverty. Urban and rural differentials and intrastate variation are of particular interest for some research and policy purposes (Pacas and Rothwell, 2020). As discussed in Chapter 5, the SPM methodology groups together all rural areas within a state, even when there may be sharp housing-price differentials across these areas. However, decisions to pursue additional geographic detail in the SPM may involve tradeoffs in terms of accuracy, transparency, and accessibility.

Owner/Renter Status

Currently, SPM thresholds are set separately for each housing "tenure" group—owners with mortgages, owners without mortgages, and renters. As illustrated in Figure 2-1, which uses the prior FCSU methodology based on CE data for respondents from the 33rd–36th percentiles, the relationships among the housing tenure groups have been fairly constant over time. Thresholds for owners without mortgages, for example, are typically about 85 percent of the thresholds for owners with mortgages or for renters.

Several methods have been explored to acknowledge differences in resource needs of homeowners and renters (Garner and Verbrugge, 2009; Törmälehto, 2017). Consumption-flow measures, such as those used to price housing services in the CPI, have been based on rental equivalence estimates for several decades (Garner, 2006). Chapter 5 explores alternative methods for considering the unique shelter-related spending needs of owners and renters in the SPM. That chapter raises a key point: homeowners incur costs in a way that affects the level of resources available to purchase other necessities.

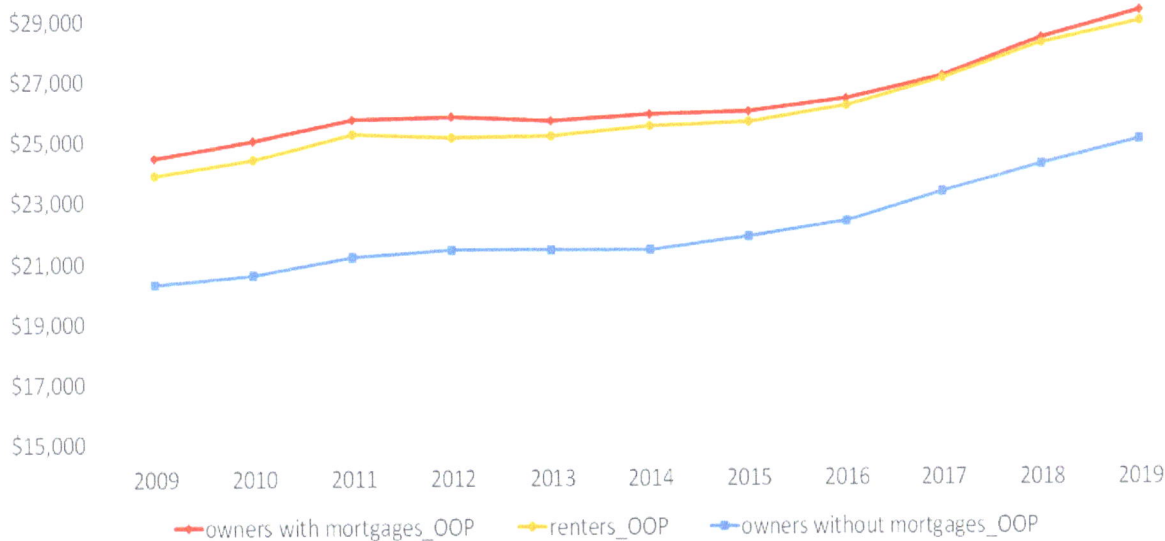

FIGURE 2-1 Published SPM thresholds (by year, for two adults with two children by housing tenure, based on out-of-pocket FCSU spending from the 33rd–36th percentiles).
SOURCE: www.bls.gov/pir/spmhome.htm.

Price Changes

In addition to the adjustments in base thresholds that reflect variation in "real factors" (such as the quantity of food or clothing purchased by CE respondents), expenditure estimates must be adjusted to account for price changes taking place over the data-collection period that factor into a given year's SPM statistics. This procedure is needed because CE data are pooled over 3 (or 5) years, a standard practice in creating a multi-year estimate.[6] As indicated above, FCSU expenditures were previously adjusted for inflation using the all-item CPI-U and are now adjusted using a more narrowly specified FCSUti CPI-U.[7]

2.1.2. Resources

The OPM resource concept is based on gross before-tax money income—meaning market income (wages and salaries, net self-employment income, net farm income, pensions, rent/interest/dividends), social insurance, cash welfare, education assistance, and financial assistance from relatives and others. In contrast, the SPM approach for estimating a family's resources takes into account these sources of money income but also includes the cash value of some in-kind benefits and subsidies, as well as tax credits, that resource units can use to meet their needs. Some one-time additions to resources, such as the 2020 stimulus payments, are also counted. As detailed in Appendix 6B, most, but not all, of the data to estimate these resource additions comes from Current Population Survey—Annual Social and Economic Supplement (CPS-ASEC). Some resource estimates rely on imputations, administrative data, and other sources. In addition to the cash assistance programs captured in the OPM, the following programs are included in SPM resources:

- Supplemental Nutrition Assistance Program (SNAP);
- Special Supplemental Nutrition Program for Women, Infants, and Children (WIC);[8]
- National School Lunch Program (NSLP);[9]
- Subsidized housing;[10] and
- Home energy assistance.[11]

Additionally, tax credits such as the Earned Income Tax Credit (EITC) and Child Tax Credit are added to estimates of available resources. One-time or transitory resource injections (and extractions)—such as capital gains and losses, withdrawals from savings, and intra-family in-kind transfers—are generally excluded from both the OPM and the SPM. Recently, the Census Bureau began counting withdrawals from defined contribution plans for people age 59 and older as resources in both the OPM and the SPM.[12]

Various adjustments are also made to the SPM to reflect expenditures that reduce the level of resources available to households. Taxes paid (federal, state, and payroll), work expenses (including child and dependent care), medical out-of-pocket (MOOP) expenses, and child support paid to another household are all subtracted from the estimation of resources. While CPS-ASEC income and demographic data are used to estimate the probability of

---

[6]For example, ACS 12-month income is reported each month; a single-year income estimate is calculated by adjusting each month's income to be in constant dollars for the calendar year. See www.census.gov/content/dam/Census/library/publications/2018/acs/acs_general_handbook_2018_ch10.pdf.

[7]The Bureau of Labor Statistics has considered alternative price-adjustment formulas, including: (1) updating the 5 years of CE quarterly expenditures using within-area specific FCSU composite expenditure indexes (as opposed to the U.S. urban FCSUti composite price indexes); and (2) converting consumer unit-level expenditures in local dollars to "national" dollars before consumer unit-level reference unit FCSU expenditures are ranked to account for differences in interarea costs (spending patterns, prices, supply) for FCSU (or at least the SU component; Garner and Munoz, 2021).

[8]CPS-ASEC does not ask respondents how much they received in WIC benefits, only whether they received benefits at all. To impute dollar amounts, the Census Bureau uses WIC program information from the U.S. Department of Agriculture on the value of WIC food packages.

[9]CPS-ASEC asks whether children "usually" ate lunch at school, and whether it was free or reduced price. The costs of school lunches are obtained from the U.S. Department of Agriculture's Food and Nutrition Service.

[10]The Census Bureau sets the value of the housing subsidy by subtracting the estimated amount paid by the tenant from the market rent value for the housing unit (see Chapter 5 for details).

[11]The CPS-ASEC asks about energy assistance received for the entire year through the Low Income Home Energy Assistance Program.

[12]Full specification of the SPM resource unit resource calculation is detailed in Appendix A, Table A-2.

families' filing statuses (e.g., married filing jointly or married filing separately), CPS-ASEC does not directly ask respondents about taxes paid. Instead, the Census Bureau estimates taxes using a model (for details of the model, see O'Hara, 2006). Subtraction of work expenses, including childcare, is capped at the amount of the work-related earnings of the lowest-earning family head (or spouse/partner). Work expenses other than childcare are imputed, and the amount is the same per week of work for all workers.[13]

While the SPM concept of resources is quite comprehensive, many transfers and benefits are underreported in surveys. As a result, estimates can often be improved using program administrative data and modeling methods (see Chapter 6). In recent decades, administrative microdata have been increasingly used by researchers and statistical agencies to supplement survey data in ways that expand what is known about family-level economic conditions. Microdata include government administrative data generated by the tax system and by Social Security and other programs,[14] as well as private administrative data such as those generated by credit reporting agencies and organizations tracking housing market transactions. In some cases, administrative data may be of higher quality than survey data because they are less subject to sampling variability and respondent reporting errors. However, administrative data are also not free from errors and, perhaps more importantly, may not match the concepts used in surveys, as administrative data collection is tied to their purpose. For example, because cash and in-kind transfers are generally exempt from taxation, taxable income as defined by the Internal Revenue Service is more restrictive than the measure of income needed to comprehensively measure economic wellbeing.

2.2. GUIDING PRINCIPLES: DESIRABLE CHARACTERISTICS OF A POVERTY MEASURE

As succinctly stated by the National Academies' report *Measuring Poverty: A New Approach* (NRC, 1995), "science alone cannot determine whether a person is or is not poor" (p. 37). Given this reality, some subjective expert judgment is required when specifying a poverty measure intended to serve a range of policy, research, and public information needs. Such judgments benefit from a process that is informed by a set of guiding principles.

In considering potential modifications to the SPM, this panel continually returned to at least four core principles—*accuracy, consistency, transparency*, and *feasibility*. While it is not possible to meaningfully weight and rank the importance of these guiding principles, the panel considered tradeoffs among them when assessing proposed changes to the SPM. In its recommendations to improve the SPM, the panel also considered specific attributes of each principle—for example, timeliness and completeness as attributes of accuracy, and accessibility (both in terms of the understandability of concepts and methods and the use of publicly available data) as an attribute of transparency—as well as operational feasibility.[15]

2.2.1. Accuracy

Perhaps the most obvious attribute needed for a poverty measure, or any economic statistic, is accuracy. Most importantly, the statistic must capture the intended, conceptual measurement objective. To achieve accuracy, the data used for measurement should have minimal bias and variance. For example, when surveys are used to estimate resources, household and item nonresponse should be low and accuracy of reported income should be high. The survey should also have sufficient sample size for reliable estimates—not just for national totals, but also for relevant population subgroups (e.g., those living in a given state or metropolitan area or specific groups defined

---

[13] In other words, work-related expenses (which, beyond transportation and childcare, also include items such as uniform fees) are a fixed value for all workers. Estimates are calculated as a weekly amount (based on calculations from the Survey of Income and Program Participation) multiplied by the reported number of weeks worked.

[14] E.g., Temporary Assistance for Needy Families, Unemployment Insurance, Workers' Compensation, SNAP, WIC, Low Income Home Energy Assistance Program, NSLP, and housing subsidies.

[15] The previous National Academies' panel (NRC, 1995, p. 3) used a related set of guiding principles—public acceptability and understandability, statistical defensibility (including consistency between threshold and resource concepts), and feasibility. The principles of the current panel also relate to a data-quality framework developed by Biemer and Amaya (2018), which includes relevance, accuracy, timeliness and punctuality, accessibility and clarity, comparability (across time and geography), and coherence (consistent standards). Similar principles apply to development of other federal statistics; for example, see National Academies (2020) for a discussion of desirable characteristics of a consumer food data system—including comprehensiveness, representativeness, timeliness, openness, flexibility, accuracy, suitability, and fiscal responsibility.

by race).[16] When other types of data are used, such as administrative records, appropriate tools must be in place to assess the quality of those data as well.[17] For example, administrative records can provide a wealth of information on safety net program participation and payments, but they must be available for comparable measurement units, have sufficient coverage of geographic areas represented by the statistic, and be linkable to core survey data (see Chapter 6).

Timeliness

Timeliness is a dimension of accuracy, the importance of which depends on policy and research information needs. A statistic with short time lags between data collection and publication more accurately reflects the current poverty situation than does a statistic that uses outdated information. Never has this been more apparent for economic statistics than during the disruption (market and nonmarket) created by the COVID-19 pandemic. Job losses (and the resultant lost income) at the onset of the pandemic were concentrated in industries that pay below-average wages, such as leisure and hospitality services, education and health services, and retail trade (Bateman and Ross, 2021). At the same time, consumers changed expenditure patterns in response to public health measures such as social distancing (e.g., spending more on food at home and less at restaurants), and prices rose more quickly for some basic item categories that comprise large percentages of outlays for low-income households. Consequently, more households found it difficult to meet their basic needs. For example, using data from the first two waves of the Census Bureau's Household Pulse Survey (April 23 and May 7, 2020), Schanzenbach and Pitts (2020) estimated that food insecurity increased significantly for most types of households over that period. The Federal Reserve Board's 2019 and 2020 Surveys of Household Economics and Decisionmaking (SHED), fielded in November 2019 and 2020 with supplements fielded in April and July 2020, found short-term fluctuations in households' financial resources during 2020. There was a five-percentage-point drop in respondents who reported they were "at least doing okay financially" from November 2019 to April 2020, followed by an increase as pandemic aid from the federal government kicked in (Lloro et al., 2022).

Related to timeliness is the *frequency* of an economic statistic—both in terms of release and reference period covered.[18] The SPM ascertains poverty for a calendar year and releases estimates annually, about 6 months after data collection ends. In some instances, however, more frequent (e.g., monthly) statistics are valuable. In the context of poverty measurement, there are important policy concerns that must be addressed using higher-frequency statistics—for example, how households spread publicly provided benefits over time, and how households fare when they exhaust (or are close to exhausting) a benefit.

Pandemic-era dislocations underscored the value of high-frequency measurement and information on short-run variability in poverty. During extraordinary times, like the COVID-19 pandemic and subsequent period of policy responses (e.g., the Coronavirus Aid, Relief, and Economic Security Act), there are clear benefits of monthly poverty measures. The Federal Reserve Board's supplements to the SHED in April and July 2020 helped provide intra-year measures of financial insecurity not normally available from the core annual survey. Directly addressing the need for monthly data, Columbia's Center on Poverty and Social Policy launched a project tracking monthly poverty rates throughout the COVID-19 pandemic. Their measure includes all (simulated) taxes and transfers, and accounts for disbursement of federal pandemic relief efforts.[19] Parolin et al. (2022) developed a framework

---

[16]Biemer and Amaya (2018) decompose survey "accuracy" into sampling error and seven types of nonsampling error: (1) frame error (under- or over-coverage); (2) nonresponse error; (3) measurement error; (4) data-processing error; (5) modeling and estimation error; (6) revision error; and (7) specification error (the difference between the true, unobservable variable and the observed indicator).

[17]National Academies (2020) states that, for most kinds of nonsurvey data, there is little in the way of "agreed-upon techniques for assessing the validity, reliability, and robustness of the inferences made" (p. 128). However, increased attention is being given to measuring the quality of administrative and commercial data. Statistical agencies are turning to quality-assessment approaches that broaden measures of error and focus on gaps in the coverage of the population of interest (e.g., BLS, 2020).

[18]The Census Bureau has recognized the value of high-frequency data, particularly during the COVID-19 pandemic. In collaboration with other federal agencies, the Household Pulse Survey was developed to "deploy quickly and efficiently, collecting data to measure household experiences during the coronavirus pandemic" that could be disseminated in near real time "to inform federal and state response and recovery planning": www.census.gov/data/experimental-data-products/household-pulse-survey.html.

[19]See www.povertycenter.columbia.edu/forecasting-monthly-poverty-data.

for producing monthly estimates of the SPM and OPM "based on a family unit's monthly income [and with only a two-week lag] ... to [among other things] better account for intra-year income volatility" (p. 1). To study the effectiveness of pandemic relief programs during 2020, Han et al. (2020) used high-frequency (monthly) CPS data to produce short-lagged, previous 12-month estimates of income and poverty.[20]

Even before the COVID-19 pandemic underscored the need for frequent estimates of short-term variability in poverty, the Census Bureau investigated the possibility of producing a monthly poverty statistic.[21] As discussed in Chapter 6, this work, which is important to continue, relies heavily on the ACS. The ACS maintains a sample size much larger than that of the CPS and therefore supports the needed estimates. Indeed, the Census Bureau pilot project involved developing methods by which ACS data could be used to support historical, sub-annual estimates of health insurance coverage or other elements of interest (Albright and Asiala, 2015).

Completeness

Completeness is another dimension of accuracy and includes which people and places are covered. A national statistic is expected to cover as many members of society as possible. For example, the SPM resource-sharing unit is an improvement over the OPM unit in that it includes foster children and other unrelated children under age 15. However, some groups—for example, people who are incarcerated or people experiencing homelessness—do not factor into the SPM (or the OPM).[22] The lack of shelter among those experiencing homelessness is a severe form of economic hardship and should inarguably be considered in estimates of poverty but, given current survey and administrative data sources, cost is a roadblock to the inclusion of these individuals. Conceptually, should people living in prisons and other institutions be included as family members when determining a family's poverty status?

It is also important for a complete poverty measure to be granular geographically, in a way that reflects political decision making at various levels (e.g., state, county, city). This feature poses challenges for statistical agencies, both due to limits regarding which data sources can be used and due to measures necessary to protect respondent confidentiality. Some state-level administrative records may provide relatively accurate information about income and program participation, for example, but if comparable data cannot be obtained from all states covered by the poverty statistic, such information may be of limited use in producing national-level estimates. The same may be true for various types of commercial data. Such data may, for example, provide accurate and detailed information about medical insurance policies, rental rates, or food prices for a subset of the population, but if they cannot be aligned to represent the full population of interest, such data are of less value (or must be combined creatively with other sources). Tracking severity levels of poverty (e.g., deep poverty, near poverty) is also needed. The Census Bureau tabulates income-to-poverty ratios (e.g., income less than 50% of the poverty threshold) for its SPM and OPM reports. Labeling the applicable ratios as "deep poverty," "near poverty," and the like could be useful to call attention to trends in and characteristics of people experiencing more or less severe poverty. These and related issues point toward the need for future poverty measurement research by statistical agencies and others (see Chapter 6).

2.2.2. Consistency

Consistency—in concepts, methodologies, and data—is an important guiding principle in poverty measurement. Consistency is particularly important for a statistical construct such as the SPM, which involves comparing threshold levels and household resources based on a range of data involving disparate measurement concepts. The National Academies' 1995 report *Measuring Poverty: A New Approach* (NRC, 1995) highlights that relative resource measures, such as one-half median family income, are consistent with threshold measures if they are estimated from

---

[20]Han et al. have continued to produce previous 12-months' poverty estimates monthly. See www.povertymeasurement.org/covid-19-poverty-dashboard/.

[21]The Census Bureau's Survey of Income and Program Participation, which features an oversampling of a high-poverty stratum, has been used to produce "unofficial" average monthly poverty rates by selected demographic characteristics. See www.census.gov/library/publications/2019/demo/p70br-165.html.

[22]Students living in college dormitories are supposed to be reported by their parents.

the same data source. When thresholds are estimated using data different from those used to estimate resources, the report notes that "explicit attention must be paid to achieving consistency between the two components" (p. 37). A poverty measure must, the report argued, "allow for reasonable comparative analyses (within the limits of available data) across time, across places, across types of families, and across population groups" (p. 38).

Census Bureau documentation emphasizes the consistency principle—particularly that, where possible, resources and thresholds are consistently defined in the construction of the SPM. The 2010 Interagency Technical Working Group on Developing a Supplemental Poverty Measure (Interagency Technical Working Group, 2011) valued consistency between threshold and resource definitions, data availability, simplicity in estimation, stability of the measure over time, and ease in explaining the methodology. One recently remedied inconsistency in the SPM resulted from the inclusion of in-kind benefits for food, rent, and energy in the estimate of resources, while the estimate of thresholds only accounted for spending on SNAP in-kind benefits—because the CE collects limited or no data on these programs. Beginning with the 2020 poverty estimates released in September 2021, the CE data used to estimate SPM thresholds include imputed values for the Low Income Home Energy Assistance Program, NSLP, WIC, and rental assistance from government sources.[23]

Among the many dimensions along which tradeoffs must be assessed, the value of statistical consistency must be weighed against accuracy criteria. Conditions and norms have changed since 1995, and even since 2011 when the SPM was instituted, so preserving the original specification indefinitely to prevent breaks in the series comes at a cost. For example, the changing budget shares of basic needs categories such as food, clothing, shelter, and utilities—relative to each other and to other expenditures—should be reflected in a poverty measure. The decision of the Census Bureau and BLS to include internet in the basic bundle beginning with the 2020 thresholds recognized important changes in the goods and services needed to participate in society and the economy.

In general, the panel weighs accuracy more heavily than avoiding series breaks. This view is consistent with that of the original guidance provided by the Interagency Technical Working Group (2011), which stressed that improved accuracy was a greater priority than historical consistency. In the panel's opinion, a headline poverty measure should always use the best methods and data available, and then strive to create a historical series. The panel also notes that certain strategies can be used in producing statistical series (e.g., extending series backward, running old and new series concurrently for a time, or creating an "anchored" version in which thresholds at a point in time are adjusted only for price changes) to minimize the impact of changes and maintain usefulness for temporal comparisons.

2.2.3. Transparency

The value of an economic statistic depends in part on the ease with which it can be interpreted and the extent to which information sources used in its production can be understood. Transparency can be increased, by: (1) reducing the number of components in the estimation formula; (2) reducing reliance on imputations or use of other complex methodologies; and (3) including careful and clear documentation to explain the measure. The OPM is quite easy to understand since its calculation relies on comparatively few components—the cost of a food diet multiplied by three for thresholds is transparent, as is money income for resources. But this simplicity comes at a high cost—simple statistics may not accurately track populations experiencing economic hardship in ways that support the intended purposes of poverty statistics. Furthermore, even though the threshold-setting and resource-estimation methods in the SPM account for the impact of a much larger set of factors than does the OPM, a high degree of transparency can still be achieved through intuitive specification (e.g., including all major expenditure categories separately in the threshold equation) and careful documentation accompanying public release of the statistic.[24]

An important aspect of transparency is the ability of the public to understand and/or use the statistical measure, its data, and its methodologies. The SPM is based on data that are generally accessible in standard, publicly

---

[23] See www.bls.gov/pir/spm/spm_2019re_changes.

[24] The call for greater transparency in official poverty measures was a common theme in public comments to the panel and is clearly an important criterion for stakeholders. A summary of these public comments is provided in Appendix B.

available data sets, such as the CPS-ASEC and the ACS, which contributes to its transparency. Accessibility of statistical systems' outputs and inputs has becoming increasingly important in a "big data" world, in which useful alternative data sources have emerged. For example, some commercial data sources may have more granular or timely data on rent payments or consumer purchases, but if those data are not accessible to policy analysts and others attempting to understand the statistics, accuracy or precision could be reduced.

Although beyond the scope of this panel, it is important to note that the Census Bureau's adoption of more stringent protections against increased threats to data confidentiality will likely erode future access to accurate, publicly available micro- and tabular data on poverty and other topics. To date, the Census Bureau has taken steps in this direction, including dropping or masking variables deemed too disclosive and, for its 2020 data products, adopting protection algorithms that satisfy *differential privacy* concepts.[25] These algorithms introduce noise into virtually every data point. For the ACS, the Census Bureau is researching construction of a synthetic public-use microdata file; this would likely require a validation server for analysts to ascertain whether their estimates from public-file data are sufficiently accurate or are too distorted for use.[26] For poverty measurement, these methods could, in some cases, reduce the accuracy of estimates requiring subnational geographic detail or details of certain populations, such as smaller racial groups.

2.2.4. Feasibility

It is obvious but crucial that production of a statistical measure must be operationally feasible. In its discussion of criteria for a poverty measure, the National Academies' 1995 report *Measuring Poverty: A New Approach* (NRC, 1995) emphasizes operational feasibility along with public acceptability and statistical defensibility. That report describes operational feasibility as occurring when "data can be collected that will in fact measure the prevalence of the conditions underlying the concept of poverty. Income and expenditures are concepts that are generally understood and can be measured and so these should be the core of the concept and measure of poverty" (p. 39).

For data to be incorporated in a statistical measure, barriers to data access must be reasonable. For example, a poverty measure would ideally include information on populations experiencing homelessness. However, official statistics are generally limited to including components for which information can be practically collected at the required frequency.[27] Estimating basic medical care needs, as proposed in Chapter 3, provides an example of an approach that would not have been operationally feasible in 1995, or even at the inception of the SPM in 2011. However, such estimation has now become possible as data and analytic barriers have been overcome.

2.2.5. Tradeoffs

In developing its recommendations, the panel regularly confronted tradeoffs between accuracy on the one hand and consistency, transparency, or feasibility on the other. In some cases, a more accurate and comprehensive SPM may require an estimation procedure that is more complex, requires additional data, or is less transparent to stakeholders than the current estimation procedure. Likewise, changing the resource measure or threshold specifications may decrease the consistency of the historical poverty series over time, if data sufficient for revising past estimates are unavailable or infeasible to access. Moreover, the cost to a household of meeting basic needs, and the adequacy of resources available to do so, depends on many factors, including area-specific cost of living, household size and composition, and program availability, to name a few.

---

[25] Census Bureau implementation of differential privacy is described here: www.census.gov/programs-surveys/decennial-census/decade/2020/planning-management/process/disclosure-avoidance/differential-privacy.html#:~:text=Differential%20privacy%2C%20first%20developed%20in,each%20release%20of%20confidential%20data.&text=By%20law%2C%20we%20must%20ensure,in%20the%20statistics%20we%20publish.

[26] See www.census.gov/library/publications/2021/decennial/2020-census-disclosure-avoidance-handbook.html.

[27] These boundaries are being pushed by research including that of Meyer et al. (2021), which combines survey data (ACS) and administrative data (from tax records and a number of benefits programs) to shed light on survey coverage of people experiencing homelessness and discusses how better to incorporate information about this hard-to-survey population into income and poverty estimates.

Attempting to consider all these factors in a more comprehensive way could quickly increase the complexity of the estimation procedure. Examples of increases in precision that could add to the complexity and data demands of the SPM include:

- Incorporating assets and debts in resource calculations;
- Seeking refined adjustments for household size, to account for scale costs that differ among needs categories (e.g., medical care, housing, food);
- Accounting for variation in the needs of households with specific characteristics, such as persons with disabilities;
- Adding granularity to housing-cost geographic adjustments, or adding dimensions to geographic adjustments (e.g., transportation or childcare); and
- Differentiating threshold costs for homeowners, as opposed to using rental rates to represent the universal basic shelter need.

In some instances, the panel has accepted a tradeoff to improve accuracy and conceptual clarity, even if the recommended approach creates new estimation and data demands. It is important to recognize that increasing complexity does not necessarily decrease transparency. For example, recommended updates to the SPM proposed in this report involve expanding the number of explicit basic needs categories represented in the measure's threshold. While this increases complexity because additional estimates are required, a more complete accounting of basic needs in the poverty threshold can increase intuition about the measure's meaning. In certain cases, added complexity in the threshold will reduce complexity on the resource side, and vice versa.

Tradeoffs also exist in terms of a measure's specificity and its generalizability to a range of applications. A measure designed to perfectly serve one purpose may be less useful for other purposes. For example, a measure optimized to accurately monitor poverty at a highly aggregated (national) level may entail an approach quite different from that of a measure designed to detect metropolitan area versus nonmetropolitan area patterns of poverty within a state or county, or one designed to determine program eligibility at a local level.

As with other desirable statistical characteristics, timeliness and frequency are subject to tradeoffs in other dimensions. Compared with annual estimates, monthly estimates will typically be based on smaller sample sizes, which can reduce accuracy. And, while poverty effects associated with COVID-19 relief programs, for example, can be included in annual measures (e.g., as part of the tax component), policy makers would benefit from more timely and frequent warnings of increasing material hardships during fast-moving economic shocks like the COVID-19 pandemic. Some people lost income but had resources available to continue living in a similar fashion; such information would be useful for measuring poverty at high-frequency intervals.[28] Given that geographic detail in poverty measurement is necessary for assessing policy variation among states for programs such as Medicaid, increasing temporal detail could compete with, and possibly deplete, resources for that important purpose. A question—relevant for a range of economic data including inflation and employment statistics—is whether the pandemic time period is an outlier, or whether greater volatility in economic conditions and household finances will become more common, increasing the need for and value of high-frequency statistics.

Tradeoffs also exist regarding the types of data used to underpin poverty estimates (see Chapter 6). For example, administrative data are often perceived to be more accurate than self-reported information on income or safety net program receipt amounts. However, for some SPM variables, administrative data would involve a longer lag, creating a potential accuracy-timeliness tradeoff. It is also important that administrative data reference the same (or a convertible) time period and population-grouping unit (household, individual, consumer unit [CU]) needed for the statistic being produced.

---

[28] The JPMorgan Chase Institute uses banking data to study intra-year variations in cash balances, income, and spending; their reports have usefully documented the situations of various types of families during the COVID-19 pandemic. The JPMorgan Chase data are not ideal for tracking everyone, however; the unbanked are of course not included in these data and thus the data may exclude families with some of the lowest incomes in the population. See www.jpmorganchase.com/institute/research/household-income-spending.

2.3. PROPOSAL FOR A NEW "PRINCIPAL POVERTY MEASURE"

Multiple data sources and statistics are required to inform the full range of questions that arise regarding a population's wellbeing and the policies designed to improve it. The OPM and the SPM are the two most prominent poverty measures in the United States. Although government safety net programs are not directed to use the OPM to establish eligibility criteria, almost two dozen federal programs (including Medicaid, WIC, NSLP, and Head Start) use a close variant of the OPM thresholds—the federal poverty guidelines—together with the OPM money income definition of resources, for this purpose.[29] However, recognizing that the official poverty thresholds/guidelines are not updated to reflect changes in societal standards, Medicaid, WIC, and NSLP accord eligibility to families with incomes higher than thresholds/guidelines—as much as 150 percent higher for WIC, 185 percent higher for NSLP, and even 300 percent higher, in the case of Medicaid. This use of the OPM, while in no way endorsed in the U.S. Office of Management and Budget Statistical Policy Directive No. 14 (see Box 2-1, last paragraph), is criticized by groups that recommend the replacement of the OPM with a statistic more fit for this purpose (e.g., NRC, 1995).

BOX 2-1
U.S. Office of Management and Budget Statistical Policy Directive No. 14

For the years 1959–1968 the statistics on poverty contained in the Census Bureau's Current Population Reports, Series P-60, No. 68, shall be used by all executive departments and establishments for statistical purposes. For the years 1969 and thereafter, the statistics contained in subsequent applicable reports in this series shall be used.

A number of Federal agencies have been using statistical series on the number of persons and families in poverty, and their characteristics, in analytical and program planning work. The basis for these series has been the classification of income data collected by the Bureau of the Census in accordance with a definition of poverty developed by the Social Security Administration and revised by a Federal Interagency Committee in 1969. This definition provides a range of income cutoffs adjusted by such factors as family size, sex of family head, number of children under 18 years of age, and farm-nonfarm residences.

The Bureau of the Census series continues the Social Security Administration definition for the base year, 1963, except that the differential between poverty levels for farm and nonfarm families is reduced from 30 percent to 15 percent. Annual adjustments in Census series are based on changes in the average annual total Consumer Price Index (CPI) instead of changes in the cost of the U.S. Department of Agriculture's Economy Food Plan.

The establishment of this standard data series does not preclude departments and agencies from more detailed analyses or from publication of tabulations for specialized needs although, where applicable, totals must agree with totals published by the Bureau of the Census. Other measures of poverty may be developed for particular research purposes, and published, so long as they are clearly distinguished from the standard data series.

The poverty levels used by the Bureau of the Census were developed as rough statistical measures to record changes in the number of persons and families in poverty and their characteristics, over time. While they have relevance to a concept of poverty, these levels were not developed for administrative use in any specific program and nothing in this Directive should be construed as requiring that they should be applied for such a purpose.

SOURCE: www.census.gov/topics/income-poverty/poverty/about/history-of-the-poverty-measure/omb-stat-policy-14.html.
NOTE: May 1978 revision; originally issued 1969.

---

[29]The federal poverty guidelines, issued each year by the Assistant Secretary for Planning and Evaluation, U.S. Department of Health and Human Services, represent a modification of the OPM thresholds using a simple equivalence scale. See Congressional Research Service (2015) for a complete inventory of federal low-income support programs and their eligibility criteria.

Development of the SPM was motivated by the need of policy and research for a statistic that could more comprehensively incorporate information about household resources and that could also track and assess the impact of various sources of market and nonmarket income on poverty. Notwithstanding this compelling statistical motivation, the SPM was not intended for—and is not specifically designed for—establishing program eligibility; nor is the OPM, as noted in Box 2-1.[30] Indeed, the OPM is outdated even for administrative purposes. The thresholds/guidelines are based on a 1955 survey at a time when food represented a larger portion of most family budgets than it does now.

The next iteration of the SPM, as specified in this report—and to which, because its role in economic statistics extends well beyond a "supplemental" one, will be referred to as the Principal Poverty Measure (PPM)—will continue to perform the essential statistical function of tracking the effects of public policies and programs on populations living in poverty. This function requires comprehensively accounting for all resources available to households, including government taxes and transfers, to compare with the cost of meeting basic needs. Due to the importance of this function, and because it is published by a federal statistical agency, the headline (flagship) measure should be the more comprehensive PPM, as opposed to the OPM. As such, the PPM is the poverty statistic that should feature most prominently in Census Bureau publications and announcements. While the language in OMB's Statistical Policy Directive No. 14 is ambiguous, it appears that the Census Bureau could simply shift the emphasis in the way the OPM and PPM feature in its P-60 reports.[31]

RECOMMENDATION 2.1: Due to its vital role in tracking the effects of public policies and programs on the size and composition of the population living in or near poverty, and its resulting status as the preferred measure of many researchers and policy makers, the Supplemental Poverty Measure should be elevated to the nation's headline poverty statistic and renamed accordingly (e.g., to the Principal Poverty Measure).

Changing the nomenclature from SPM to PPM will underscore its elevation in Census Bureau publications and, overall, help to provide clarity to users. The current OPM could become the Basic Poverty Measure, or Basic Income Poverty Measure. The various alternative constructs of the PPM being developed by the Census Bureau and BLS could be referred to as Experimental Poverty Measures.

A version of the new PPM threshold estimates could be useful for some program eligibility purposes. The Census Bureau already produces versions of the SPM to examine how poverty rates change when certain income sources are added to or subtracted from resources, and similar exercises can continue with the PPM. Even if a version of PPM threshold estimates is developed that provides a picture of poverty before government tax and transfer assistance, some government agencies will benefit from maintaining their standard operating procedures, which they can only do if the Census Bureau continues producing threshold statistics using its current methods. For this reason, it would be useful for the OPM (perhaps with the new name) to remain in the P-60 as an alternative measure. It may also be useful for BLS and the Census Bureau to be provided with the resources to create consistent measures that extend back prior to the start of the SPM (or before 2014), rather than simply creating a "series break" or relying on existing poverty researchers to create the backcasts.

2.4. MODERNIZING POVERTY THRESHOLDS

Specification of basic needs as conceptualized in the proposed PPM requires periodic reexamination of changes in the population's consumption patterns, social and economic norms, perceptions of wellbeing, and goods and

---

[30]If thresholds alone were used, however, the SPM could be used for program eligibility in poverty guidelines established by the U.S. Department of Health and Human Services. Currently, use of the OPM for eligibility relies mainly on threshold estimates, although the resource definition varies by program. For example, some programs subtract housing costs, some exclude other income, some subtract other expenses. Programs rarely use money income as estimated in the OPM.

[31]The Census Bureau has already taken significant steps in this direction. The OPM and the SPM are now presented in the same report, and much more attention is given to the SPM in the report's analyses, including presentation of historical poverty tables.

services needed for full participation in the labor market; this reexamination must take into account changes in poverty-reduction policies as well as the information available to evaluate those policies. The recent addition of internet service as a threshold component is evidence that Census Bureau measurement experts agree with this need to update poverty statistics. A good case can be made for further expansion of threshold categories, as the basic needs of most families today extend beyond FCSUti.

Explicit inclusion of high-expenditure family budget items in the threshold equation arguably makes a poverty measure more transparent.[32] Currently, major household budget items—most notably medical care and work-related needs such as childcare and commuting—are accounted for by subtracting expenditures from estimates of resources available to the SPM resource unit to cover FCSUti expenses. Basically, according to the SPM, a family is considered to be living in poverty if its income after taxes and transfers, minus work expenses, childcare, and MOOP costs, is less than the FCSUti threshold (set based on housing tenure type, geographic location, and number of children and adults in the household). However, as discussed in later chapters, the impact of receipt (or nonreceipt) of program benefits on poverty can sometimes be most accurately estimated by accounting for the need in the poverty threshold.

RECOMMENDATION 2.2: For the Principal Poverty Measure, the set of threshold categories should be expanded beyond the current food, clothing, shelter, utilities, telephone, and internet (FCSUti) to explicitly recognize that the minimum basic needs—as well as policies designed to help households meet those needs—have evolved since the establishment of the Supplemental Poverty Measure.

Although a comparatively minor point, adding categories beyond FCSUti will necessitate a change in nomenclature. This report will refer to "FCSUti plus any added categories" as the "basic bundle threshold."

It is important to consider the potential impact that transitioning from the SPM to the PPM will have on measurement complexity. While more will be said on this matter in terms of medical care, childcare, and housing in Chapters 3–5, respectively, it is worthwhile to distinguish between conceptual complexity and data/implementation complexity. In the panel's view, including a more comprehensive set of basic needs categories in the threshold will improve transparency because it will eliminate the necessity to explain why major needs (such as medical care and childcare) are excluded from the threshold "because they are accounted for on the resource side." A more comprehensive accounting may also allow the threshold number on its own to represent the budget level necessary to obtain all basic needs—that is, without additional information embedded on the resource side. Furthermore, as will become apparent in later chapters, the PPM approach advanced in this report also creates more consistency with the treatment of government programs in resource estimates. For example, the current SPM does not explicitly consider the substantial government subsidies used to purchase health insurance or childcare. Conceptual advantages notwithstanding, the PPM's more transparent approach may, in some cases, create data needs and increased estimation complexity for the Census Bureau.

2.4.1. Medical Care and Childcare

Wimer et al. (2016) argued that a better reflection of whether minimum standards of medical care and childcare are being met is among the most needed improvements in poverty measurement. In line with this assessment, Chapters 3 and 4 make the case for adding medical care and eventually childcare to the set of basic needs categories. Transportation is a potential candidate as well but, as with childcare, more research and improved data are first required. In contrast, the state of research is such that the proposed approach to medical care is currently ready to be incorporated into the PPM.

---

[32] As noted earlier, the initial designation of "FCSU" was not intended to suggest that there are no other important basic needs. These other items are included in the 0.2 multiplier (or accounted for on the resource side), and the SPM is transparent regarding the components in this multiplier.

Medical Care

The negative impact of medical care costs on the financial wellbeing of households and the positive impact of Medicaid on pulling people out of poverty are well established (Lin et al., 2021; Creamer, 2022). Even so, the current SPM does not directly value publicly or privately provided health insurance.

RECOMMENDATION 2.3: The basic needs categories of the Principal Poverty Measure should be expanded beyond food, clothing, shelter, utilities, telephone, and internet to include medical care as a separate threshold category, represented by the cost of insurance to cover that care.

Once the cost of a basic insurance plan is added as a basic need in the PPM threshold, the value of an insurance plan provided by an employer or by the government could be added to the household's resources in a parallel manner. The state of research into development of a health-inclusive poverty measure (HIPM), which carefully details how the threshold need and insurance resources are valued, is sufficiently advanced such that the Census Bureau could immediately begin implementing this recommendation. A detailed description of the considerations involved in making this transition—based on methods and analyses from Korenman and Remler (2016) and Korenman et al. (2019)—is presented in Chapter 3. Additionally, the Census Bureau is already well along in its research investigating the practical implications (e.g., data needs) of moving toward a health-inclusive SPM (Creamer, 2022).

Childcare

As with medical care, childcare represents a large and rapidly growing component of family budgets. Among families that pay for childcare, this expense currently represents 16 percent of direct family expenditures, making it the third-largest component after housing (29%) and transportation (18%). Of course, childcare costs are even higher, and represent a larger share of the household budget, for families with preschool-aged children.

Childcare is also receiving increased attention in the policy arena. The welfare reforms of the 1990s saw a major expansion in childcare support for working parents and parents enrolled in education, as part of a work-based safety net. Policies that support universal, educationally oriented preschool and prekindergarten to promote child development and school readiness have also greatly expanded. If the goal of the PPM is to measure the wellbeing of households and the effects that government policies have on family wellbeing, then childcare would need to be included in the threshold.

RECOMMENDATION 2.4: The Census Bureau should recognize and initiate research on how to incorporate childcare needs—which are a basic and regular expense for many families—into the Principal Poverty Measure as an explicit threshold category for families with children.

Rather than being deducted from resources as a work expense as done currently, childcare would, under the PPM, ideally be treated more analogously to other threshold categories, particularly the new medical care component. Specifically, childcare would be recognized as a basic need for families with young children. Once a basic childcare need is added as a threshold category of the PPM, childcare subsidies received would be added to estimates of a family's resources. The (ultimate) reorganization of SPM threshold and resource components in the PPM is summarized in Table 2-1. Moving toward this ideal will require considerable time and resources. Before the Census Bureau can incorporate a methodological modification to the treatment of childcare into the PPM, more research will be needed (see Chapter 4). For potential shorter-term modifications, this research will need to investigate options for estimating the basic need for paid childcare to be included in the threshold. Other difficult topics, such as how to value unpaid care in household resources and how to define childcare needs in families that do not use paid care, are longer-term projects. While several practical steps must be completed, as described in the HIPM literature for medical care, these data and conceptual challenges are surmountable.

TABLE 2-1 Comparison of OPM, SPM (Current), and PPM (Proposed)

Concept	Official Poverty Measure (OPM)	Supplemental Poverty Measure (SPM)	Principal Poverty Measure (PPM)
Measurement Units	Families (individuals related by birth, marriage, or adoption) or unrelated individuals	Resource units (official family definition plus any coresident unrelated children [age 15 and under], foster children, and unmarried partners and their relatives) or unrelated individuals	Households, consisting of one or more resource units of related and unrelated individuals of all ages
Poverty Threshold	Three times the cost of a minimum food diet in 1963	Based on 83% of median expenditures on food, clothing, shelter, housing utilities, other utilities (telephone and internet), multiplied by 1.2; using CUs with children	Basic needs budget using share of median expenditures on food, clothing, telephone/internet (using all CUs), times a multiplier, *plus housing needs based on Fair Market Rents, health insurance needs based on basic insurance, and childcare based on service costs*
Threshold Adjustments	Vary by family size, composition, and age of householder	Vary by resource unit size, composition, and housing tenure; with geographic adjustments for differences in housing costs	Vary by household size and composition; *geographic adjustments are built into housing, medical care, and childcare needs*
Updating Thresholds	Consumer Price Index for All Urban Consumers: all items	5-year moving average of expenditures on FCSUti, lagged 1 year and adjusted by a FCSUti CPI-U price index	Update health, housing, and childcare with available data; *spending updated using 3-year moving average of expenditures on FCti lagged 1 year and adjusted by a FCti CPI-U price index*
Resource Measure	Gross before-tax regular cash income	Sum of cash income, plus noncash benefits that resource units can use to meet their FCSUti needs, minus tax payments net of refundable tax credits, work expenses, childcare expenses, nonpremium MOOP expenses, and child support paid to another household	Sum of cash income plus noncash benefits that households can use to meet their FCti needs, plus *childcare subsidies, health insurance benefits and subsidies,* and imputed rental income flow for homeowners; minus tax payments net of refundable tax credits, work expenses, nonpremium MOOP expenses, homeowner costs, and child support paid to another household

SOURCE: Extended from Fox (2020).

Implementation

As indicated above, construction of the PPM will require substantial modifications to current SPM methods, particularly in the handling of medical care, housing, and potentially childcare. Appendix 2A summarizes, algebraically, how the two measures differ. Medical care and childcare are not ignored in the current SPM but, as depicted in the equations in Appendix 2A, these expenditures are not represented in the set of threshold needs; rather, MOOP expenses and out-of-pocket childcare are incorporated indirectly as subtractions from resources. For the ideal PPM (Equations 2.3, 2.4, and 2.5 in Appendix 2A), medical care (represented by a basic health insurance plan) and childcare explicitly appear as threshold needs.[33] Subtracting these costs from resources is conceptually equivalent to increasing the thresholds for each individual household. While shifting aspects of the calculation from the resource side to the threshold side will raise threshold levels, other features of medical care and childcare revisions (such as adding health insurance benefits and childcare subsidies to estimates of households' resources) mean that, on balance, these modifications to the SPM will not necessarily change measured poverty rates.[34] However, these modifications are needed to show the impact of medical benefits and transfers on poverty.

---

[33] This respecification of the threshold reflects the presumption that the barriers to including childcare, discussed in Chapter 4, can be overcome.

[34] The rationale for incorporating housing into the threshold using Fair Market Rents is discussed later in this chapter and explained in detail in Chapter 5.

In both the SPM and the PPM, households experience poverty if the value of their calculated resources is less than that estimated for the threshold. Since some items (e.g., the basic health insurance plan; see Chapter 3) are included on both sides of the inequality, poverty status will be the same for family units with no out-of-pocket costs for housing and medical care under both the SPM and the PPM. For example, for renters with health insurance and a standard childcare expense, the PPM inequality is similar to the SPM inequality. Hence, even though the new PPM threshold will be higher than the SPM threshold, after adjusting for the differing treatment of resources, there will be no difference in poverty status in these cases. Family units that do not have sufficient health insurance or childcare subsidies, or that have substantial housing maintenance expenses, will be those most likely to experience poverty as measured by the PPM but not the SPM.

As an additional consideration, expanding the basic bundle threshold categories will impact the application of equivalence scales in the PPM and, potentially, the size of the threshold multiplier. The panel suggests that the Census Bureau reexamine the equivalence scales to reflect the respecification of the basic bundle—which, instead of applying to FCSUti as it currently does in the SPM, would apply to FCti (food, clothing, and telephone/internet) in the PPM (see Chapter 6). Similarly, changing the FCSUti to the "basic bundle threshold" will directly impact the contents of the catch-all multiplier, currently set at 0.2, which means that the multiplier will need to be updated to reflect the new specification.

Given the recommendations above, the threshold multiplier could be recalculated based on the new FCti bundle, and adjusted to account for new spending needs beyond those considered in the National Academies' 1995 report (NRC, 1995). Originally, these needs included personal care, household supplies, education, reading, and nonwork-related transportation costs (50% of total transportation costs). Murphy et al. (2022) suggest that nonwork transportation needs differ for metropolitan and nonmetropolitan area households and could be higher than the costs used in 1995 calculations. The 1995 report recommended a multiplier between 15 and 25 percent. At that time, BLS and the Census Bureau decided to use the average of the recommendations—both for the share of the median (between 78% and 83% of the median) and the multiplier. More recent spending patterns may suggest a larger multiplier.

RECOMMENDATION 2.5: The Census Bureau and Bureau of Labor Statistics should conduct a review of the basis for the 20-percent multiplier. This review should include:

- **Assessing whether a multiplier set at a different level better matches current spending patterns on the basket of goods currently included in the Supplemental Poverty Measure threshold;**
- **Evaluating the spending categories included in the threshold multiplier, specifically whether transportation should be a larger share and should vary by metropolitan and nonmetropolitan residence status;**
- **Recalculating the multiplier based on the new basic needs bundle; and**
- **Developing a plan for updating the multiplier for future changes in spending patterns.**

The PPM threshold concept recommended by the panel involves a widened set of calculations for a larger number of components than exists in the current SPM, with implications for the multiplier for "a little more" and for the equivalence scale used to estimate comparable needs for families of various sizes and compositions. The end result should be a set of thresholds that more accurately reflect families' differing needs for basic levels of food, clothing, housing, medical care, childcare, and other necessities in contemporary America.

2.4.2. Other Basic Needs?

In the future, other basic needs categories could be considered for explicit inclusion in the PPM threshold bundle, as opposed to being handled in the multiplier or exclusively on the resource estimate side. Transportation is an obvious candidate for explicit inclusion given its prominence in household expenditures, although additional methodological research and data development would be needed. In the current SPM, commuting costs are treated like childcare—they are subtracted from income/resources using a flat weekly deduction applied

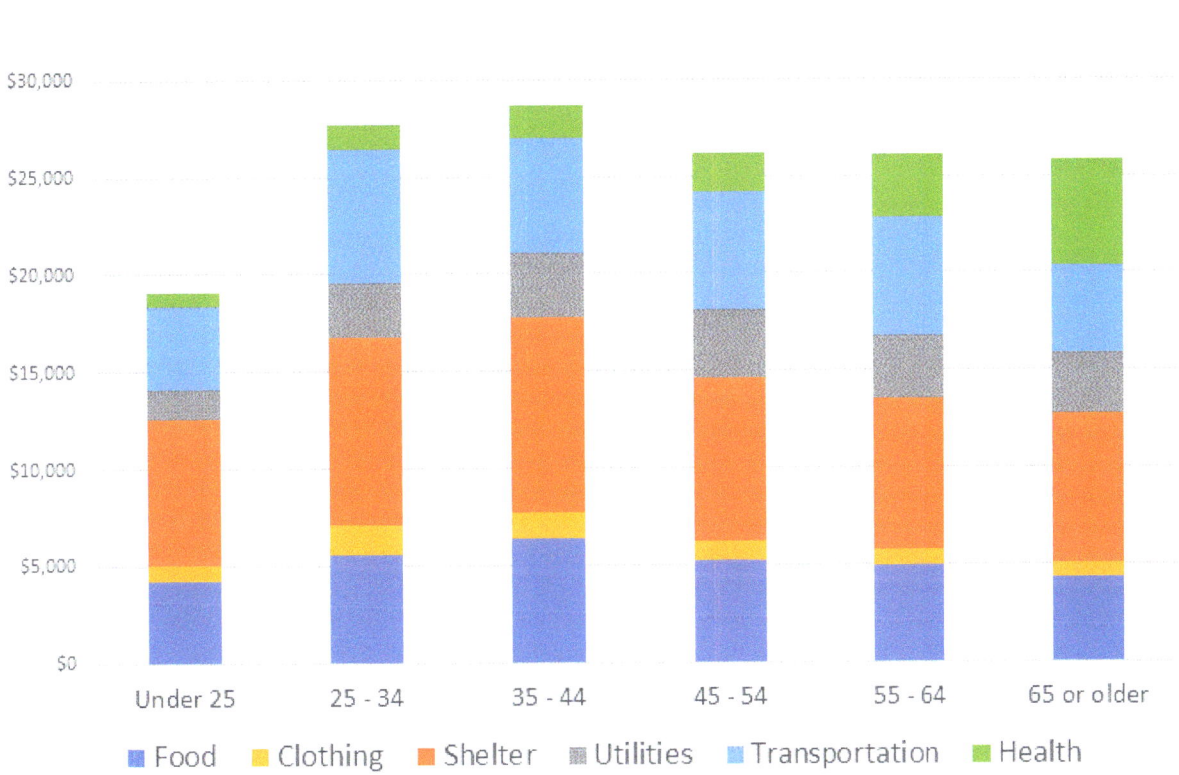

FIGURE 2-2 Average expenditures for select basic needs categories (2020–2021), for consumer units with incomes less than $40,000/year, by age.
SOURCE: Panel calculated using published Consumer Expenditure Survey crosstab tables (www.bls.gov/cex/tables.htm).

to all individuals based on the number of weeks of the year they worked, as reported in the CPS-ASEC. The deduction is calculated from Survey of Income and Program Participation (SIPP) data on commuting expenses and other miscellaneous work expenses. Nonwork-related transportation is currently included in the 20 percent multiplier added to FCSUti.

There are two relevant considerations related to treating transportation as a separate expenditure/budget category in the PPM bundle. First, as illustrated in Figure 2-2, transportation represents a much higher share of consumers' expenditures than does clothing, which would argue for its inclusion as a separate category. Second, it is logical to distinguish between work- and nonwork-related transportation. People who do not work may, on average, have lower transportation costs, but the same is true for people who do not have to take their children to school every day.[35]

Additionally, families face money and time tradeoffs between housing and commuting—as illustrated by inexpensive but time-intensive options such as walking and biking—which may be captured by adding transportation as an explicit category of the threshold. To improve the accuracy of the PPM, variation in transportation costs faced by families across geographic locations, and across housing and job situations, could one day be

---

[35] Murphy et al. 2022 find that commutes represent only a small proportion of total travel. The CE previously asked separate questions about work and nonwork transportation, but these questions are now combined.

incorporated. The Census Bureau is already conducting relevant research;[36] and, while it is too early to incorporate this nascent research into the PPM, results already highlight the importance of transportation costs on families' financial wellbeing.[37]

2.4.3. Alternatives to an Exclusively Expenditure-Based Approach to Thresholds

The method for estimating current SPM thresholds—the minimum level of resources required to cover basic needs—is primarily based on expenditures as reported in the CE. However, even the current approach is a hybrid of sorts, in that it relies on expert judgment in some important respects. For example, the appropriate subset of CE consumer units on which estimates are based must be determined, as well as the percentage of average expenditures chosen to represent basic needs levels. For housing, the method of establishing separate thresholds for renters and homeowners is also the byproduct of expert deliberations. The National Academies' report *Measuring Poverty: A New Approach* (NRC, 1995) acknowledged expert judgment as an inherent characteristic of poverty measurement, stating "although judgment enters into nearly all aspects of the poverty measure—from how to value in-kind benefits to how to specify the particular form of an equivalence scale—questions of the threshold concept and level are more inherently matters of judgment than other aspects of a poverty measure" (p. 99). The report goes on to discuss concepts underlying expert budgets, relative thresholds, subjective thresholds, and other characteristics. The subjective elements of poverty measurement allow room for a wide range of statistical constructs; various countries, states, and cities have developed significantly different approaches. As just one example, New York City's Center of Economic Opportunity reports that their alternative poverty threshold—which is grounded in analyses of the Self Sufficiency Standard and income adequacy developed by the Center for Women's Welfare at the University of Washington—was about 127 percent greater than that of the SPM in 2018.[38] In a process so dependent on judgment, the criteria for an authoritative poverty measure described above—consistency, transparency, and operationally feasibility—become crucial.

Incorporating a medical care need into PPM thresholds—as recommended above and detailed in Chapter 3—moves the approach further toward a hybrid model wherein a mix of survey-reported spending levels and nonsurvey information is used to estimate and set the cost of basic needs. The proposed PPM would reflect the cost of a basic health insurance plan in the threshold (see Chapter 3). For people with insurance benefits from an employer or the government, the value of the basic plan (adjusted for some types of premium expenditures) would be added to household resources. (As noted earlier, for those with health insurance plans from employers or the government, there would be no change in poverty status if less than the capped amount is spent on premiums and cost sharing.) For those without insurance or with direct-purchase insurance, the basic plan value is not included on the resource side, but any health insurance subsidy is included. The availability of community-rated premiums for benchmark plans from Affordable Care Act (ACA) Marketplaces enables the determination of each household's health insurance need (in dollars), which is required for this revision of the PPM threshold. Thus, even though most threshold categories in the current SPM are calculated based on CE-reported values, medical care need would rely on market information and expert judgment about which insurance plan(s) should serve as the benchmark. It is worth noting that, by introducing medical care based on the ACA Silver plan, and possibly childcare—based on something like Child Care and Development Fund reimbursement rates—into the threshold, the PPM threshold will be estimated in part using programmatic changes and not directly linked to changes in the distribution of the population's actual reported expenditures. As such, the hybrid methodology of the PPM could be viewed as less quasi-relative than the current SPM. The panel favors applying this hybrid approach on a case-by-case basis when the accuracy versus (methodological/data) consistency and complexity tradeoffs warrant it. While the bar should be

---

[36] In his presentation to the panel, Burrows (2022) reported on research showing meaningful geographic variation in transportation costs. He also discussed pros and cons of various data sources (American Housing Survey, ACS, SIPP) that could be used to estimate commuting costs.

[37] The Center for Neighborhood Technology has a tool to estimate local transportation expenses, which could be used to develop the poverty threshold (www.htaindex.cnt.org/). A growing body of research (e.g., Murphy et al., 2022) covers transportation insecurity and its correlation with poverty status, which could help justify accounting for transportation expenses in the poverty threshold rather than including them in the multiplier.

[38] See www.fpwa.org/wp-content/uploads/2021/03/NY2021_SSS.pdf.

set high for approving a methodological shift of this kind—that is, for switching estimation of a threshold category away from the expenditure basis—the panel's assessment is that medical care clearly meets the necessary criteria in terms of methodological development and data needs.

RECOMMENDATION 2.6: Due to both conceptual and data problems, the current Supplemental Poverty Measure approach that relies on subtracting medical out-of-pocket expenditures from resources does not adequately capture the medical care needs for most people. The current expenditure-based model should therefore be replaced by a cost-of-insurance approach, which comes closer to reflecting the basic needs of households.

It is reasonable to question whether increasing the methodological diversity in the way thresholds are established for specific needs categories might negatively affect PPM transparency. However, due to the paramount importance of accuracy, the cost-benefit assessment would also do well to consider problems with setting thresholds based on expenditure data, as currently practiced, and with defining a household's "need" implicitly (via an expenditure subtraction from resources) as the amount the household spends on a good or service. Critics argue that this approach is logically flawed, in that it fails completely to identify unmet need, which is particularly glaring in the cases of childcare and medical care (e.g., Korenman and Remler, 2016). In some cases, using data on expenditures as in the SPM can embed the shortcoming that unmet needs—for example, for childcare or medical care—go unrecognized in the poverty measure threshold.

It should also be noted that the proposed PPM approach to establishing need is based on a low-cost plan available to a household of a particular age composition in a particular residential location. This approach reflects social norms embedded in policies regarding the meaning of "basic care." The ACA defines essential care that must be covered by insurance; the ACA was designed to make insurance covering basic care affordable and accessible through either Medicaid or ACA premium subsidies for the purchase of a benchmark Marketplace plan. This makes the conceptual underpinnings of the HIPM basic need somewhat different from the expert judgment described in the National Academies' 1995 report (NRC, 1995).

Including medical care need in the PPM as described above suggests a possible alternative estimation method for other needs categories, such as childcare or housing. As detailed in Chapter 4, the proposed PPM approach to the treatment of childcare includes basic-level costs on the threshold side. These costs could be approximated based on consumer expenditures; alternatively, if appropriate levels could be determined, a basic need for childcare could be used. One possibility could be based on market rate surveys conducted by each state as part of the Child Care and Development Fund—a federal program that helps low-income families obtain childcare so that they can work, seek education, or participate in training (see Chapter 4). As noted above, in either case, childcare subsidies, and possibly the value of various types of "free" childcare, would need to be accounted for in PPM household resource estimates.[39]

In addition to medical care and childcare, the method for obtaining the threshold cost of a basic unit of shelter should also be revisited. Currently, the housing portion of the FCSUti threshold is calculated using data from the CE. However, as developed in Chapter 5, a method based on the use of Fair Market Rents (FMRs), established by the U.S. Department of Housing and Urban Development for the housing choice voucher program, provides an alternative. FMRs are designed to capture the cost to rent a moderately priced, standard-quality dwelling unit in the local housing market. As with ACA insurance plans, it is an attractive feature that FMRs are linked to policy—e.g., subsidy caps for housing choice voucher recipients—in a way that reflects the cost of renting a basic (standard) housing unit in a given area.

For the foreseeable future, other elements of the PPM threshold—most notably the food component—will continue to be estimated based on survey estimates of expenditures. However, alternatives are worth exploring. There are no major conceptual difficulties with the current approach for estimating food expenditures based on actual budgets which, in some ways, makes the proposition for methodological revision less compelling than for the cases of medical care or childcare. Nonetheless, the Census Bureau could consider estimating the "F" in "FCSU"

---

[39]The proposed PPM would ideally subtract net childcare costs from resources—the actual price minus any subsidy received by the family.

based on the U.S. Department of Agriculture's (USDA's) Thrifty Food Plan (TFP),[40] for example. One advantage of this option is that it would create consistency with the proposed PPM approach to housing, health insurance, and childcare in that the TFP (like FMRs, the ACA benchmark plan, and federal childcare reimbursement rates) is established by the government and updated regularly.[41] While the construction of the TFP is complex in practice, as a matter of interpretation the TFP is transparent in the sense that it indicates how much it would cost, based on observed food prices, for a household of a given size to eat a minimally nutritive diet on a low-income budget. The TFP also is available for various types of families (including gender and age of children), which helps to determine appropriate equivalence scales. The recently reevaluated TFP addresses many shortcomings of the previous TFP, reflecting the food consumption patterns of a broader set of Americans and taking some time-saving substitutions of prepared foods into account.[42]

While using the TFP to represent food needs for PPM thresholds is appealing due to its consistency with the approaches for measuring housing, health insurance, and childcare needs, there are potential drawbacks to this approach. Unlike the other needs-based approaches, the cost of the TFP is the same across the 48 contiguous states, and the only region-specific plans are for Alaska and Hawaii. (USDA is currently updating the TFPs for food costs and consumption patterns that differ in these two states.) Also, the TFP is based only on "at-home" food consumption, not foods purchased and consumed from restaurants or eating places—which account for roughly half of all food expenditures in the United States[43]—although the share is smaller for lower-income households (Saksena et al., 2018). The TFP uses the food consumption patterns and food prices for a sample of households with incomes below 350 percent of federal poverty levels. The current food portion of the FCSU is based on the food consumption patterns of a nationally representative sample and includes food expenditures from all food sources.

Further research could assess these tradeoffs in methods of accounting for food needs in a threshold. This research could compare the current thresholds to the revised TFP and potentially to the USDA's Low- or Moderate-Cost Food Plans. The USDA's Low-Cost Food Plan is used in the Economic Policy Institute's Family Budget Calculator, which does not add money for food eaten outside the home.[44] Currently, the complication of food eaten at home versus away is one issue that could complicate using the TFP in the PPM threshold. A potential way to address the critique that the TFP does not consider food from all sources (and thus does not completely represent common consumption patterns) would be to apply a multiplier to TFP levels to allow for slightly great costs.

2.5. ALTERNATIVE CONCEPTS OF RESOURCES

Respecification of the basic bundle threshold will necessitate updating the method of estimating household resources. Alternative conceptual frameworks for estimating resources available to households and families have been considered for poverty measurement. One contrasting characteristic of the various frameworks is their treatment of assets and debt, which may accumulate over very long periods of time and which can impact the ability of households to meet basic needs in the short run. For example, access to assets may allow a family to cover purchases of large-ticket items, particularly if the expenses are extraordinary and unexpected. Assets can help households to smooth consumption when income is erratic. Conversely, debt—perhaps most notably credit card debt—constrains the capacity of low-income families to cover their current basic expenditures (Fitzgerald and Moffit, 2022). For these reasons, multi-period resource measures that include assets (and their liquidity) and debts are important for understanding chronic poverty or intergenerational poverty.

---

[40] The TFP estimates the cost of food needs for a representative family, balancing nutritional guidelines, caloric needs, and some food consumption patterns at a budget, or low-cost, level. The TFP is used as the base for setting SNAP maximum benefit levels. The TFP assumes food is prepared at home (as opposed to purchased at a restaurant or food service venue) and does not consider the time costs of preparing food (Ziliak, 2016).

[41] The TFP is now updated every 5 years as specified by the Agricultural Improvement Act of 2018 (P.L. 115-334), www.ers.usda.gov/agriculture-improvement-act-of-2018-highlights-and-implications/.

[42] See www.fns-prod.azureedge.us/sites/default/files/resource-files/TFP2021.pdf.

[43] See www.ers.usda.gov/data-products/chart-gallery/gallery/chart-detail/?chartId=104043.

[44] See www.epi.org/resources/budget/.

While these arguments are sound, this panel agrees with the recommendation of the National Academies' 1995 panel not to expand the resource bundle to include additional assets and debts (NRC, 1995)—at least not for the flagship poverty measure. This decision was based mainly on issues of transparency and feasibility. More research is needed to establish whether the increased complexity of data collection required to expand the scope of the PPM in this way can be justified, and whether the accuracy of available asset data is sufficient. Moreover, there is little evidence that families with low incomes have sufficient capital gains (realized or unrealized) and savings to allow income smoothing to an extent necessary to impact the PPM. Among older people with low incomes, retirement savings and home equity are possible exceptions. Indeed, the CPS-ASEC, and therefore the current SPM, already captures retirement income (in the form of lump-sum payments) in addition to annuities.

These questions about treatment of assets and debt are important ones—particularly as they relate to the duration of family episodes in poverty—and they are worthy of attention in a longer-term, aspirational measurement program, perhaps for an experimental statistic. Fitzgerald and Moffit (2022) provide an example of this kind of research with their Supplemental Expenditure Poverty Measure, which uses BLS data supplemented with bank and credit card information to generate estimates of the actual and potential spending power available to households.

Research that comprehensively seeks to measure the intertemporal role of assets and debt in families with low incomes would also be valuable for understanding population flows into and out of poverty (within and across years). Such research would also be useful for studying the risk of experiencing material deprivation. The Census Bureau could perform research on measures of assets and debt that would, for example, elucidate hardships related to education loans, a topic currently of great interest to policy makers. The SPM and the OPM do not consider education loans as income, either as an addition when received or a subtraction when repaid.[45]

Using data from their Consumer Credit Panel, a recent report by the Federal Reserve Bank of New York (Mills et al., 2022) found that "Americans residing in low-income areas hold auto and student loan balances comparable to those residing in wealthier areas" (p. 2). This translates into considerably higher nonhousing debt-to-income ratios among low-income borrowers. Research could also tackle conceptual questions about treatment of interest payments. For example, should interest paid on certain categories of debt (e.g., medical, credit cards) be subtracted from income/resources? What about legal debt or child support debt—how can these forms of debt be consistently treated? Also, some debts, such as child support owed, may not always accrue interest but may be binding in terms of payment (i.e., wage garnishing).[46] These questions suggest the need for a well-reasoned guiding principle regarding the types of assets and debts that should be included for resource estimates in an experimental poverty measure. Regularity of flows is one principle; the EITC would conform to this principle, albeit with a 1-year lag.

For its new poverty measure, the UK Social Metrics Commission (2020) concluded that assets that can be freely liquidated into cash should be included as an available resource, on the same weekly basis as income—by dividing the stock of assets by 52, to reflect the number of weeks in a year. Similarly, in the Commission's view, obligated debt repayments should be considered an inescapable cost that reduces the overall level of a family's available resources.[47] However, practical data constraints also shape the scope of a poverty measure—a reality not lost on the Commission. Although the Commission had a comparatively broad view of which categories of debts and assets would ideally be included, data were not always of a level that allowed those inclusions, and the Commission strongly recommended updating the data infrastructure to allow robust measures to be added in the future.

---

[45] The OPM and the SPM *do* include educational subsides and scholarships; the CPS-ASEC explicitly excludes loans.

[46] Some states do allow for interest on child support arrears. Child support obtained through wage garnishing is already included in the SPM—assuming the person who pays the child support reports it as a payment in the CPS-ASEC, and the person who receives the child support reports it as income.

[47] An overview of the UK Social Metrics Commission treatment of assets and debt in the determination of resources available for a new experimental poverty measure was provided in a presentation to the panel (Joyce, 2022).

2.6. UNIT OF ANALYSIS

2.6.1. Grouping Concepts/Definitions

In estimating a poverty measure, the total amount of resources and threshold needs hinges on the unit of analysis, which is defined as the group of "people whose economic resources are to be pooled in determining poverty status" (NRC, 1995, p. 301). The resource unit of the current SPM differs somewhat from other units commonly used in economic statistics such as consumer units (CUs), households, families, and individuals. The SPM resource unit is broader than the OPM resource unit—among other differences, the SPM's single-family unit includes cohabitating partners and their children, as well as foster children.[48] In addition, as discussed below, the SPM resource unit differs slightly from the CU in the CE used to calculate the thresholds.

The conceptually ideal measurement unit hinges on the extent and characteristics of resource sharing in the "household"—that is, how household members pool economic resources to meet their material needs as a unit. In some cases, the precise breakdown is less important. For example, as discussed in Chapter 3, incorporating health insurance into the PPM requires using CPS-ASEC information on health insurance coverage to form health insurance-sharing units. As demonstrated by Korenman et al. (2019), these (sometimes smaller) subunits can be aggregated up to the SPM resource unit to construct a HIPM based on the SPM resource unit.

Although more research on resource sharing is needed, relevant insights have already been gleaned in the literature. Short and Smeeding (2005), for example, used data from the SIPP to compare the SPM resource unit of analysis with that of the CE CU. They showed that cohabiting couples met the criteria established by the CE for CUs, defined as a family (related by blood, marriage, cohabitation, or adoption) or two or more individuals who share at least two of three major expenses: housing, food, or other living expenses. This important finding supported the use of the CE to estimate thresholds for the SPM (Provencher, 2011).

The poverty rates of people living in cohabitating families (particularly children) are the most affected by the differing unit definitions used by the OPM and the SPM. Studies by Bauman (1999), Carlson and Danziger (1999), Iceland (2000), and Short (2009) evaluated how the potential to share resources affects consumer behavior, such as decisions about housing arrangements. Mykyta and Macartney (2012) showed that the number of shared households in the United States increased by 11.4 percent between 2007 and 2010—the period that included the housing market crash and subsequent recession. Sharing residences lowered official poverty rates through the pooling of resources.[49]

2.6.2. Consumer Units versus Household Units

In revisiting the unit of analysis issue, the central question facing the Census Bureau is whether to maintain the current SPM approach or to switch to the household and to include additional unrelated people therein. Such a respecification offers several advantages. First, most international statistical organizations use the household as the poverty unit; this practice is also recommended by the *Canberra Handbook on Household Income* (UNECE, 2011). Second, the household is a more intuitive concept, improving transparency, and is more straightforward to implement across surveys (e.g., in the ACS). However, as mentioned above, the CE uses a CU to construct its thresholds which, as detailed in Chapter 6, complicates the construction of a household threshold. This is because about 3 percent of households contain multiple CUs—that is, those that do not share expenses for two of the categories of food, housing, and other goods—and the CE only collects data from one CU per household. In 2020, 4.3 percent of households had more than one SPM resource unit, and almost three-quarters of those were households with two SPM resource units. Similarly, in the CE in 2017, 2.5 percent of CUs were in multi-CU households; about half of those consisted of two CUs in the household, and 88 percent of the CUs were single-person CUs. Of the

---

[48]The SPM followed the recommendation in NRC (1995) that the definition of the poverty measurement unit be broadened to include cohabitating couples and their children. That panel further recommended that additional research be conducted on the extent to which roommates and other household and family members share resources, in an effort to determine if the unit of analysis should be modified further.

[49]The authors define a shared household as a household containing at least one resident adult who is not a student, spouse, or partner of the householder. In 2010, shared households accounted for 18.7 percent of all U.S. households.

CUs with children, only 0.4 percent were multi-CU households and, hence, using the household would have had a minimal impact on the SPM thresholds. For the PPM, however, all CUs (including singles) would be included in the household. One could assume that the other CUs in the household are the same single CUs, and hence adjust the total spending on food and clothing (which have fewer economies of scale than housing), which would likely have minimal impact on the median. In addition, the thresholds implicit in the FMR and the equivalence scale for FCti may need to be examined when there are other CUs in the household. Including unrelated individuals age 15–17 in the PPM unit will also bring the unit closer to the household concept.

In selecting the unit of analysis, the main issue is whether poverty is best reflected in multi-SPM units using a measure that pools their resources or one that separately calculates their resources. In 2020, the poverty rate was 9.1 percent. However, the poverty rate for people living in single-SPM households was 8.4 percent, and the poverty rates for people living in multi-member SPM households were much higher—21 percent for two-member households and 31 percent for 3-member households. Although only a small share of the population lives in multi-SPM households, these groups experience much higher poverty rates than the general population. A likely reason for this observation is that SPM units in multiple-unit households have low incomes, so they double up and share to economize on housing. This does not necessarily mean that these SPM units share resources other than housing.

Combining multi-household SPM units into household units may decrease the poverty rate. Perhaps the target measure of poverty is somewhere between the current measure and a household-based one; hence, additional research is needed to evaluate the economic deprivation faced by multi-SPM households, and whether they share resources and costs. This information becomes even more important for the proposed PPM, which may reflect a variety of arrangements within PPM units for sharing resources (such as housing and, in some cases, childcare).

RECOMMENDATION 2.7: The Bureau of Labor Statistics (BLS) and the Census Bureau should move toward using the household as the Principal Poverty Measure (PPM) unit. These agencies should study the impacts on measured poverty for people living in multi-PPM units, and BLS should determine the appropriate methods to calculate thresholds at the household level, including the possibility of using only single-consumer unit households in the estimation of FCti (food, clothing, and telephone/internet).

While additional research is needed to support expanding the current SPM resource unit to the entire household, the panel recommends that additional household members be included in the SPM resource unit. Currently, an SPM resource unit includes all related family members within a household plus resident cohabitors, unrelated children under age 15, and foster children under age 22. Unrelated adults are considered a separate SPM resource unit, as are unrelated children age 15–18. Since the CPS-ASEC collects income information for every household member age 15 and older, the poverty status of these older unrelated children can, in principle, be determined. However, when these children live in multi-SPM households, they likely share income and expenditures with the other SPM resource units. Given the inclusion of foster children over the age of 15, other categories of unrelated children should ideally be treated in a parallel fashion. Research should involve exploring various equivalence scales for multi-PPM households.

The Census Bureau could also research how a range of family or household arrangements (e.g., educational situations in which older children stay in school longer and live at home) might affect the status of individuals who potentially share resources within the SPM/PPM unit. Additionally, social programs differ in the age cutoffs used for determining the eligibility of young adults (e.g., health insurance for children under 26; EITC for full-time students up to age 23), which might dictate that a higher age threshold would more accurately capture these resource impacts.

Appendix 2A

Algebraic Representations of the Supplemental Poverty Measure and the Principal Poverty Measure

This appendix presents details of the arrangement of variables representing threshold (basic needs) and household resources in the Supplemental Poverty Measure (SPM) and the Principal Poverty Measure (PPM). Equations 2.1 and 2.2 summarize the current construction of the SPM, and Equations 2.3 and 2.4 highlight the differences in the proposed PPM. As depicted in Equation 2.1, medical care and childcare are not represented in the set of threshold needs; rather, as indicated in Equation 2.2, medical out-of-pocket (MOOP) care and out-of-pocket childcare (CCOOP) are incorporated indirectly as subtractions from resources. For the ideal PPM (Equations 2.3, 2.4, and 2.5), medical care, represented by a basic health insurance plan (BHP), and childcare (CC) explicitly appear as threshold needs.[1] As described in Chapter 2, while shifting aspects of the calculation from the resource side to the threshold side will raise threshold levels, adding health insurance benefits and childcare subsidies to estimates of households' resources means that, on balance, these modifications to the SPM will not necessarily change measured poverty rates.[2] A family unit lives in poverty under the SPM if the value yielded by Equation 2.2 is less than that yielded by Equation 2.1; a family unit is living in poverty under the PPM if the value yielded by Equation 2.4 (a or b) is less than that yielded by Equation 2.3.

- SPM Threshold: $\text{Scale}_{\text{SPM},j} * \text{FCSUti}_t * (\text{Mu}) * G_g$ (Eq. 2.1)
- SPM Resources: $I_i + R_i - T_i - \text{Work}_i - \text{CCOOP}_i - \text{MOOP}_i - \text{CS}_i$ (Eq. 2.2)
- PPM Threshold: $\text{Scale}_{\text{PPM},j} * \text{FCti} * (\text{Mu}) + \text{FMR}_{gj} + \text{BHP}_{gj} + \text{CC}_{gj}$ (Eq. 2.3)
- PPM Resources [owners]: $I_i + R_i - T_i - \text{Work}_i + (\text{REQ/FMR}_{gj} - \text{HOOP}_i) +$
  $(\text{BHP}_{gj} - \text{PremMOOP}_i - \text{NonPremMOOP}i) + \text{Csub}_i - \text{CS}_i$ (Eq. 2.4a)
  [household with health insurance benefits]

---

[1] The equations simplify the needed calculations. For example, there would be consumer units in which children receive Medicaid but the parents are uninsured. The housing variable, Fair Market Rent (FMR), is introduced in Chapter 2 and described in detail in Chapter 5. These equations reflect the presumption that the barriers to including childcare in the proposed PPM, discussed in Chapter 4, can be overcome.

[2] The rationale for incorporating housing into the threshold using FMRs is discussed in Chapter 2 and explained in detail in Chapter 5.

$$I_i + R_i - T_i - \text{Work}_i + (\text{REQ/FMR}_{gj} - \text{HOOP}_i) + (\text{Msub}_i - \text{NonPremMOOP}_i)$$
$$+ \text{Csub}_i - \text{CS}_i \quad \text{(Eq. 2.4b)}$$
[household uninsured or direct purchase]

- PPM Resources [renters]: $I_i + R_i - T_i - \text{Work}_i + (\text{BHP}_{gj} - \text{PremMOOP}_i - \text{NonPremMOOP}i)$
$+ \text{Csub}_i + \text{Rentasst}_i - \text{CS}_i$ (Eq. 2.5a)
[household with health insurance benefits]

$$I_i + R_i - T_i - \text{Work}_i + (\text{Msub}_i - \text{NonPremMOOP}_i) + \text{Csub}_i - \text{CS}_i + \text{Rentasst}_i \quad \text{(Eq. 2.5b)}$$
[household uninsured or direct purchase]

NOTES: $\text{Scale}_{\text{SPM},j}$ and $\text{Scale}_{\text{PPM},j}$ are the SPM and PPM equivalence scales for family j which signifies differences in family type/size; FCSUti_t (food, clothing, shelter, utilities, telephone and internet) is estimated as 83 percent of the averages of the 47th–53rd percentile range of the FCSUti distribution by owner (tenure) type t; Mu is multiplier (now at 1.2 but would likely be different for the PPM); G_g is the geographic adjustment for area g (rebased for the housing share); I is income of family i; R is government transfers; T is taxes; Work is work-related expenses; CCOOP is out-of-pocket childcare cost for family i; MOOP is all out-of-pocket spending on insurance, cost sharing, and over-the-counter medications for family i; CS_i is child support paid by family i; g is geographic area; FCti is median of expenditures on the food, clothing, and telephone/internet threshold component; FMR is fair market rent applicable for household i in geographic area g; REQ/FMR is the rental equivalence for the homeowner, which initially is estimated using the appropriate FMR; Rentasst is the household's rental assistance, BHP is the basic health insurance plan; CC is childcare cost; HOOP is out-of-pocket housing costs that apply to homeowners and which is capped at the imputed rental income; For renters ($\text{REQ/FMR}_{gj} - \text{HOOP}_i$) = 0; PremMOOP is premium payments, which are capped at the at the BHP or Medicaid/Veterans Health Administration limit; Csub is childcare subsidy; Msub is medical subsidy (zero if unsubsidized); NonPremMOOP is medical out-of-pocket cost share spending, which is capped at the BHP or Medicaid limit; for those without insurance, NonPremMOOP also includes direct purchase of medical services.

3

Challenging Categories: Medical Care

In this chapter, the panel proposes a new way to more fully incorporate health insurance and medical care into a revised Supplemental Poverty Measure (SPM) which, for reasons explained in Chapter 2, is called the Principal Poverty Measure (PPM) in this report. Chapter 3 builds on the concept of a health-inclusive poverty measure and discusses measurement aspects and implementation decisions for putting the concept into practice. In the context of this chapter, the term "inclusive" conveys that—unlike the SPM—the PPM explicitly adds a need for health insurance to the threshold while "transfers" of health insurance, including those provided by the government and employers, are counted as resources.

3.1. BACKGROUND/MOTIVATION

The demand for medical care, unlike most goods, is uncertain. That is, while households can usually predict how much food they will need over the course of a month, this is far less true for medical care. Although individuals with chronic conditions will, on average, have predictably higher spending than those without such conditions, everyone faces the risk of unexpected illness or injury which creates unavoidable uncertainty about the need for medical care. While there is no way for individuals to insure their good health against the risk of unexpected medical events—that is, to guarantee that one's underlying health status can be returned to its baseline level—individuals *can* insure against the risk of unexpected medical spending. Most individuals prefer to pay a predictable health insurance premium to mitigate the risk of unpredictable spending on medical care because they are risk averse.[1] Nonetheless, most health insurance policies in the United States do not cover all costs of medical care: they require cost sharing in the form of copayments or coinsurance, such that consumers bear some of the costs of care (intended to deter unnecessary use of medical care).

Medical care expenditures are a large and increasing share of GDP (19.7% in 2020, up from 5.6% in 1965), with average per capita expenditures in 2020 equaling $12,530 (Catlin and Cowan, 2015; Hartman et al., 2022). Nearly 70 percent of this spending is financed by insurance (Hartman et al., 2022). The federal government spends more than $1.2 trillion annually on medical care—nearly all of it on insurance—accounting for more than 15 percent of federal outlays and dwarfing the next largest in-kind transfer program (the Supplemental Nutrition

---

[1] Economists tend to view health insurance as providing protection against financial risk and value it as the expected loss in utility from the occurrence of adverse health events. Economic theory says that individuals are willing to pay a premium equal to that expected utility loss; a basic exposition can be found in the public finance textbook by Gruber (2022).

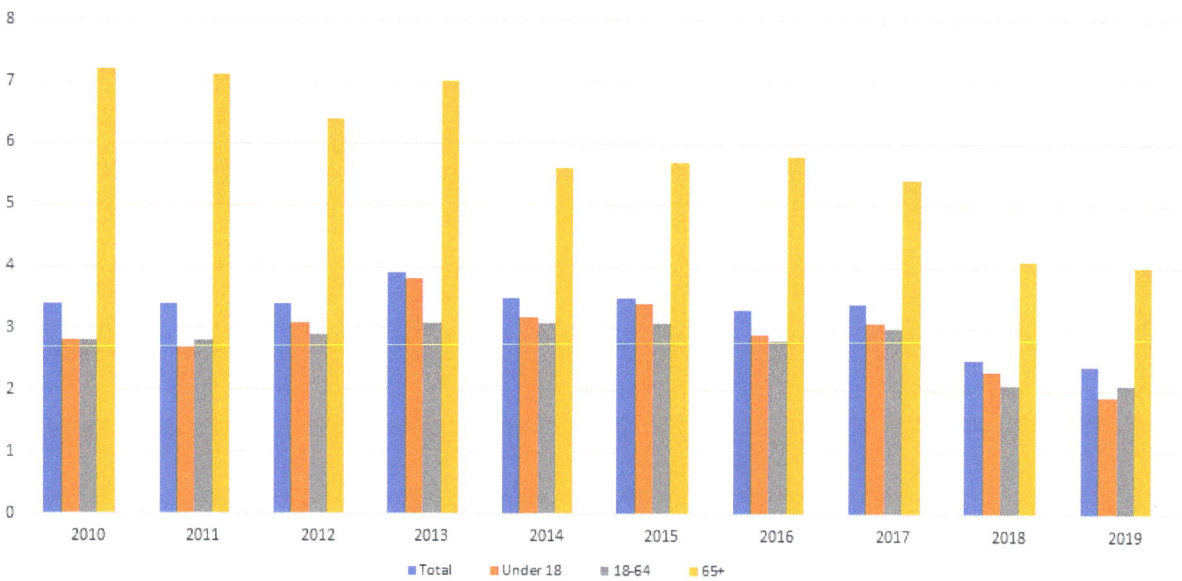

FIGURE 3-1 Percentage point increase in poverty rate due to subtraction of medical out-of-pocket spending from resources.
SOURCE: U.S. Census Bureau yearly SPM reports.

Assistance Program [SNAP]). The high level and rapid growth of health insurance and medical care spending underscores the importance of explicitly and accurately incorporating this basic need into the measurement of poverty. The 1995 National Academies of Sciences, Engineering, and Medicine report, *Measuring Poverty: A New Approach* (NRC, 1995), acknowledged the desirability of including medical care in the measurement of poverty but identified two key obstacles: variability in the need for care across the population, and the fact that health insurance benefits cannot be repurposed to pay directly for nonmedical needs such as food and housing. That panel's compromise solution, reflected in the current SPM, was to deduct medical out-of-pocket (MOOP) spending on both health insurance and medical care from resources, without explicitly including a need for those goods in the threshold. MOOP expenses in the SPM include household payments for health insurance premiums plus household payments or copayments for other medically necessary items, such as prescription drugs, doctor visits, hospital visits, dental services, vision aids, medical supplies, and over-the-counter, health-related products that are not covered by insurance. As shown in Figure 3-1, accounting for MOOP expenditures in the estimate of a households' resources typically raises the SPM poverty rate by about 3 percentage points overall; the increase is largest for those age 65 and older.

The current SPM approach likely understates the impact of government health insurance spending on measured poverty because the only channel through which these outlays can affect poverty is an indirect one—via the deduction of MOOP expenditures from resources.[2] This fails to capture potentially important effects of government health insurance programs. For example, consider an uninsured individual who forgoes medical care entirely because of its high cost. If this individual gained Medicaid coverage that allowed them to obtain treatment, the SPM poverty rate would not fall. If this individual obtained subsidized coverage through an

---

[2] As a reminder, the SPM income (resource) measure is cash income *plus* in-kind government benefits (such as SNAP and housing subsidies) *minus* nondiscretionary expenses (taxes, MOOP expenses, and work expenses). The SPM thresholds are based on a broad measure of necessary expenditures—food, clothing, shelter, utilities, telephone, and internet (FCSUti), but not health coverage—and are based on recent, annually updated expenditure data. The SPM thresholds are adjusted for geographic differences in the cost of living.

Affordable Care Act (ACA) Marketplace plan that allowed them to obtain treatment, their spending on premiums and copays would be deducted from their SPM resources, potentially pushing them below the poverty threshold and thereby *increasing* the poverty rate, as public subsidies for the purchase of coverage would not be counted as resources. These examples make clear that the treatment of health insurance and medical care by the SPM should be revised, if it can be done validly and practically. Specifically, a basic need for medical care should be included in the measure's threshold and the value of transfers like Medicare, Medicaid, employer health insurance benefits, and health insurance premium tax credits in household resources. The approach described in this report offers a partial solution, proposing a method to incorporate *health insurance* into poverty measurement in a way that solves these problems, including modifying the SPM deduction from resources to incorporate the costs of medical care that are not fully covered by insurance.

3.2. TREATMENT OF HEALTH/MEDICAL CARE IN THE SUPPLEMENTAL POVERTY MEASURE: STRENGTHS AND LIMITATIONS

The current treatment of medical care in the SPM has advantages: it is relatively easy to implement, allows for a consistent expenditure-based definition of the needs threshold, and captures important effects of health coverage expansions via reductions in MOOP expenses.[3] The SPM's treatment of medical care also captures variation in spending that is driven by differences in medical care needs; holding insurance constant, households with higher needs will have higher spending. But the current SPM approach has three significant flaws. First, the value of health insurance provided by government or employers affects SPM poverty only indirectly, through its effect on MOOP spending. Second, because neither health insurance nor medical care are included as a need in the threshold, the SPM does not capture the unmet need for care of persons who are uninsured or underinsured. Third, the deduction of MOOP spending from resources is not limited, implying that all MOOP spending represents a "basic need" whereas, in reality, some MOOP spending on care or insurance cannot be accurately characterized as necessary expenditures. That is, the current approach implies that a family's health need is simply equal to whatever the family spends out of pocket on insurance and medical care.

There are several alternatives to the SPM approach to medical care. Table 3-1 compares the Official Poverty Measure (OPM) and the SPM to four additional approaches found in the literature (for additional details, see Appendix 3A): (1) the health-inclusive poverty measure (HIPM; Korenman and Remler, 2016); (2) the SPM-MOOP in threshold (SPM-MIT) which, as its name suggests, includes a need for spending on health insurance and medical care in the threshold but may not capture the unmet need for those without insurance (Garner et al., 2014); (3) a two-index method which constructs a medical care economic burden and medical care economic risk index in addition to the nonmedical index (Institute of Medicine and National Research Council 2012b); and (4) the Full-Income Poverty Measure (FPM) which includes the value of health insurance transfers from government or employers in household resources; these values are also included in needs, to the extent that such transfers existed in 1963, because the distribution of the FPM in that year is used to define the initial FPM thresholds that are then updated for inflation (Burkhauser et al., 2020).

Among these alternatives, this panel's preferred approach, described in greater detail below, builds on the HIPM developed by Korenman and Remler (2013, 2016) and Korenman, Remler, and Hyson (2019). The National Academies' report *Roadmap to Reducing Child Poverty* recommended that relevant statistical agencies review the HIPM for adoption (National Academies 2019, Recommendation 9.8), and the Census Bureau has explored in depth the feasibility of implementing a health-inclusive concept in the SPM (Creamer, 2022). The HIPM approach, which explicitly incorporates the value of health insurance transfers into poverty measurement, builds on similar innovations in the SPM for incorporating other in-kind transfers.

---

[3] According to the Social Security Administration, "MOOP is measured using the CPS/ASEC which collects information on amounts paid for (1) health insurance premiums; (2) over-the-counter, health-related products; and (3) medical care (hospital visits, medical providers, dental services, prescription medicine, vision aids, and medical supplies). Caswell and O'Hara (2010) concluded that CPS/ASEC estimates of MOOP expenditures compare favorably to estimates from the Medical Expenditure Panel Survey (MEPS) and the Survey of Income and Program Participation (SIPP). The MEPS, in particular, devotes considerably more effort to collecting MOOP expenditures than does the CPS/ASEC."

TABLE 3-1 Six Approaches to Poverty Measurement and Their Treatment of Health Insurance/Care/Benefits/Costs

Approach	Thresholds	Resources	Key References
1. Official Poverty Measure (OPM)	Medical care/health insurance not explicitly included in threshold	Medical care/health insurance not included in resources	• Orshansky (1969) • National Research Council (1995)
2. Supplemental Poverty Measure (SPM)	Medical care/health insurance not explicitly included in threshold	Health insurance premiums and other household MOOP spending subtracted from resources	• National Research Council (1995) • Short (2011) • Fox and Burns (2021a)
3. Health-Inclusive Poverty Measure (HIPM)	SPM thresholds, *plus* health insurance need	SPM resources, *plus* net health insurance transfers, *minus* capped nonpremium MOOP costs	• Korenman and Remler (2016) • Korenman, et al. (2019) • Remler and Korenman (2022)
4. SPM with MOOP in Threshold (SPM-MIT)	Predicted MOOP spending included in threshold	SPM resources; MOOP spending is *not* subtracted from resources	• Short and Garner (2002) • Garner, Short, and Gudrais (2014) • Garner and Munoz (2021)
5. Two-Index Method: Nonmedical SPM; Medical Care Economic Burden; Medical Care Economic Risk	SPM thresholds	*Nonmedical:* SPM resources, *not* subtracting MOOP spending *Medical Care Economic Burden (retrospective):* MOOP costs minus resources available for medical care (= excess of nonmedical resources over SPM threshold; zero for nonmedically poor) (separately for premiums and non-premium MOOP expenditures) *Medical Care Economic Risk (prospective):* Use burden measure as proxy until further R&D	• National Research Council (1995) • National Research Council and Institute of Medicine (2012a)
6. Full-Income Poverty Measure (FPM)	Absolute thresholds fixed at the 19.5th percentile of 1963 "full income" distribution, which includes the value of health insurance transfers at that time; inflated using BEA PCE Price Index	"Full income" includes SPM cash and noncash income, plus health insurance transfers; no MOOP costs subtraction	• Council of Economic Advisers (2019) • Burkhauser et al. (2020)

One challenge identified by the National Academies' 1995 panel was that transfers of health insurance are not fully fungible. In the view of the current panel, the conceptual framework of the HIPM provides the best available solution. In particular, the panel prefers the HIPM-based approach to the approach used in the FPM which essentially treats health insurance benefits as equivalent to cash—that is, available to meet any need, medical or nonmedical. The FPM approach implies, for example, that a couple who receives Medicare is not poor, even if they have no other income or resources (Remler and Korenman, 2023); and, as a corollary, FPM poverty is reduced if prices for medical care rise due to increases in the cost of medications, for example, or an increase in useless procedures whose cost is counted as income to beneficiaries even if there is no change in real benefits to the patient (Case and Deaton, 2020). The panel also feels that the conceptual framework of the HIPM is preferable to that of the SPM-MIT as the latter implies medical care need is limited to MOOP expenditures. By excluding the value of health insurance benefits from resources, the SPM-MIT does not reflect the impact of public health insurance transfers on poverty estimates, such as those published annually in the Census Bureau's SPM reports (e.g., Fox, 2020).

Finally, the HIPM approach has an advantage over the two-index approach in that the latter fails to capture how health benefits reduce poverty since medical care enters the measure as a separate index. The medical care economic risk index also employs complex imputations of health-related financial risk that require detailed information on health conditions and health insurance. While such information may be available in health surveys such as the Medical Expenditure Panel Survey, it is not collected in the social and economic surveys used to measure poverty (such as the Current Population Survey Annual Social and Economic Supplement [CPS-ASEC], American Community Survey, or Survey of Income and Program Participation). Research using this approach is valuable and could be particularly useful for understanding poverty of populations with special care needs and expenses, as well as the influence of new technologies on health-related financial risk. The poverty measurement approach proposed below does not adjust for individuals with special needs such as limited sight or hearing, or persons with other disabilities who may have health needs beyond those covered by health insurance, including Medicare. The recommendations discussed in this chapter are intended to improve the SPM by incorporating health insurance needs and benefits. They do not address other aspects of health or medical care. Clearly, research into other health care issues in poverty measurement should continue. But, at this time, the practical advantages of a health-inclusive poverty measurement approach for an official statistic that must be produced on a regular schedule are major and would increase the measure's accuracy.

A critical assumption underlying the proposal for a PPM that is health inclusive is that the basic need for medical care has two parts: a need for health insurance and a need for resources to cover any required cost sharing. The basic need for health insurance can be represented by the price of an insurance policy: that is, the premium. As noted above, most individuals prefer to pay a predictable health insurance premium to mitigate the risk of unpredictable spending on medical care because they are risk averse. In economists' terms, people willingly pay (and reduce current income by the amount of the premium) to avoid possible loss of far larger amounts if they need expensive medical care.[4] Thus, the price of insurance—reflecting both the risk of needing medical care and the expected cost of that care—represents a large fraction of the health care need.

The insight that a substantial portion of health care needs can be represented by an insurance premium, combined with laws that require guaranteed issue and community rating of health insurance premiums, make it possible to incorporate a basic need for health insurance as part of the revision of the SPM to the PPM. Guaranteed issue means that health insurers cannot refuse to cover enrollees based on their health status, age, or gender while community rating means that all persons of a given age group face the same premium (and coverage) in a given market area. We find this logic compelling. But what premium should be used? The current ACA establishes a Marketplace along with an essential benefits package which meet these requirements. The essential benefits package includes a set of 10 categories of services that plans must cover including doctors' services, inpatient and outpatient hospital care, prescription drug coverage, pregnancy and childbirth, mental health services, and dental care for children. To the extent that health insurance requires cost sharing, which the ACA benchmark plans all require, there remains a need for MOOP spending on medical care, which is addressed separately below.

RECOMMENDATION 3.1: For the Principal Poverty Measure, the current approach to medical spending in the Supplemental Poverty Measure should be replaced with one that includes health insurance in the estimates of both the needs threshold and resources.

The proposed approach within the PPM incorporates key modeling elements developed by Korenman and Remler (2016). As described below, one reason this innovation is possible is that the legal and regulatory framework of the 2010 ACA—namely, the specification of the benchmark health insurance plan and the requirement for community rating of premiums and guaranteed availability of coverage—dramatically simplify the process of specifying health insurance needs. "Benchmark plan" is the term used to describe the second-lowest-cost Silver plan available in the exchange. The benchmark plan also specifies an annual maximum for out-of-pocket spending on medical care (patient cost sharing), which can be used to limit (cap) subtractions from resources.

---

[4]Risk aversion is tied to the concept of declining marginal utility of income so that the loss of a thousand dollars to a person with $15,000 "hurts" more than the same dollar loss to a person with $100,000.

3.3. INCORPORATING HEALTH INTO THE PRINCIPAL POVERTY MEASURE

As noted, the health insurance and medical care components of the recommended PPM would follow the HIPM approach (Korenman and Remler, 2016; Korenman et al., 2019). Specifically, the PPM would add the price of the benchmark health insurance plan (that is, the unsubsidized premium) to the poverty threshold to represent the health insurance need. The PPM would also add a value for health insurance benefits provided by government or employers to household resources, up to the price of the benchmark plan.[5] Because the PPM threshold includes a need for health insurance, resources in the PPM do not deduct all out-of-pocket spending on insurance premiums. This is a departure from the SPM. As in the SPM, resources in PPM do include a deduction for medical out-of-pocket spending that is *not* on premiums, which we refer to here as nonpremium medical out-of-pocket (NP-MOOP) spending; unlike the SPM, the deduction of NP-MOOP spending is capped. Equations in Appendix 2A contrast the basic needs thresholds and resource estimation approaches as specified in the SPM and the PPM.

To address the remaining need for cost sharing, the PPM would deduct NP-MOOP spending, such as deductibles and copays, from resources. The deduction from resources is similar to the current SPM, but with two important differences. First, because a need for health insurance is explicitly included in the threshold and health insurance transfers are counted in resources, only out-of-pocket spending on *medical care* would be deducted from resources in the PPM; out-of-pocket spending on *premiums* by those who purchase health insurance directly from an insurer or on the ACA Marketplace is not deducted from resources in the PPM. Second, unlike the SPM, which allows an unlimited deduction for health insurance and medical care, the PPM would cap the deduction of NP-MOOP spending at the out-of-pocket maximum for ACA plans (or less, depending on the household's health insurance type, as explained below). The conceptual justification for the NP-MOOP deduction is the same in the PPM as the SPM. Nondiscretionary spending on necessities not explicitly represented in the threshold reduces resources available to meet those threshold needs.

In the proposed PPM, unlike the SPM, the NP-MOOP subtraction is capped at available out-of-pocket maxima in the benchmark plan in an attempt to limit the deduction to spending that could be considered necessary. However, some spending below the NP-MOOP limit could also be for care that is discretionary, and some care above the maximum could be for nondiscretionary care. The PPM does not attempt to define or measure nondiscretionary spending below the out-of-pocket limit. The PPM procedure of capping the NP-MOOP deduction from resources is, therefore, a pragmatic compromise between the SPM assumption that all NP-MOOP spending is nondiscretionary and attempting to make judgments about whether specific medical care expenditures are or are not discretionary. If the health insurance plan included in resources were "full," in the sense of not requiring any cost sharing, there would be no subtractions from resources for NP-MOOP expenditures.

There are other possible approaches to dealing with the remaining need for cost sharing. For example, the benchmark plan has an actuarial value of 70 percent, meaning that, on average, households will pay out of pocket for 30 percent of the cost of their care. The PPM could incorporate the need for cost sharing by inflating the benchmark premium to 100 percent of actuarial value and would make no deductions for actual NP-MOOP spending (Remler and Korenman, 2022). This method fully incorporates the average anticipated need for medical care into the need for health insurance. As noted by Remler and Korenman (2022), one drawback of such an approach is that it is based entirely on the anticipated, or ex ante, need for care as measured by the benchmark premium. Actual NP-MOOP expenses reflect the realized, or ex post, need for care. Some households, such as those including a family member with a disability, may consistently face higher than average NP-MOOP costs based on realized need beyond that reflected in their premiums. Others may have to pay considerable NP-MOOP costs in any given year due to serious injuries or other health shocks. Many, even most, people will be healthy in a given year and need substantially less than the average cost-sharing amount. Subtracting actual NP-MOOP spending (even capped, as proposed for the PPM) will capture these need-based differences in a way that the ex ante expected cost-sharing approach would not.

On the other hand, a threshold need that includes both the insurance premium and expected cost sharing would allow a more complete accounting of the impact of health insurance benefits on poverty. For example, Medicaid has

---

[5] As envisioned by Korenman and Remler (2016), a health insurance sharing unit is a subunit of the PPM unit consisting of persons covered by the same health insurance policy (or policies), one of whom is designated by the CPS-ASEC as the policy holder. Poverty status is determined for each PPM unit ("household") by aggregating resources and needs of the health insurance units to the PPM unit (household) level.

very low copays and would meet nearly all medical care and insurance needs. Employer-provided health insurance generally has an actuarial value higher than 70 percent and could be credited for meeting a larger portion of the full insurance-plus-care need.[6]

3.3.1. Threshold Health Insurance Need

That medical care is a basic need seems self-explanatory; the harder question, in terms of measuring poverty, is *how much* medical care should represent the modern standard. A key insight of the HIPM research is that a substantial portion of the basic need for medical care can be represented by the value of an insurance policy. In practice, this requires choosing an insurance policy to represent the basic need and, inevitably, not everyone will agree on which specific plan best represents the basic need. Because of differences in health insurance coverage options that depend on age and disability status, the policy that represents the basic need must vary based on those characteristics. For nondisabled individuals younger than age 65, the ACA benchmark plan presents a straightforward option for establishing the dollar level that should be added to the PPM threshold to reflect the need for health insurance. The ACA benchmark provides a practical and conceptually valid answer to the question: how much cash income would an uninsured person need to obtain a basic health insurance policy? Thus, in implementing the health-inclusive element of the PPM, the panel proposes adding the unsubsidized age-specific cost of the ACA benchmark Silver plan in an individual's region to the threshold for individuals under age 65.[7]

RECOMMENDATION 3.2: For individuals under age 65 (excluding those who have Medicare due to disability), the Affordable Care Act (ACA) benchmark health insurance plan should be used to represent the basic health insurance need for a typical American household (or the designated resource-sharing unit for poverty measurement). The ACA defines a benchmark plan as the second-lowest-cost Silver plan available in the health insurance Marketplace in an individual's geographic area. The Silver plan for those age 65 and over who are not covered by Medicare is also the basic health insurance need.

Using the ACA benchmark plans may limit the ability to construct a consistent pre-2014 historical series for the PPM. The panel recognizes this limitation but does not believe it is a strong enough reason to preclude recommendation of these revisions.

For Americans age 65 and older, as well as those who are younger but qualify for Medicare on the basis of disability, the threshold need for health insurance is defined as the full cost, including the government contribution, of Medicare, if the recipient were to choose the cheapest Medicare Advantage plan that includes a prescription drug plan (MAPD plan) available in their location (e.g., county of residence, if that information is available; if not, state of residence).

RECOMMENDATION 3.3: For the population age 65 and older covered by Medicare, as well as those under 65 who qualify for Medicare based on disability, the basic need level should be set based on the full cost of a Medicare Advantage plan that provides prescription drug coverage. The cost of this plan should be calculated as per-recipient federal spending on Medicare Parts A, B, and D, *plus* the lowest-cost out-of-pocket premium for the Medicare Advantage plan that includes a prescription drug plan.

As detailed below, the MAPD out-of-pocket premium is the additional premium required for the MAPD plan above the required Part B premium.

---

[6]Remler and Korenman (2022) provide estimates and further discussion of these issues. They have not developed similar methods for incorporating Medicare, however.
[7]Marketplace premiums may also vary by smoking status. The HIPM proposed by Korenman and Remler (2016) used the premium for nonsmokers. The PPM could allow the threshold need to vary by smoking status. The panel has not made a recommendation on this feature.

3.3.2. Resources

The National Academies' 1995 panel, in discussing challenges to incorporating medical care in poverty measurement, highlighted the challenges associated with determining how much of the value of health insurance transfers should be considered fungible—that is, a resource that can be used to meet other needs. This panel shares those concerns and, therefore, the proposed PPM approach, like the HIPM, caps the value of the health insurance transfer included in resources at the amount included in the needs threshold. Thus, mathematically, the PPM approach to including these transfers in resources cannot lift an SPM-poor household out of poverty, since an equal or greater amount has been added to the threshold.

RECOMMENDATION 3.4: The definition of resources in the Principal Poverty Measure should include a value for any health insurance benefits or subsidies received from an employer or from the government but must also reflect the fact that such transfers cannot be used to pay for nonhealth needs. This is achieved by capping the value of the transfer that is added to resources at an amount that is less than or equal to the health insurance need that is added to the threshold.

Finally, NP-MOOP costs should also be deducted from resources, subject to a cap. This is similar to the SPM approach, with the addition of a cap for individuals who are not Medicare eligible. Starting in 2025, it will also be possible to cap the deduction for cost-sharing expenses for Medicare recipients, since the Inflation Reduction Act of 2022[8] caps prescription drug out-of-pocket spending at $2,000.[9] The cap is operationalized by using the out-of-pocket limits specified in ACA Marketplace plans or other information about health insurance status and household characteristics. For example, many households covered by Medicaid with no cost sharing required would have their deduction for NP-MOOP spending capped at zero. This approach allows the PPM to capture variation in actual medical care spending needs associated with worse health status, as noted above, without implicitly deeming an unlimited amount of NP-MOOP spending to be necessary.

RECOMMENDATION 3.5: Medical out-of-pocket spending should be subtracted from resources in the Principal Poverty Measure. For individuals who are not covered by Medicare, this subtraction should be capped at the out-of-pocket maximum for Affordable Care Act Marketplace plans or lower, depending on health insurance status and other household characteristics. Out-of-pocket spending by Medicare recipients can also be capped starting in 2025, due to changes enacted under the Inflation Reduction Act, and the panel recommends doing so.

To give specific examples of how health insurance benefits and cost-sharing amounts are calculated for the resource measure, several illustrative scenarios follow (additional details of each are presented in Appendix 3B):

- For those with *employer-sponsored health insurance*, the value of the threshold need is added to resources as the health insurance benefit value (regardless of the actual value of their coverage). Reported out-of-pocket premiums paid by the household, capped at the value of the threshold need, are subtracted from the health insurance benefit value to form a net health insurance benefit amount. This amount—the benchmark premium minus capped out-of-pocket spending on health insurance premiums—is intended to stand in for the net value of the health insurance transfer from the employer. Reported nonpremium out-of-pocket expenses, capped at the benchmark maximum out-of-pocket expense, are also subtracted from resources.[10] Hence, for a family with employer-provided insurance spending less than the caps, the family's poverty status under the PPM and the SPM

---

[8] See www.congress.gov/bill/117th-congress/house-bill/5376/text.

[9] The $2,000 cap is adjusted for inflation annually after that time. In 2024, the cap will be $3,250, accomplished by eliminating the 5 percent beneficiary coinsurance requirement above the catastrophic coverage threshold.

[10] Most employer plans have better coverage than the benchmark Silver plan, and lower out-of-pocket limits (benchmark out-of-pocket limits are quite high). The ACA defines minimum value for employer plans and if an employer does not offer a plan with minimum value, an employee can decline the employer plan and buy the benchmark Marketplace plan and get a premium subsidy, if eligible. If the employer offers a plan of minimum value that is "affordable" coverage as defined by the ACA, then the employee would not be eligible for subsidies for Marketplace plans. See, for example, Norris (2021).

will be the same (see line 2a in both Panel 1A and 1B in Appendix 3B). Veteran's Tricare is treated the same way. Those who are offered an employer plan but no subsidy (e.g., under COBRA) would have the benchmark plan value added to resources and a large premium payment subtracted, resulting in a zero health insurance benefit value. This process correctly shows that they will be poor if they lack sufficient cash income to meet the health insurance need in the threshold and the additional income and benefits to meet their other basic needs.

- For those with *subsidized ACA marketplace coverage*, the amount of the ACA premium subsidy is added to resources. Nonpremium out-of-pocket expenses, capped at the maximum out-of-pocket for the benchmark plan, are subtracted from resources.[11] (See line 2c in Panel 1B in Appendix 3B.)
- Those with *unsubsidized ACA marketplace coverage* and those who buy insurance directly from an insurance company outside the Marketplace receive no health insurance transfer, and thus no net health insurance benefit amount is added to their resources, nor is out-of-pocket *premium* spending subtracted from their resources, since their need for health insurance is already captured by the need included in the threshold.[12] Nonpremium out-of-pocket expenses, capped at the benchmark maximum out-of-pocket, are subtracted from resources (see line 2d in Panel 1B in Appendix 3B). Note that this is quite different from the way such a household would be treated in the current SPM, which does not include a threshold need for health insurance but would subtract all premium and nonpremium out-of-pocket spending from the household's resources (see line 2d in Panel 1A in Appendix 3B).
- For those with *Medicaid*, the value of the threshold need is added to both the threshold and to resources. In most cases, no premium is required, and cost sharing is limited. But in cases requiring a small premium and/or cost sharing, these are deducted from resources.[13] The panel considers this to reflect incomplete insurance so, consistent with those getting a subsidy to purchase coverage on the Marketplace, cost sharing is taken as a reduction to resources, while the value of Medicaid is added to resources. For those covered by VA Health Care, the approach is the same.
- For those with *Medicare*, to form a net health insurance transfer value, the value of the threshold need is first added to resources. Recall that threshold need value is defined as equal to the full cost of Medicare: actuarial value (per-beneficiary federal spending on Medicare Parts A, B, and D) plus the lowest-cost MAPD out-of-pocket premium in the county of residence. For the net transfer value, the beneficiary's required Part B premium is then subtracted from resources, as is additional reported premium spending, capped at the lowest-cost MAPD additional premium amount. (The Part B premium is zero for those with incomes below 132% of the federal poverty level.) To capture the need to pay for cost sharing, nonpremium out-of-pocket expenses are also subtracted from resources, and for Medicare beneficiaries, there is currently no cap on the amount that may be subtracted.[14] This will change in 2025, when a cap will apply to Medicare beneficiaries; at that time, Medicare beneficiaries should be treated consistently with the approach recommended for those with employer coverage, other private coverage, and ACA coverage, in which NP-MOOP expenses are capped.
- For those with *no health insurance*, nothing is added to resources. Nonpremium out-of-pocket expenses, capped at the benchmark maximum out-of-pocket, are subtracted from resources.[15] The logic behind this

---

[11] For those eligible for ACA cost-sharing subsidies, the PPM nonpremium MOOP costs cap is lowered according to a sliding scale based on income.

[12] Those able to purchase a plan as a result of the ACA do benefit from the existence of an ACA Marketplace and from community rating and guaranteed issue, but if they do not qualify for a subsidy, they must still have sufficient cash income to purchase the benchmark plan.

[13] Medicaid NP-MOOP amounts could be capped either using state-specific policy parameters or, more simply, at 5 percent of income according to federal requirements.

[14] An MAPD plan was chosen as the threshold need plan for the PPM (and the HIPM before it) because these plans limit out-of-pocket spending on medical care. However, MAPD plans have not limited out-of-pocket spending on prescription drugs (those with very high expenditures may pay 5% copays on marginal expenditures). If the CPS-ASEC collected separate spending amounts for out-of-pocket spending on medical care and prescription drugs, the medical care portion of the cost-sharing deduction could be capped. Moreover, due to Medicare changes in the Inflation Reduction Act, out-of-pocket spending on prescription drugs will be capped at $3,250 in 2024 and $2,000 in 2025 and indexed thereafter (Cubanski et al., 2022). Thus, the deduction from resources for cost-sharing expenses for Medicare recipients in the PPM should also be capped beginning with calendar year 2024.

[15] Uninsured individuals are matched to a benchmark plan, based on individual characteristics and geography, to determine the maximum out-of-pocket payment.

approach is that a person should not be deemed poor if they have sufficient resources to meet their nonhealth needs, purchase the benchmark plan, and pay for their medical cost-sharing expenses up to the maximum out-of-pocket limit under the benchmark plan. If an uninsured person spends more than the maximum cost-sharing amount out of pocket, such expenditures would be considered discretionary in the sense that they could have been avoided by purchasing the basic insurance plan and are therefore capped at the out-of-pocket maximum. While there is room for debate on this point, the approach reflects a consistent and practical choice for determining a basic need for medical care for the purpose of poverty measurement.

3.3.3. Future Considerations

The proposed approach raises three questions that the panel leaves for future research: (1) How should free and reduced-price care be incorporated into poverty measurement? (2) Does poverty measurement—either the SPM or the PPM—adequately account for the greater needs of households that include individuals with disabilities? and (3) What happens to PPM poverty if there are changes in the policies on which this approach implicitly relies (specifically, the specification of a benchmark plan, and its guaranteed availability at a community-related premium)?

On the first question, regarding free care: conceptually, free and reduced-price medical care should be counted as a resource for households that use it, or households that have the option of using it. For example, one might impute a resource value reflecting the availability of free care from a Federally Qualified Health Center in a given geographic area.[16] At this point the panel does not recommend including free care in the measure, but suggests that free care, as well as reduced-price care, be studied in the future.

On the second question, the panel deems it important to study ways to better incorporate the needs of individuals with a variety of disabilities into the measurement of poverty. These needs may include specialized equipment, aides, housing modifications, and counseling—many of which are not covered by health insurance. Research should continue to develop ways to incorporate these needs, both medical and nonmedical, into poverty measurement. In the panel's opinion, this is not a reason to defer the adoption of the PPM to improve the accuracy of poverty measurement.

Finally, what happens to PPM poverty if there are changes in policy? Changes in the benchmark plan—for example, revisions over time to the generosity of coverage—are likely, but they present no methodological challenge since the PPM incorporates these changes into both resources and needs. More problematic would be changes in the ACA guaranteed issue and community rating regulations, since these are required for the determination of the threshold health insurance need specific to each household. Without guaranteed issue, there is no assurance that a person with a given amount of income could purchase an insurance policy that meets their basic health needs. Without community rating, insurance premiums could once again depend on detailed health characteristics (e.g., preexisting conditions), and determining the basic plan premium would require access to the detailed health information and actuarial models used to set private insurance premiums. Indeed, this would represent a return to the conditions that led the National Academies' 1995 panel to exclude health needs and health insurance benefits from the recommended approach that became the SPM.

In this chapter, the panel's case has been made that the Census Bureau should move forward with development of a PPM that incorporates an explicit need for health insurance in the threshold, adds the value of health insurance transfers to resources, and modifies the deduction of MOOP spending from resources so that only *nonpremium* MOOP expenses are deducted. Medical care is a major component of individual spending, whether directly or in the form of health insurance. It is a major and growing component of the U.S. gross domestic product. Medicaid and Medicare are by far the government's largest in-kind transfer programs, and health insurance is the largest nonwage benefit provided by employers. To accurately measure poverty, it is necessary to include the need for care and the value of these transfers. This chapter describes the best way to do so, using the framework of the health-inclusive poverty measure. The panel recommends that the PPM incorporate this approach.

---

[16] Korenman et al. (2018) present estimates using alternative approaches to incorporating implicit insurance values of free care to the uninsured in HIPM estimation for the state of New York.

Appendix 3A

Alternative Approaches to Accounting for Medical Care in a Poverty Measure

The approach recommended in this report for incorporating medical care into the measurement of poverty builds on the Health-Inclusive Poverty Measure (Korenman and Remler, 2016; Korenman et al., 2019; Remler and Korenman, 2023b). Alternative approaches have been proposed, including the incorporation of medical out-of-pocket spending into Supplemental Poverty Measure (SPM) thresholds; multiple-index methods that treat health risk and needs as a distinct dimension of poverty; and a full-income approach. Table 3-1 provides an overview of the treatment of health and medical care in these three measures as well as in the Official Poverty Measure (OPM), the SPM, and the HIPM. Here, this issue is reviewed in greater detail.

Official Poverty Measure: The OPM does not explicitly treat health, medical care, or health insurance as needs. Government transfers of health insurance and employer payments for health insurance on an employee's behalf are not treated as household resources; and medical out-of-pocket (MOOP) spending is not deducted from resources. Thus, the OPM mostly ignores medical care, and changes in the OPM over time reflect neither increases in households' medical care cost burden nor any offsetting effects of public health insurance programs such as Medicare and Medicaid.

Supplemental Poverty Measure: SPM thresholds do not include a need for medical care, particularly care paid by insurance. Instead, they include an implicit need for care or insurance paid for out of pocket, by subtracting health insurance premiums and other MOOP expenses (e.g., copays, deductibles) from resources. Expansions of public health insurance coverage or increases in medical care costs are reflected in the SPM only as far as they affect household out-of-pocket spending. There are no adjustments for underspending by those who are not insured or underinsured. In contrast, since premiums are subtracted from resources while subsidies are not included in resources, those who receive subsidized benefits could appear to experience higher levels of poverty.

Health-Inclusive Poverty Measure: The HIPM proposed by Korenman and Remler (2016), described in detail in National Academies of Sciences, Engineering, and Medicine (2019) and Korenman et al. (2019), accounts for health insurance/medical care in calculating thresholds and resources. Specifically, a need for health insurance, as a proxy for medical care, is explicitly added to the SPM's expenditure-based threshold, while the value of health insurance benefits received from the government or an employer (e.g., Medicare, Medicaid, employer-provided coverage) is added to resources and a capped amount of MOOP spending is subtracted from resources. The HIPM and the proposed approach for incorporating it into the Principal Poverty Measure are described in detail in Chapter 3.

Supplemental Poverty Measure with MOOP in Threshold (SPM-MIT): The SPM-MIT is conceptually similar to the SPM, as the name suggests. The main difference is that, instead of subtracting MOOP costs from household resources, a measure of the need for MOOP spending is added to the threshold, as originally proposed by Bavier (2000) and implemented experimentally by Short and Garner (2002) and Bavier (2006). One advantage of this approach relative to the SPM is that the threshold need for MOOP spending in the SPM-MIT is a predicted measure of a household's expected need for medical spending, based on family size, age, and health insurance status (Garner et al., 2014)—in contrast to actual MOOP costs subtracted from resources in the SPM. This addresses a key concern about the SPM's treatment of uninsured households, which may have significant unmet needs for medical care that would not be captured by subtracting actual MOOP expenditures from resources. However, like the SPM, the SPM-MIT is limited in its ability to capture the impact of any expansion of public health insurance programs on poverty; the SPM-MIT will capture such impacts only as far as they affect expected MOOP spending.

Two-Index Measure: In 1995, the National Academies panel recommending the SPM wanted to include medical care in the measure of poverty but recognized multiple validity problems in doing so. The panel suggested using a two-index measure, in which the second index would capture the medical care economic risk (MCER) to the population relative to the adequacy of their health insurance coverage to pay for their medical care needs. The Institute of Medicine and National Research Council (2012b) developed recommendations to estimate the proportion of the population at risk of incurring high MOOP expenses in relation to their resources as a second index to accompany the SPM, to better measure economic vulnerability. The SPM would serve as the core measure of poverty and include MOOP expenses as a deduction from resources, while MCER would serve as a second index that would capture the economic risk from having no or inadequate health insurance. The poverty status of an individual or family could then be determined by the core index or by a combination of the two indices. Using two indices would remove the issue of fungibility of health insurance as a resource in the core measure.

Technically, the MCER could be based on individual risk aggregated up to families. Individuals could be divided into a set of categories used for predictions of economic risk based on age group, sex, and broad measures of health. Such an approach would be useful to measure reductions in economic risk from medical expenditures due to changes in policy, such as the Affordable Care Act, Medicaid, and Medicare. However, this approach implicitly requires using the two indices together to measure poverty, which may not be politically viable; the approach does not address underutilization of care by the un- and underinsured; and it is difficult to measure accurately with current data sets.

Full-Income Poverty Measure: Burkhauser et al. (2020) define a Full-Income Poverty Measure (FPM) to evaluate the impact of the War on Poverty. The year 1963 is treated as the benchmark for this evaluation, which can be used to capture the impact of a wide range of antipoverty programs, including those that provide in-kind benefits (e.g., Medicare and Medicaid) and those that are administered through the tax code (e.g., the Earned Income Tax Credit). As Burkhauser et al. (2020) discuss, neither the OPM nor the SPM is suitable for this purpose, not only due to the failure to fully incorporate the value of in-kind transfers (the OPM excludes all in-kind transfers and the SPM excludes Medicare and Medicaid), but also due to changing thresholds over time, which deviate from the standard used in 1963.[1]

In the FPM, resources include market income *plus* cash transfers, the market value of in-kind transfers (including Medicare and Medicaid), the market value of employer contributions to employees' health insurance premiums, and tax credits—*minus* federal income and payroll taxes. Thus, in terms of its treatment of health and medical care, FPM resources are more inclusive than resources in the SPM, which reflect Medicare, Medicaid, and employer-provided insurance only as far as they reduce households' MOOP spending.

On the threshold side, the FPM sets the threshold to achieve the official poverty rate in 1963 of 20 percent. This threshold is then updated annually using the Personal Consumption Expenditure price index. A need for health insurance or medical care is not explicitly included in the threshold; these goods are implicitly included in

---

[1] The specific reasons why the OPM and the SPM are not suitable for this purpose differ from each other, and interested readers are referred to Burkhauser et al. (2020, pp. 25-27).

the baseline threshold to the extent that they were being consumed in 1963. This approach embraces the idea that the correct yardstick for measuring the success of the War on Poverty is its effectiveness in reducing what would have been considered poverty in 1963, updated for rising average prices.

Over time, due to technological advances in medical care, an absolute poverty threshold that includes medical care becomes less meaningful. The 1963 medical care "good" held constant in the absolute threshold bundle becomes inexpensive to purchase (if it is even available). The health insurance benefits included in resources valued in today's dollars buy care that is far more valuable than the now inexpensive but antiquated care of 1963 represented in the threshold. As a result, over time, a growing health benefit far exceeds the threshold medical care need and is assumed available to meet nonmedical needs. This distortion of the FPM is the result of an interaction between absoluteness of the medical care need in the threshold and the fact that health insurance benefits are not truly fungible resources; and, over decades, the distortion can grow large. The result can be seen in FPM trends between 1963 and 2017: the value of Medicare benefits for an eligible couple in 2017 exceeds the entirety of the couple's FPM threshold. Obviously, while Medicare benefits are a highly valuable resource, they alone cannot meet all basic medical care needs, as implied by FPM analyses. Thus, the current panel does not view the FPM's treatment of health insurance as a viable alternative to the SPM for ongoing poverty measurement.

Two remaining approaches to modifying the poverty measure are not included in this Appendix because they do not explicitly deal with health or health insurance. These are: (1) the SPM-absolute measure (Wimer et al., 2016) which anchors the SPM threshold to keep it absolute rather than allowing it to change with the 33rd percentile of food, clothing, shelter, and utilities (no specific treatment of medical care or insurance is considered that differs from the SPM); and (2) the Meyer and Sullivan (2012) estimate of consumption poverty with and without including medical spending. Meyer and Sullivan prefer to exclude MOOP spending, arguing that it likely represents substantial need or lack of good insurance (p. 142), and that medical spending might better be viewed as an investment similar to education, and thus should be excluded from a consumption-based measure. They also explore using a fungible value of public health insurance.

Appendix 3B

Examples of PPM versus SPM Treatment of Health Insurance and Medical Care

This Appendix provides simple examples to illustrate how the Principal Poverty Measure (PPM) and the Supplemental Poverty Measure (SPM) differ in their treatment of health insurance and medical care. Consider first *individuals under the age of 65 who do not have Medicare* (Example 1). These individuals may have employer-sponsored coverage, Medicaid, subsidized Marketplace coverage, unsubsidized Marketplace (or other nongroup) coverage, or they may be uninsured. In each example, the hypothetical values for total premiums and out-of-pocket spending for premiums and medical care are first introduced.

Panel 1A shows how individuals with each type of coverage would be treated under the SPM. None of the individuals have an addition to needs under the SPM. Actual out-of-pocket spending on premiums, which depends on insurance type, is subtracted from resources. Actual out-of-pocket spending on medical care, which is assumed in this example to be the same regardless of insurance type, is also subtracted from resources. Panel 1B shows how individuals with each type of coverage would be treated under the PPM.

Regardless of insurance type, the *benchmark premium*—here assumed to be $5,000—is added to needs. The *net value of health insurance transfers* is added to resources. This value depends on insurance type, as shown in Panel 1B. For individuals with employer-sponsored coverage or Medicaid, the net transfer value is calculated by subtracting the individual's actual out-of-pocket spending on premiums from the benchmark premium; the amount subtracted is capped at the value of the benchmark premium so that the net transfer value will always be greater than or equal to zero. For individuals with a premium tax credit for Marketplace coverage, the net value of the health insurance transfer added to resources is the value of the tax credit. Individuals with unsubsidized private coverage or no coverage at all are not receiving a health insurance transfer, so nothing is added to their resources. Finally, actual nonpremium out-of-pocket spending on medical care (MOOP), which is assumed in this example to be the same regardless of insurance type, is also subtracted from resources for all individuals; this subtraction is capped at the out-of-pocket spending limit for the benchmark Silver Marketplace plan.

For most individuals with insurance benefits, the SPM and the PPM yield the same poverty status. This is because the inclusion of the benchmark premium in the PPM needs threshold is largely offset by the addition of health insurance transfers to resources. For individuals without health insurance benefits, however, more of these individuals will likely be counted as poor by the PPM than by the SPM, because the PPM needs threshold includes the benchmark premium, but there is no addition to resources. In addition, for individuals with all insurance types, the fact that the subtraction of MOOP spending from resources is capped under the PPM but not the SPM may result in some individuals with very high MOOP spending being classified as nonpoor under the PPM approach while they would have been classified as poor according to the SPM.

CHALLENGING CATEGORIES: MEDICAL CARE

Example 2 illustrates how the SPM and the PPM treat Medicare beneficiaries. The SPM adds nothing to the threshold and deducts actual out-of-pocket spending on health insurance premiums and medical care from resources. The PPM, in contrast, adds an imputed Medicare premium to the need threshold. The value of the imputed premium is based on the average government outlays for Medicare Parts A, B, and D, plus the lowest out-of-pocket premium for a Medicare Advantage plan that includes prescription drug coverage (MAPD plan). This quantity is intended to reflect the average cost of a plan that provides a standard package of benefits. The PPM then adds to household resources the net value of the health insurance transfer from the government, calculated as the imputed Medicare premium minus the individual's out-of-pocket premium for Part B. Finally, actual nonpremium MOOP spending is also subtracted from resources for all individuals. (In 2025, it will be possible to cap these subtractions according to changes passed in the Inflation Reduction Act. The Act limits the maximum out-of-pocket spending on prescription drugs in 2025 to $2,000, indexed to inflation. Thus, MAPD plans will have identifiable maximum out-of-pocket limits for medical care and prescription drug spending.)

Example 1: Single individual, age less than 65 and not Medicare eligible

Assumptions
- Benchmark premium is $5,000
- Out-of-pocket spending on premiums varies with coverage type:
  - Employer-sponsored coverage: $1,200
  - Medicaid: $60
  - Marketplace coverage with a tax credit: $1,000; value of tax credit is $4,000
  - Marketplace coverage without a tax credit: $5,000
- Regardless of coverage type, non-premium MOOP spending is $500

Panel 1A Supplemental Poverty Measure	Resources ($)	Needs ($)
1. Threshold adjustment: None		
2. Resource adjustment for health insurance premiums: Subtract actual out-of-pocket premium spending (uncapped) from resources (choose *one*):		
a. Individual has *employer-sponsored coverage*	−1,200	
b. Individual has *Medicaid*	−60	
c. Individual has *subsidized Marketplace coverage*	−1,000	
d. Individual has *unsubsidized private coverage*	−5,000	
e. Individual is *uninsured*	0	
3. Resource adjustment for out-of-pocket medical care: Subtract reported MOOP spending (uncapped)	−500	

Panel 1B Principal Poverty Measure	Resources ($)	Needs ($)
1. Threshold adjustment: Add benchmark premium to needs threshold		+5,000
2. Resource adjustment for health insurance premiums: Add net value of any transfer from government/employer (choose *one*):		
a. Individual has *employer-sponsored coverage*: Add imputed net value of transfer		
Add benchmark premium	+5,000	
Subtract actual out-of-pocket premium spending (capped) from resources	−1,200	
b. Individual has *Medicaid*: Add imputed net value of transfer		
Add benchmark premium	+5,000	
Subtract actual out-of-pocket premium spending (capped) from resources	−60	
c. Individual has *subsidized Marketplace coverage*: Add value of tax credit	+4,000	
d. Individual has *unsubsidized private coverage*: No premium adjustment	0	
e. Individual is *uninsured*: No premium adjustment	0	
3. Resource adjustment for out-of-pocket medical care: Subtract reported MOOP costs (capped)	−500	

Example 2: Single individual with Medicare based on age or disability

Assumptions

- Imputed Medicare premium is $10,000 (calculated as average government outlays for Parts A, B, and D of Medicare, plus the lowest out-of-pocket premium for a Medicare Advantage plan that includes prescription drug coverage)
- Out-of-pocket premium spending on Part B is $1,800
- Out-of-pocket spending on medical care is $1,000

Panel 2A: Supplemental Poverty Measure	Resources ($)	Needs ($)
1. Threshold adjustment: None		0
2. Resource adjustment for health insurance premiums:		
Subtract actual Part B premium	−1,800	
3. Resource adjustment for MOOP spending: Subtract reported MOOP spending (uncapped)	−1,000	
Net effect of health insurance on (resources − needs) = (−$1,800 − $1,000) −0 = −$2,800		

Panel 2B: Principal Poverty Measure	Resources ($)	Needs ($)
1. Threshold adjustment: Add imputed Medicare premium to needs		+10,000
2. Resource adjustments for health insurance premiums:		
Add average total value of Medicare spending to resources	+10,000	
Subtract actual Part B out-of-pocket premium	−1,800	
3. Resource adjustment for out-of-pocket medical care: Subtract reported out-of-pocket medical care or prescription drug spending (currently uncapped)	−1,000	
Net effect of health insurance on (resources − needs) = (10,000 −1,800 − 1,000) −10,000 = −$2,800		

4

Challenging Categories: Childcare

4.1. BACKGROUND AND MOTIVATION

Among those who pay for childcare, out-of-pocket childcare costs as a percent of household budgets have increased more than any other budget element since the 1960s. According to Lino et al. (2017), childcare costs represent 16 percent of family budgets among families who pay for childcare, the third-largest component after housing (29%) and transportation (18%). Childcare costs represent an even larger share of the household budget for low-income families with preschool-aged children (U.S. Census Bureau, 2011; Mattingly and Wimer, 2017).

Moreover, the federal government spends a substantial amount on childcare subsidies, the value of which is not currently tracked in either the Official Poverty Measure or Supplemental Poverty Measure (SPM). In 2019, the two largest federal programs, the Child Care and Development Fund (CCDF) and Head Start, provided $20 billion in childcare support for low-income families (Congressional Budget Office, 2021). The impact of these important policies affecting resources to families with low incomes is not adequately captured in the current methodology, and that is a major motivation to improve this component of poverty measurement. Additionally, in recent years, the Child and Dependent Care Tax Credit—a nonrefundable tax credit that reduces federal income tax liability based on child- and dependent-care expenses incurred by taxpayers who work or are looking for work—provided about $4 billion in annual support for low- and middle-income families (Congressional Research Service, 2021). As detailed in Chapter 2, Child and Dependent Care Tax Credits are included in estimates of available resources in the current SPM.

The recommendations in this chapter are intended to contribute to a more complete and transparent accounting of childcare costs and resources, while recognizing that development of an approach for implementation as part of the proposed Principal Poverty Measure (PPM) will require a considerable amount of additional research.

4.2. CURRENT SUPPLEMENTAL POVERTY MEASURE TREATMENT—STRENGTHS AND WEAKNESSES

The SPM has a very simple approach to incorporating childcare costs: if both parents (or single parents[1]) work, the SPM deducts the amount paid for childcare from resources, as a work-related expense (capped at the amount

---
[1] Throughout this chapter, "parent" is used as shorthand for any person acting in a parental capacity. For example, in some cases, a child's caregivers may be grandparents or other relatives.

of earnings of the lowest-paid parent).[2] Amounts are estimated from the Current Population Survey Annual Social and Economic Supplement (CPS-ASEC), in which respondents are asked if they pay for childcare and, if so, how much they pay while the parents are working. The SPM, then, treats childcare costs the way it treats work-related expenses such as commuting costs.[3]

The current SPM approach is simple to implement using data available in the CPS-ASEC. However, the approach has several shortcomings if the goal is to comprehensively assess the impact of childcare needs and costs on a family's wellbeing and/or to capture the impact of government spending in this domain. The current method makes overly simplistic assumptions about families' childcare needs and costs. One simple-to-correct flaw is that parents who are not working are assumed to have no childcare costs, even if they are engaged in activities such as education and training. This assumption is inconsistent with childcare subsidy rules, which recognize education/training as an activity requiring childcare.[4] Similarly, an employed parent is assumed to have no need for childcare, and therefore no childcare costs, if a nonemployed parent is in the home—even if that parent is unable to provide care due to disability, ill health, or some other limitation.

To address these problems, the panel recommends correcting the current approach by: (1) treating parents who are engaged in education or training the same way as parents who are employed; and (2) not assuming that a parent who is not working and is disabled is available to provide childcare while the other parent is working or engaged in education. This correction would be consistent with childcare subsidy rules that consider educational activities equivalent to work for the purposes of subsidy eligibility and would also more accurately reflect families' childcare needs. The panel sees this as an issue that could be addressed in the near term and thus recommends it for immediate action.

RECOMMENDATION 4.1: In households with children under the age of 13 (or, in line with current childcare subsidy rules, up to age 18 if disabled), parents who are in education or training should be treated like parents who are employed, and a parent who is not working and is disabled should not be assumed to be available to provide childcare while the other parent is working or in education/training.

More consequentially, a large proportion of childcare is omitted from the current SPM because the SPM's specification only addresses paid childcare used by employed parents. Uncompensated childcare provided by working parents (e.g., parents who work opposite schedules), friends, or family is unrecognized, as is care provided by parents who are not in the labor force. Childcare purchased by nonemployed parents is also omitted from the current measure. In all these scenarios, the current SPM treatment of childcare understates childcare needs and expenses and therefore overstates financial resources.

These omissions derive from a conceptual flaw: the current approach views childcare as a need only if parents are working in the labor market, and it takes childcare into account only if parents pay for it in the market. However, an alternative view—one that the panel endorses—is that *all* households with children have a need for childcare. Some parents meet that need by purchasing childcare in the market, some use fully or partially subsidized care, some rely on unpaid care provided by friends or family members, some provide care themselves, and of course many use a mix of modes or switch modes over time. Ideally, PPM thresholds in the future would include a childcare need for all households with children in a way that parallels the treatment of food, shelter, utilities, and (in the panel's proposal) medical care. Specifically, a need for childcare should be included for all households with one or more children under the age of 13 (or with disabled children up to the age of 18). These age groups are selected in line with current childcare subsidy rules. Achieving this conceptual ideal, however, depends on whether the need can be conceptually well defined and feasibly measured.

Balancing the inclusion of a childcare need in the threshold, the PPM would ideally also account for childcare subsidies on the resource side. This would address the second shortcoming of the current measure—that childcare

---

[2] Childcare expenses are currently subtracted as reported (after capping).

[3] Equation 2.2 in Appendix 2A describes how these out-of-pocket costs are subtracted from resources available to a household.

[4] For instance, under the Child Care Development Block Grant Act, states can use Child Care and Development Fund resources to offer childcare to low-income families so that parents can work or attend job training or educational programs.

assistance is not systematically accounted for in the resource estimate, and thus the effect of childcare policies is invisible. This is problematic since one of the primary purposes of the SPM/PPM is to gauge the effects of policies on poverty and, as discussed above, the federal government spends a substantial sum on childcare assistance. Additionally, once a valuation approach is agreed upon, the receipt of unpaid care would ideally also be valued as a resource (just as the rental value of a home owned free and clear would be included as a resource in the panel's proposal).

4.3. AN IMPROVED APPROACH

Given the above-described shortcomings, an updated approach to account for childcare in the SPM is warranted. An updated approach, once developed, would improve the accuracy, consistency, and transparency of the updated poverty measure. Importantly, although an updated approach will require considerable additional research and development, the construct envisioned here is now more feasible than it would have been when the SPM was originally designed. The increased availability of state- and even county-level databases on childcare prices (some of which are discussed below) is a key reason for this greater feasibility. As outlined in Chapter 2 and stated in Recommendation 2.4, the panel proposes ultimately broadening the number of explicit basic needs categories beyond the current food, clothing, shelter, utilities, telephone, and internet (FCSUti) to include childcare (along with medical care).[5]

The panel recognizes that, in contrast to the proposed approach to medical care, full implementation of the PPM approach to childcare requires further research and possibly new data. For this reason, the panel believes it prudent to distinguish three stages of revision: (1) changes that should be made immediately to fix problems with the current SPM approach to childcare (Recommendation 4.1); (2) changes that the Census Bureau could make in the near future after further research to bring *paid* childcare and childcare subsidies into the threshold and resources respectively; and (3) changes that would require considerable research and discussion to address the issue of *unpaid* childcare.

Action on stages 2 and 3 begins with the recognition that households with children vary considerably in whether or how much they use paid childcare and the types of care used. Defining a childcare need and assigning the appropriate dollar amount to meet that need is complex, as it is for medical care need, and research on the former is at an early stage. For this reason, additional research is needed to build consensus on the conceptual issues and to develop practical methods for implementation, as has been done for medical care. The recommendations in this chapter, therefore, reflect incremental steps that, along with future research, could improve the accuracy, consistency, and transparency of childcare in the SPM.

4.3.1. Broadening the Concept of Childcare Need

To more accurately capture families' childcare needs, the panel recommends the following. First, as stated in Recommendation 2.4, a set of childcare needs should be developed for the threshold for households with children under the age of 13 (or up to age 18 if a child is disabled)—as is done with other elements of the FCSUti bundle. This would increase transparency in the SPM by making explicit the full range of basic needs categories faced by households, and it would also increase consistency with the handling of other costs. Consistent with the incremental approach endorsed by the panel, the childcare need would initially be assigned only to households that use paid childcare—but ideally, in the future, this need would be assigned to all households with children.

RECOMMENDATION 4.2: For households with children under the age of 13 (or up to age 18, if disabled) that are using paid childcare (paid out of pocket and/or subsidized), a basic childcare need should be included in the threshold. In the near future, the Census Bureau should conduct research to develop and implement a methodology for defining the amount of this basic childcare need, varying by age and number of children, geographic location, and hours of paid care used.

---

[5]Childcare may actually be a more consistent expense for families than some other threshold categories. For example, medical care and clothing both tend to be temporally "lumpy" purchases, but childcare is a constant and smooth purchase.

Childcare costs for paid care vary substantially by age, number of children, types of care (home-based, center-based), quality, hours, and geographic location, among other dimensions. Some of these elements (e.g., type, quality, and hours of care) are subject to parental choice and can vary considerably even within the course of a year, while age, number of children, and geographic location are relatively more fixed. For this reason, the panel recommends establishing a basic need defined by age and number of children and geographic location.

One option for establishing the basic childcare need is to use state and federal policies directing reimbursement rates for subsidized care. Each state collects considerable data on childcare costs through childcare market rate surveys and sets reimbursement levels as part of their Child Care and Development Fund (CCDF) programs. Another option for informing threshold need amounts that the Census Bureau might explore is the National Database of Childcare Prices (NDCP). The NDCP is an official federal (U.S. Department of Labor) data source that provides price information at the county level by type of provider and age of children.[6] These market rate surveys, along with data from other recent research, provide a data infrastructure that may be useful for establishing a basic childcare need.[7]

Implementing Recommendation 4.2 would make the treatment of paid childcare consistent with that of other threshold components like food and shelter. There are, however, issues that must be addressed before the PPM can transition to this approach. States vary in the percentile of market rate survey childcare costs used for their programs, so the Census Bureau would need to weigh options to address this; for example, the PPM could apply a uniform percentile based on CCDF, or a modification of CCDF, across states. Before this can be resolved, the presumption that CCDF payments are sufficient to purchase childcare deemed adequate by most people requires further scrutiny. For example, childcare centers that operate with state or federal subsidies may report prices paid that understate their overall costs.[8] Other options for data on childcare costs exist, such as relying on Consumer Expenditure Survey data as the SPM currently does for several important threshold categories. These are important research questions in need of attention.

4.3.2. Estimating Childcare Resources

Just as childcare needs should enter the PPM threshold, financial assistance that defrays the cost of childcare should be added to household resources. Thus, the calculation of resources should include the value of childcare subsidies and childcare tax credits received by households. Here, too, the panel recommends an incremental approach, starting with households that use paid childcare before ultimately including all households with children.

> **RECOMMENDATION 4.3:** To accurately assess a household's ability to meet its needs, for households that have children and that use paid childcare, in the near future, the Census Bureau should research, develop, and implement a methodology for valuing assistance received by the household for childcare, so that it can enter into the calculation of the household's available resources.

Childcare resources vary substantially across households. Therefore, for households that use paid childcare, resources would include the value of any subsidies or tax credits received. Such subsidies may come in the form of vouchers funded by states or by the federal government, or through an array of childcare-assistance programs, and may also include the value of childcare tax credits. Accounting for these resources would require new CPS-ASEC

---

[6] See www.dol.gov/agencies/wb/topics/childcare.

[7] Examples include the University of Washington's Self Sufficiency Standard, the ALICE Project (www.unitedforalice.org/), Massachusetts Institute of Technology's living wage project (livingwage.mit.edu/), and the Economic Policy Institute's Family Budget Calculator (www.epi.org/resources/budget/). In one application of these data, Danielson and Thorman (2019) used California's 2016 Regional Market Rate survey to add preschool care costs to poverty thresholds for all families with 3- or 4-year-olds. While federal guidelines recommend payment rates as part of CCDF, states vary considerably in their practices (Borowsky et al., 2022). In light of this variation, the Urban Institute's CCDF Policies Database, which collects detailed information about program rules in states and territories, may be a useful resource for implementing the panel's recommendations.

[8] See www.stlouisfed.org/on-the-economy/2022/oct/estimating-affordability-child-care-us-states.

questions, updates to current methods, and imputation.[9] The panel recommends that the CPS-ASEC ask respondents what types of childcare they used, for how many hours, and whether a government agency helped pay for that care; separately, if government assistance was received, the question set should include whether that assistance covered the full cost or a portion of the cost.[10] With this information, the Census Bureau could impute the value of the subsidy. Researchers have developed standard questions about childcare type and subsidy receipt that the Census Bureau could draw on for this purpose. The panel endorses this approach, rather than one that asks parents the value of the subsidy, because parents are unlikely to know or be able to report accurately on subsidy (or copayment) amounts (e.g., see Shantz, 2019).

Census Bureau research should investigate options for estimating the value of subsidies received by households with very young children enrolled in pre-K or Head Start, as this may also require additional survey questions. Children in states with universal programs have access to benefits that presumably cover the majority of the childcare need that would be included in the PPM threshold.

In addition, to implement Recommendation 4.3, the Census Bureau will need to revisit its approach to childcare tax credit receipt. Currently, the Census Bureau models the Child and Dependent Care Tax Credit (CDCTC) in its tax model for the SPM, but this portion of the credit is not broken out separately from tax liability or refundable tax credits. To assess the resource side of childcare in a transparent and comprehensive manner in the PPM, the CDCTC would ideally be combined with other childcare subsidies received, to create a measure of total childcare assistance.[11] However, the CDCTC interacts with other parts of the tax calculation and may not be easily separated out, particularly for the American Community Survey-based estimates that rely on the TAXSIM model used in the SPM. Another option that could therefore be explored would be to include the CDCTC benefits in the PPM through their effect on reducing positive tax liability.

The question of whether to cap, at the threshold need, the value of childcare subsidies and tax credits included in resources also requires further research. One could argue that the cap is not needed because childcare subsidy programs (presumably) already provide subsidies based on need, and the CDCTC reduces federal tax liability regardless of the definition of that need. But crediting families the value of a subsidy that goes beyond the amount of need would be inconsistent with the approach proposed by the panel for medical care and housing. Additionally, while the panel recommends that this question be studied, cases in which subsidies exceed need are likely uncommon, and the amounts are likely to be small.

4.3.3. Long-Term Changes to Address Unpaid Childcare

Moving beyond market childcare, the calculation of household resources would ideally include—in addition to childcare subsidies and tax credits—the value of unpaid childcare, just as the threshold would ideally include the need for childcare for all households with children, regardless of whether they use paid care. The panel recognizes that tackling this issue will require extensive future discussion and research, as indicated in Recommendation 4.4.

RECOMMENDATION 4.4: Recognizing that many households with children do not use paid childcare and are providing care for their children themselves, whether through parental care or care by other relatives or friends, future discussion and research are needed on the topic of unpaid childcare and whether and how such care should be reflected in poverty measurement.

---

[9]The childcare questions in the CPS-ASEC are:
  1. Did anyone in this household PAY for the care of their children while they worked in (year)?
  2. Which children needed care while their parents worked?
  3. What is the easiest way for you to tell us how much you and others in this household paid for childcare while they worked in (year): weekly, etc.?
  4. How much did they pay for childcare?
  5. How many payments did they make during (year)?
  (www2.census.gov/programs-surveys/cps/datasets/2022/march/asec2022_ddl_pub_full.pdf).

[10]The question of employer-assisted childcare is also pertinent. However, the share of employers that provide childcare assistance is very low, and most of that assistance is in the form of information and referral or help with emergency childcare.

[11]Wheaton and Stevens (2016) describe the multiple approaches to modeling taxes used in the SPM, which include the CDCTC.

TABLE 4-1 SPM versus Proposed Long-Term Approach

	SPM	Proposed Approach
Threshold	Childcare need not included	Childcare need included for all households with children under age 13, or age 18 if a child has a disability (with amount varying by number and age of children, and by geographic area)
Resources	Value of tax credits included	Value of subsidies and tax credits included (capped at value of childcare need)
		Ideally, a valuation of unpaid care
Childcare Costs	Deducted from resources (capped at the lower-paid parent's earnings)	Not deducted from resources
Who Benefits?	Both working parents (or a single parent who is working)	All households with children under age 13

SOURCE: Panel generated.

Estimating the value of resources for households that do not use paid childcare (or that use paid childcare for only a portion of the time for which care is needed) is a major challenge, and an appropriate and transparent method would have to be developed. Consider cases in which parents provide care themselves (e.g., by splitting shifts or having one parent home full-time) or use unpaid care provided by friends or family. These households receive no government subsidy (or only a partial subsidy if they use a mix of paid and unpaid care) but may well be benefitting from unpaid care (e.g., a grandparent as caregiver) or parental care—that is, they are in essence subsidized from their own or other households' resources. Parents who provide care may also earn less as a result, although this impact would be captured in the PPM resource calculation.[12]

Although an extensive literature exists on valuation of nonmarket home production (e.g., NRC, 2005, Chapter 3; Suh and Folbre, 2015), further research is needed to probe the conceptual issues and to explore potential approaches to including childcare in the resource calculations for households with children that do not use paid care or that use a mix of paid and unpaid care. One possible approach to be explored by the Census Bureau for valuing unpaid childcare, for example by parents, family, or friends, would be to assume that the value of the care is equal to the need level established in the threshold. This approach would eliminate the problem of valuing different parents' unpaid care differently based on factors such as education level or hourly wage rate.

4.3.4. Implications of Proposed Long-Term Changes and Need for Future Research

As stressed in this chapter, moving to a more comprehensive measure of childcare needs and resources will require considerable further research and development. Table 4-1 summarizes and compares the main elements of the recommended approach, which would include childcare in the set of threshold needs and would account for childcare receipt in resources, with the current approach of the SPM.

Two example household types serve to illustrate how childcare needs and resources might be defined under the proposed future approach. Household 1 has two preschool-aged children, ages 1 and 4, and lives in a moderately expensive childcare market in the Northeast. Their threshold would reflect the CCDF-approved reimbursement rate for family day care for the 1-year-old (the most common type of care used for 1-year-olds) in their area, and the CCDF rate for center care for the 4-year-old (the most common type of care used for 4-year-olds). Alternatively, the threshold amounts could be defined as the weighted average of the reimbursement rate for the various types of care used by children of the given age. On the resource side, the household would receive credit for the imputed value of any childcare subsidy or tax credit reported, as well as the value of any unpaid care received from friends or family or that the household itself provides, capped at the amount of their childcare need. The unpaid care would be valued at the CCDF reimbursement rate for in-home childcare for a child of the given age in that geographic area.

---

[12]Parents may choose to provide care themselves in light of the perceived benefits of doing so, as well.

Household 2 has two school-aged children, ages 8 and 12, and lives in a relatively inexpensive childcare market in the Southeast. Their threshold would reflect the CCDF-approved reimbursement rate for afterschool childcare for the 8- and 12-year-old children. On the resource side, the household would receive credit for the imputed value of any childcare subsidy or tax credit reported, as well as the value of any unpaid care received from friends or family or that the household itself provides, valued at the CCDF reimbursement rate for in-home childcare for a child of the given age in that geographic area.

Clearly, moving toward such an ideal measure of childcare will require considerable future research. The current approach of assigning childcare needs (and benefits) only to families that are employed and use paid care is incomplete. All young children need care, and school-aged children need care outside of school hours—but these needs are met in various ways. However, the panel also recognizes that broadening the definition of childcare need, assigning value to that need, and assigning value to resources families receive to meet that need are all complex steps that require more research.

Future research is also needed regarding the ages and circumstances for which childcare need should be assumed. For instance, Recommendations 4.2 and 4.3 assume that all children need care through age 12—a universal need is not assumed for children age 13 or above. Research might consider situations in which families utilize care for their children age 13 and above outside of school hours or during summers. As alluded to above, solutions for families that use a mixture of paid and unpaid care—which suggests adjusting estimates by hours of care—should be investigated.

This research on childcare could be extended to consider parallel contexts in which care for disabled or elderly adults is taken on by younger family members, or in which adults are caring for adult children with disabilities. To what extent do the costs of care for elderly parents mirror the costs of childcare? How much do public programs defray such costs? Future research in this arena may shed light on a basic need for care—and its poverty implications—at later stages in life.

5

Challenging Categories: Housing/Shelter

5.1. CONCEPTUAL MEASUREMENT GOAL

Housing is typically the largest component of a household's spending. Harvard University's Joint Center for Housing Studies estimated that, in 2020, 30 percent of U.S. households were cost burdened—that is, paying more than 30 percent of their incomes for housing. The figure for renters was even higher, with 46 percent cost burdened in 2019—down from 50 percent in 2011, but well up from the 40 percent estimated in 2001 (Joint Center for Housing Studies, 2020). Rent burdens vary considerably across the country, as shown in Figure 5-1. As depicted in Figure 5-2, housing costs subsume an even higher share of monthly income for households with low incomes.

Given its magnitude, the methodological choice for handling housing in a poverty measure—both in terms of establishing basic need and including housing in the estimate of resources—can have a major impact on who is counted as poor, on geographic variation in poverty rates, and on the overall poverty rate. Conceptually, a poverty measure should reflect whether households have adequate resources to obtain a basic level of shelter, month to month and year to year, while still being able to afford necessities such as food, clothing, transportation, and medical care. The most straightforward way to represent this basic need is to first establish the amount of money required, in a given location for a given family size, to rent a house or apartment deemed to be of acceptable quality. Next, to determine whether a family/household can meet this threshold for shelter (in addition to the other items in the basic needs bundle), income, and other available resources must be estimated. The calculation of available resources should include any government assistance received to pay for housing and any implicit rent earned by homeowners.

In the Supplemental Poverty Measure (SPM), housing costs are prominently reflected in the needs—food, clothing, shelter, utilities, telephone, and internet (FCSUti)—threshold. The shares of the threshold accounted for by out-of-pocket expenditures on shelter and utilities for the 2015 SPM reference unit (two adults with two children) were 50.5 percent for owners with mortgages, 41.1 percent for owners without mortgages, and 49.8 percent for renters (Renwick and Garner, 2020). In the panel's assessment, the treatment of housing in the current SPM thresholds is less conceptually clear and transparent than it could be, and there are four primary concerns with the current calculation. First, the SPM does little to adjust housing costs for basic quality. Second, the SPM groups together all nonmetropolitan areas in a state, ignoring what may be large costs differentials across counties. Third, the shelter needs defined in the SPM do not draw on the U.S. Department of Housing and Urban Development's (HUD's) Fair Market Rents (FMRs), which are used for HUD's programs and already provide a threshold cost

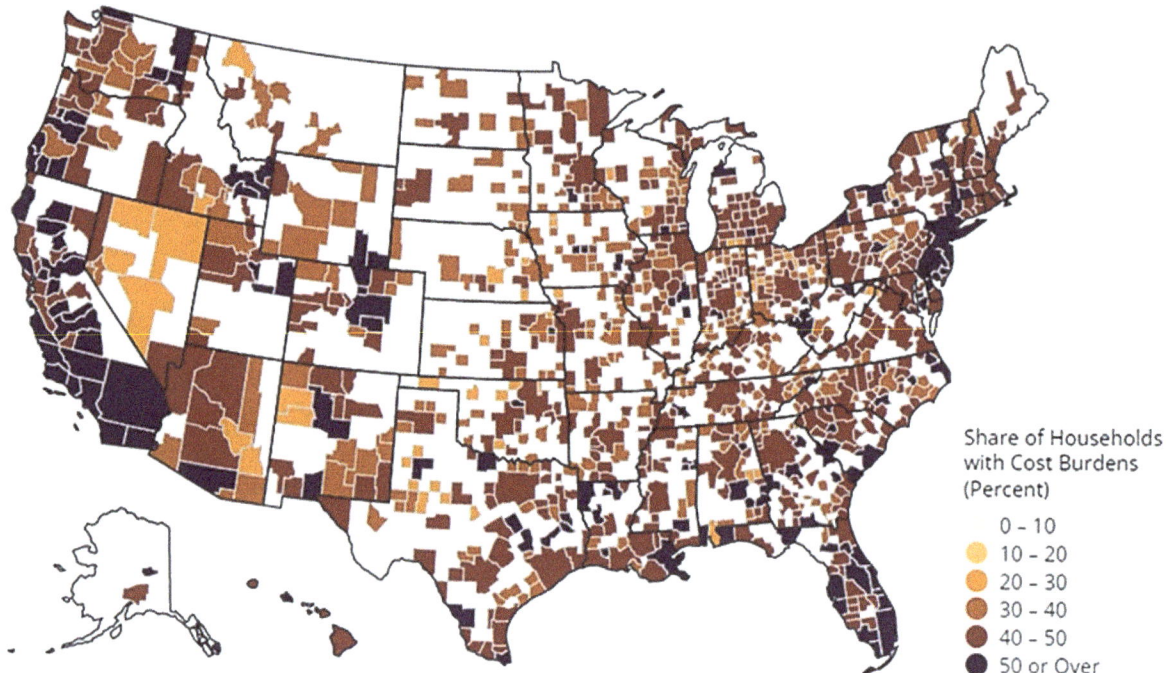

FIGURE 5-1 Share of renter households burdened by housing costs in 2019, by metropolitan area.
SOURCE: Harvard Joint Center for Housing Studies, based on American Community Survey 1-year estimates (www.jchs.harvard.edu/son-2019-cost-burdens-map).

of decent, affordable housing each year in every local market in the country. Finally, the SPM uses distinct needs thresholds for renters, homeowners with mortgages, and homeowners without mortgages—even though tenure choice is endogenous (at least to some extent) and all three groups face the same basic need for shelter.

While the basic need for shelter is the same for all households of the same size and composition, the resource calculation should ideally reflect the fact that homeowners have an asset (a home) that delivers a flow of rental

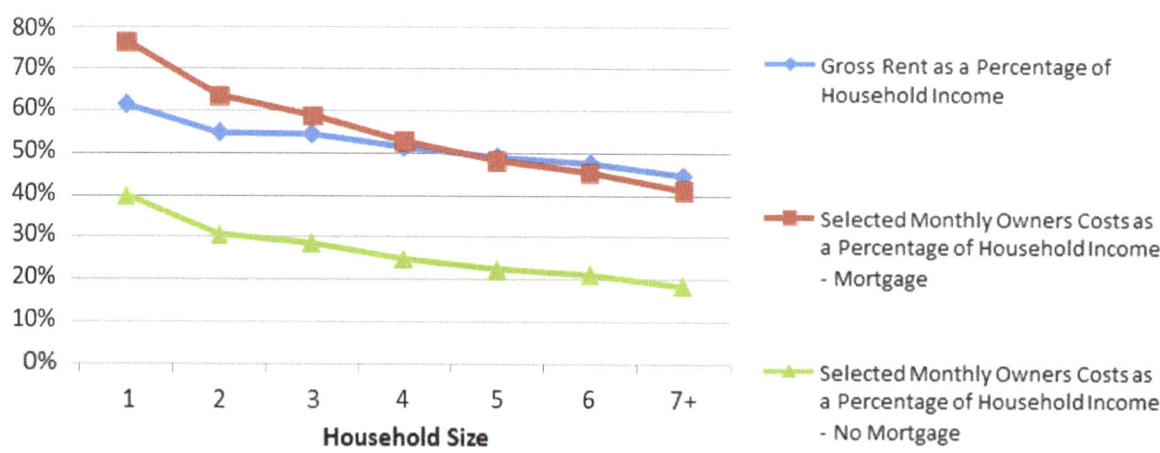

FIGURE 5-2 Housing costs, as a percentage of income, for households with income less than 200 percent of the official poverty level.
SOURCE: Renwick and Garner (2020), using 2014 American Community Survey 5-year data (www.census.gov/acs).

CHALLENGING CATEGORIES: HOUSING/SHELTER

income, whether they are renting it out to someone else or to themselves. Imputed or implicit rent is an estimate of the amount of income that homeowners earn from effectively renting their residences to themselves. While this can be confusing, ignoring this implicit rent leads to inequitable treatment of households in a poverty measure. Imagine two households with the same incomes who own identical homes. One of them lives in their home, while the other rents their home to another family and then uses that rental income to rent a similar house nearby. These two households still have the same level of resources. But if implicit rent is not counted, then homeowners who choose to rent out their homes will appear to have an additional source of income—rental income—compared to homeowners who live in their own homes. However, the two households have the exact same level of resources to spend on nonhousing goods.

Incorporating implicit rent into resource calculations is not without precedent. Several European countries—including Iceland, Luxembourg, the Netherlands, Slovenia, and Switzerland—tax the flow of implicit rent for homeowners (as if they were paying themselves; Andrews et al., 2011). In the United States, the implicit rent that homeowners pay to themselves is already included in calculations of gross domestic product. In making this calculation, the Bureau of Economic Analysis (BEA) estimates the amount that homeowners would pay in rent—using the rent of comparable units in the same local market—if they were renting their homes instead. Any imputation of implicit rental income should also take into account and deduct the user costs incurred by home ownership (e.g., property taxes, maintenance and repairs, and mortgage interest).

In the current SPM, the threshold reflects expenditures on food, clothing, shelter, and utilities and is scaled (by family size) for each specific tenure type (homeowner without mortgage, homeowner with mortgage, and renter).[1] Further adjustments are made to account for the multiplier—which accounts for other goods and services, such as personal care and nonwork transportation—and for geographic differences in housing costs.[2] Resources available for a family include all sources of income, plus any government transfers, minus taxes paid, work-related costs, childcare, and/or medical out-of-pocket expenses.

Data permitting, the recommended SPM revision—which, for purposes of this report, is called the Principal Poverty Measure (PPM)—follows the approach introduced in Chapter 2. The cost estimate for area-specific basic rent is captured on the threshold side, as determined by HUD's annual estimated FMRs in the local area for all households of the same size and composition (regardless of whether households own or rent). For homeowners, implicit rent is denoted on the income/resource side of the PPM as an additional income flow, based on an estimate of the rental equivalence of their home, or how much rent they would earn if they rented it out; out-of-pocket costs incurred by ownership are subtracted. Implicit rent (rental equivalence) is of course not included as income in the resources available to renters.

If conceptualized as described above (and as detailed in Appendix 2A), the three separate thresholds now used in the SPM for the three tenure modes (homeowner without mortgage, homeowner with mortgage, and renter) would no longer be required; the basic shelter need in a given location would be ascertained in the same way for all household types. The resource side of the PPM would capture differences (due to housing tenure type) in required monthly outlays for shelter. This simplification—the establishment of a single threshold—represents another advantage of adopting an implicit rental income approach.

5.2. DEFINING AND ESTIMATING HOUSING/SHELTER NEEDS

5.2.1. Setting Thresholds—Current Approach

The housing portion of the threshold in the SPM is calculated by the Bureau of Labor Statistics (BLS) using the Consumer Expenditure Survey (CE). First, BLS constructs the distribution of FCSUti for all consumer units (CUs) with at least one child.[3] Then, using the subset of CUs within the 47th–53rd percentiles of the FCSUti

---

[1] As described in Chapter 2, the threshold is estimated as 83 percent of the averages of the 47th–53rd percentile range of the FCSUti distribution.

[2] Appendix 2A depicts the SPM and the PPM algebraically. Equations 2.1 and 2.2 show the SPM specification. Equations 2.3 through 2.5b show the PPM specification.

[3] For 2021, the estimation sample was expanded from CUs with exactly two children to CUs with any number of children.

distribution, the housing portion of the threshold is determined by the share of the FCSUti expenditure around the median comprised by shelter and utilities (excluding phone and internet). Current practice sets the threshold at 83 percent of CUs' average expenditures from this percentile range. For CUs living in metropolitan areas, the SPM's measure of need is geographically adjusted based on local housing costs. For those living in nonmetropolitan areas, the geographic adjustment is based on housing costs for all nonmetropolitan counties within the state (Renwick and Garner, 2020).

As described above, the SPM thresholds are based on actual (surveyed) expenditures. Prior to geographic adjustments, the shelter and utilities portion of the SPM threshold for renters was, for 2020, approximately $13,400 per year (44.4% of the overall threshold of $30,150), or $1,117 per month.[4] These levels are comparable to several calculations of housing costs based on alternative data sources. For example, the national median two-bedroom rent from the 5-year American Community Survey (ACS; 2016–2020) was $1,080 per month. This estimate uses the variable for "gross rent." which includes utilities even if they are not included in rent.[5]

The shelter and utilities portion of the threshold is also used to determine the share that is geographically adjusted using ACS data. As part of the 2021 SPM revisions, the Census Bureau shifted from centering the thresholds at the 33rd percentile to 83 percent of the average expenditures of CUs within the 47th–53rd percentiles (Fox and Burns, 2021a).

5.2.2. Setting Thresholds—Proposed Approach

For low-income households, rental housing is typically a more attainable goal than is purchasing a home, as it requires a security deposit rather than a down payment. Not surprisingly, then, renting is the dominant tenure mode for families with low incomes. In this sense, renting represents the baseline housing need. The FMRs used by HUD for the housing choice voucher program are an obvious candidate to represent the cost of obtaining a basic unit in the rental market. FMRs are designed to capture the cost to rent a moderately priced, standard-quality dwelling in the local housing market. FMRs are estimated annually and become effective on October 1 for U.S. Office of Management and Budget (OMB)-defined metropolitan areas, some HUD-defined subdivisions of OMB metropolitan areas, and each nonmetropolitan county. The steps involved in calculating FMRs include:

1. Calculating 40th percentile gross rents for standard-quality, two-bedroom rental units from the 5-year ACS;
2. Adjusting to the recent year by multiplying benchmark rent by the recent mover factor, using recent in-mover rents from the 1-year ACS;
3. Making additional inflation adjustments to get current-year two-bedroom rents;[6] and
4. Multiplying the two-bedroom rents by equivalence scale adjustments, to get FMRs for housing units with more/fewer bedrooms.

Additionally, HUD does not allow an area's FMRs to decline by more than 10 percent annually. These steps are described in greater detail in HUD documentation.[7]

Among the advantages of the HUD approach to valuing the cost of basic housing are its simplicity, transparency, consistency, and feasibility. The FMR estimate is conceptually clear and simple, in that it is the baseline cost that

---

[4] These are the revised figures: www.bls.gov/pir/spm/spm_2019re_changes.htm.

[5] Data on gross rent were obtained from answers to Housing Questions 14a–d and 18a in the 2020 ACS. Gross rent is the contract rent plus the estimated average monthly cost of utilities (electricity, gas, and water/sewer) and fuels (oil, coal, kerosene, wood, etc.) if these are paid by the renter (or paid for the renter by someone else). Gross rent is intended to eliminate differentials that result from varying practices with respect to the inclusion of utilities and fuels as part of the rental payment. The estimated costs of water/sewer and fuels are reported on a 12-month basis but are converted to monthly figures for the tabulations. Rental units occupied without payment of rent are shown separately as "No rent paid" in the tabulations. Calculation is from ACS tables (www.census.gov/programs-surveys/acs/data/data-tables.html).

[6] HUD is currently considering using other private-market data to adjust to recently rented units or to inflate to current year rents in areas where 1-year ACS and/or BLS metropolitan Consumer Price Index data are not available.

[7] See www.huduser.gov/portal/sites/default/files/pdf/fmr-overview.pdf.

any household, family, or CU must be able to afford to obtain basic shelter. For these reasons, the PPM threshold calculation methodology would benefit from adopting the FMR approach to estimating the cost of obtaining basic housing in the rental market.

RECOMMENDATION 5.1: The Principal Poverty Measure housing thresholds should be set based on shelter costs for renters only. Rental levels should be based on the U.S. Department of Housing and Urban Development's annual Fair Market Rent estimates for various shelter unit sizes, which are anchored to the 40th percentile of gross rent for a recently available "standard-quality" two-bedroom unit in a given local area (metropolitan area or nonmetropolitan county).

Transparency of the approach is enhanced by eliminating adjustment for housing tenure type, which is complicated. The FMR approach, based on the ACS—which is available from HUD on an annual basis for every county—is also feasible within the confines of the Census Bureau's data-publication timelines.

The proposed approach lends consistency to the PPM in that it introduces a threshold that is already used by HUD to estimate local rents for those who receive housing assistance. Specifically, HUD uses FMRs to set subsidy levels for the housing choice voucher program, assuming that the measure captures the cost of renting a decent-quality, two-bedroom housing unit in the local area. The FMR-based approach to housing would also be conceptually similar to this report's proposed approach to medical care (Chapter 3), in that it would use a preexisting standard of basic need and cost already used by the government for other purposes.

In terms of accuracy, the FMR measure standardizes unit quality to some extent (trimming both substandard units at the bottom and luxury units at the top before calculating the 40th percentile of rents) and attempts to exclude subsidized rental units. In this sense, the FMR measure should capture rents for decent-quality, private-market homes. HUD also adjusts FMRs for housing units with specific numbers of bedrooms and uses an inflator to try to capture current rental costs.

It is worth noting that FMRs are designed to measure rental housing costs for recent movers, not established renters. The rationale for HUD's focus on recent movers is that a key purpose of the FMR measure is to estimate market rents for standard-quality units that would be paid by housing choice voucher holders. This focus is the key reason that HUD has not previously supported the use of FMRs for the SPM. The rents of recent movers are typically higher than those paid by established renters, and this difference is generally larger in more rapidly appreciating areas. However, an argument can be made that the rents paid by recent movers are a better measure of the available market rents in a local area, and thus more accurately capture housing costs for those actively seeking housing. Total rents paid include those paid by longstanding renters who may enjoy long-tenure discounts and are more likely to live in subsidized or rent-restricted homes.

The Census Bureau could also use an alternative, tailored version of the FMR measure that omits the adjustment for recent movers. Another option would be to use the median rent (or some other percentile of the full rent) of homes that housing choice voucher holders occupy, which must pass housing-quality inspections.

Recommendation 5.2: The Census Bureau should evaluate the impact of adjusting Fair Market Rent (FMR) values for recent movers and determine whether FMRs are an appropriate measure of housing need in the Principal Poverty Measure. It would be useful to compare the current Supplemental Poverty Measure housing component to the current FMRs as well as a measure of FMRs that omits the adjustment for recent movers across geographic areas.

5.2.3. Impacts of Shifting from Consumer Expenditure Survey-Based Expenditures to Fair Market Rents

The proposed method for including housing in the PPM differs from that currently used in the SPM in that the expenditure-based estimates of housing in the SPM threshold are replaced with the FMRs for particular geographic areas. For cases in which the FMR value is equal to the housing share estimated using the CE for a geographic area, there will be no impact on the threshold or the poverty rates for renters. In 2020, the national housing component of the SPM threshold for renters (with two adults and two children) was $1,117 per month. For the

250 metropolitan areas in the Current Population Survey Annual Social and Economic Supplement (CPS-ASEC), the average monthly housing components are almost identical to the average FMRs for two-bedroom rental units: $1,048 versus $1,043 in 2020. However, many metropolitan areas—about 70 percent—have FMRs that are lower than rent levels appearing in the housing component of the SPM. Many of the remaining 30 percent are large cities, where the higher FMRs could be due to the adjustments for recent movers or for the particular municipalities (Housing and Urban Development Department, 2020). For example, in New York City, the geographically adjusted housing component of the threshold for renters (with two adults and two children) is $1,585 (monthly), while the FMR for two-bedroom rental units is much higher, at $1,951. However, for Jackson, Mississippi, the SPM housing component is $932 and the FMR is similar, at $911. For homeowners, both with and without mortgages, the geographic impact will depend on the actual housing costs they incur. As these costs are currently built into the median calculations of FCSUti, the actual costs are expected to be similar, on average, to the current shares in the thresholds. For example, the SPM threshold for a homeowner without a mortgage in New York City is $28,805, while their new threshold using the FMR is $35,813. However, as described below, their housing costs will be subtracted from resources, which could be more or less than the difference of $7,008. Hence, while the thresholds are different, the difference in poverty status may be minimal.

5.2.4. Handling Housing Tenure Status

The current SPM specifies three separate sets of poverty thresholds based on owner/rental status or "tenure"— homeowners with a mortgage, homeowners without a mortgage, and renters. These separate thresholds reflect that housing expenditures, intuitively and as estimated from the CE, differ across these three groups. However, consistent with Recommendations 5.1 and 5.5, it will no longer be necessary to distinguish between renters and homeowners on the threshold side of the PPM.

> **Recommendation 5.3: The Principal Poverty Measure should discontinue the practice of maintaining separate thresholds for homeowners with a mortgage, homeowners without a mortgage, and renters. While owners without mortgages face lower monthly housing costs, these differences can be accounted for on the resource side.**

The rationale for such a methodological switch again rests on simplicity and transparency, as well as on the belief that, in contrast to the number of children in the household, for example, tenure status should not be treated as a factor that changes the minimum cost of the basic shelter needed. Little difference is found in monthly costs between owners with mortgages and renters and, conceptually, the basic shelter need is the same regardless of renter or owner status. The PPM should control for cost-of-living differences, not householders' consumption choices. Also, tenure status is not a fixed attribute—people transition into and out of home ownership.

5.3. ADJUSTING SHELTER AND UTILITY THRESHOLDS

5.3.1. For Housing Unit Size

The SPM currently assumes that all CUs, regardless of size, require the same fraction of the overall thresholds for shelter and utilities. Moving to the proposed method—using FMRs to adjust for differences in shelter and utility costs for CUs of varying sizes, and then creating a new equivalence scale specific to food and clothing— offers two key advantages. First, the current method implicitly assumes that economies of scale for housing are the same as economies of scale for FCSUti thresholds as a whole, which is likely inaccurate. One would expect greater economies of scale for shelter and utility costs than for food and clothing. In the past, the Census Bureau has deemed that separate equivalence scales would not materially change poverty estimates.[8] Still, there are likely

---

[8]Renwick and Garner (2018), investigating the potential impact of adjusting the housing portion of the thresholds independently, find that "the choice of housing share or the choice of equivalence scale (as estimated) has very little impact on the measure of the impact of housing assistance on overall poverty rates. Even the impact on the poverty rates of those reporting housing assistance is relatively small" (p. 17).

differences in the economies of scale for housing as compared with the other threshold needs categories and, given that the FMR measure has a built-in equivalence scale, it would be relatively simple and sensible for the Census Bureau to use this measure.

The second argument for using the equivalence scale built into the FMR measure is that it is specific to local markets. In its adjustments for housing and utility costs by number of bedrooms, HUD uses market-specific ratios of rents for two-bedroom units versus smaller units, as well as for two-bedroom units versus larger units. This may be important since it is possible that the marginal cost of an additional bedroom is significantly greater in some local markets than in others. Thus (as depicted in Equation 2.3, Appendix 2A), the Census Bureau would adjust the threshold for a CU of a given size and type using an equivalence scale that applies only to food, clothing, and internet/phone since, in its calculation of FMRs, HUD already adjusts for housing unit size, as proxied by number of bedrooms. The "scale" adjustments (on average) for additional bedrooms are:[9]

0 1.00
1 1.11
2 1.38
3 1.82
4 2.08

HUD goes on to state that the FMRs for units with more than four bedrooms increase by 15 percent for each bedroom—much smaller than the three-parameter scale suggests.[10]

A similar approach is used elsewhere. For example, the Economic Policy Institute's (EPI's) Family Budget Calculator consists of seven components: housing, food, transportation, childcare, medical care, taxes, and "other necessities." The housing portion of the budget calculator is based on FMRs and adjusts for family size:

> HUD makes rental rates available for studio apartments and one-bedroom through four-bedroom apartments. The EPI family budgets assume that a one-adult household occupies a studio apartment and that a two-adult household occupies a one-bedroom apartment. Families with one or two children occupy a two-bedroom unit. Families with three or four children occupy a three-bedroom unit. Rental costs include shelter plus all tenant-paid utilities, excluding telephone service, cable or satellite service, and Internet service. Telephone service costs are included in "other necessities" within the family budgets. (Gould et al., 2018)

One minor complication of using FMRs to adjust for economies of scale in shelter and utilities is that the HUD calculation is based on number of bedrooms, not household size. The Census Bureau will need to research and test approaches for mapping FMRs based on number of bedrooms needed into PPM shelter units based on household size. Although HUD allows local agencies to set allowable unit sizes, HUD's documentation describes parameters for households with various numbers of members (e.g., households with three people should not live in homes with fewer than two bedrooms or more than three). HUD guidelines state that Public Housing Assistance Assessments may develop occupancy standards consistent with the following rules:[11]

- No more than two people would be required to occupy a bedroom;
- Persons of different generations, persons of the opposite sex, and unrelated adults should not be required to share a bedroom;
- Husband and wife share the same bedroom;
- Children of the same sex share a bedroom; and
- Children, with the possible exception of infants, would not be required to share a bedroom with persons of different generations, including their parents.

---

[9] These are averages using 2019 FMR data: avg(FMR by size) / avg(FMR for studio).
[10] See www.hudexchange.info/programs/home/home-rent-limits/.
[11] Documentation of HUD adjustments for family size can be found at www.hud.gov/sites/documents/74651C5PIHH.PDF.

One potential mapping between household (or SPM unit) size and number of bedrooms, which is consistent with these guidelines, might be as follows:

(Adults, Children)	Bedrooms
1, 0	0
2, 0	1
2, 1	2
2, 2	2
2, 3	3
2, 4	3
2, 5	4
1, 1	2
1, 2	2
1, 3	3

Alternatively, the Census Bureau could assign CUs average FMRs based on the minimum and maximum number of bedrooms allowed by HUD.

Recommendation 5.4: The Census Bureau and Bureau of Labor Statistics should consider using Fair Market Rents (FMRs) to adjust for differences in shelter and utility costs for consumer units of varying sizes, and then create a new equivalence scale specific to food and clothing. The Census Bureau should research whether using separate equivalence scales for housing still makes little difference for a version of the Principal Poverty Measure using the geographically specific adjustments to consumer unit sizes embedded in the FMRs.

5.3.2. For Geographic Differences in Rental Prices

It makes sense to adjust SPM (and PPM) thresholds for differences in costs of living, and housing cost is the most important component of cross-area variation. Other budget categories such as food and medical care also vary, but typically by less than housing cost. The conceptual goal of these adjustments is to ensure all families, regardless of location, can purchase comparable basic bundles of necessities—food, shelter, clothing, and utilities. To some extent, cost-of-living differences across locations may reflect differences in underlying amenities. For example, people may pay more to live in parts of the country that offer more moderate climates or better transportation infrastructure. If differences in rent reflect amenity differences to some extent, this counsels against geographic adjustments for cost of living. But such amenities do not directly translate into household economic resources, and to the extent that they do, they are captured in regional differences in income. Finally, cross-regional moves are relatively rare; Child Protective Services' annual mobility estimates indicate that only about 1.5 percent of households move across state lines each year (U.S. Census Bureau, 2021a).

Evidence suggests geographic adjustment also has a substantial effect on the spatial distribution of poverty, pushing it from the southern United States to the coasts. The adjustment also substantially decreases poverty rates for children living outside of metropolitan statistical areas and increases it for children living inside these areas (Renwick et al., 2017).

Current Method

The SPM method adjusts the housing portion of FCSUti to account for differences in living costs across 342 metropolitan and nonmetropolitan areas in the United States; the largest component of this adjustment depends crucially on the median rent of the area. Pacas and Rothwell (2020) find that, as currently estimated, most of the geographic adjustment in the SPM is explained by median rent differences as opposed to the housing tenure component. Geographic adjustments, which are estimated using ACS data, are based on a formula that accounts for the percentage of residents within an area who are owners with a mortgage, owners without a mortgage, or renters (see Renwick, 2018, for full specifications of this calculation). As represented by SPM expenditure data, housing accounts for about 40 percent of a typical family's budget. The SPM geographic adjustment therefore only applies to 40 percent (the SU) of the FCSU threshold. The assumption, driven in part by data constraints, is that cost of living for other categories (and thus the remaining 60% of the budget) is homogenous across regions.[12]

Proposed Changes/Additions

Geographic adjustment of shelter threshold amounts in the PPM should be consistent with the broader methodology proposed above, using FMRs to represent the basic housing need.

Recommendation 5.5: Principal Poverty Measure thresholds should continue to reflect geographic differences in housing costs. Geographic adjustments should apply to owners and renters based on official Fair Market Rents, which are set at the individual metropolitan area or nonmetropolitan county level.

Using FMRs to make geographic adjustments in cost of living offers several advantages. First, FMRs incorporate cost differences at the metropolitan area and nonmetropolitan county level, so the Census Bureau will not need to make further geographic adjustments. Second, FMRs offer more refined sub-state-level geographic adjustments, particularly for nonmetropolitan areas.[13] One problem with the current approach is that the geographic adjustments are applied separately for geographies identified in the CPS Public Use Microdata Sample files (i.e., those with populations large enough to surpass current Census Bureau disclosure safeguards). This effectively means that, while adjustments are made for large metropolitan areas and an agglomeration of smaller metropolitan areas within a state, only a single adjustment is made for all nonmetropolitan areas within a state. However, housing costs may vary significantly within a state's geographic units, despite the fact that they are currently treated homogenously. Mueller et al. (2021) demonstrate the wide variability between median rents of nonmetropolitan counties within the same state, a pattern that is not adequately captured in the current SPM geographic adjustment.

Ideally, then, the Census Bureau should aim to estimate the PPM at the county level for nonmetropolitan areas within a state and then explore ways to make data publicly available while meeting disclosure standards. Even with the shift to FMRs, the disclosure issue will remain for nonmetropolitan counties. To optimize data value, chosen disclosure procedures should minimize impacts on the resulting geographic distribution of poverty. For metropolitan areas, the Census Bureau could use FMRs at the level of core-based statistical areas;[14] for nonmetropolitan areas, county-level FMRs could be used. If the FMR approach is not adopted, then the PPM could be estimated with county-level adjustments and the Census Bureau could explore how to generate publicly available data that meet disclosure standards while minimizing the effect on the resulting geographic distribution of poverty.

5.4. VALUING RESOURCES

While the basic housing need can be assumed to be similar for households (or SPM resource units) of a certain size living in a certain location, the kinds and amounts of resources that can be marshalled to meet this basic, monthly expense vary considerably by shelter type. Specifically, homeowners maintain an asset allowing them the means to shelter themselves. Some households receive resource enhancements toward meeting housing costs, in the form of government assistance. Properly accounting for these resources is crucial for accurate measurement of poverty.

---

[12]This and other methodological issues having to do with geographic price adjustments are comprehensively addressed by Ziliak (2011).

[13]It worth noting that the New York City poverty measure uses an FMR approach for making geographic cost adjustments (www.nyc.gov/assets/opportunity/pdf/NYCgovPoverty2020_Appendix_B.pdf), as do Fitzgerald and Moffit (2022). The SPM method (which compares median rents based on ACS data) would be problematic for the New York City poverty measure, due to the prevalence of housing-affordability programs in the city.

[14]Core-based statistical areas are metropolitan or micropolitan statistical areas describing a group of counties (or sometimes just one county) around an urban core.

5.4.1. Rental Income for Homeowners

Alternatives to the Current SPM Method

The SPM does not currently account for implicit rental income in its calculation of resources. Key arguments against incorporating implicit rental income into a poverty measure are: (1) it is difficult for people to understand the concept; and (2) accurate calculation requires reliable data about the market rent that could be charged for any given home. Further, average or median measures of market rent may systematically overstate the implicit rental income for demographic groups that tend to own lower-valued properties, including Black households. However, there is a good argument to be made that homeowners' resources should include the implicit rent they pay to themselves, as an annual flow of benefits from an owned asset. Homeowners receive a benefit from "renting to themselves," or, perhaps more accurately stated, from not having to pay monthly rent, which frees up resources to cover other needs.

To be sure, incorporating implicit rent into resources is operationally challenging, as the rental value (or rental equivalence) of a home is not observed.[15] The approach requires an estimate of the dollar amount that homeowners would pay for their home if they were renting it; this estimate is typically based on the rent charged for comparable units in the same local market. As such, the rental equivalence is potentially different for every homeowner, depending on the size, location, and features of each home.[16] BEA takes this approach in estimating the valuation of shelter services provided through owner-occupied housing for calculation of gross domestic product. BEA imputes a value based on the rents charged for similar tenant-occupied housing, minus related expenses such as maintenance and repairs, property taxes, and mortgage interest.

Unfortunately, the current CPS-ASEC asks few questions about housing characteristics. The survey simply collects the self-reported market value of the owned home, the number of units in the structure, and the type of living quarters (e.g., house, apartment, mobile home, etc.). Given current data availability, the Census Bureau could take three specific approaches to estimate rental equivalence. The first and simplest option would be to use the FMRs for the local market and CU size. The second option would use the number of units in the structure, type of living quarters, and geographic location reported in the CPS-ASEC to estimate a rental equivalence based on gross rents charged for units in similarly sized buildings and in the same type of living quarters in the local market. A third option would use the ratio of market values self-reported by CPS-ASEC respondents to average prices in the area based on the ACS; this ratio would be used to inflate the local FMR to account for the quality/size of that owner's home.

In addition to simplicity and ease of implementation, the first option has the advantage of consistency with the use of FMRs in calculating the threshold cost of renting an acceptable-quality home. Applying FMRs directly as the implicit rent would also have the virtue of consistency with the proposed approach to medical care described in Chapter 3, wherein the Affordable Care Act benchmark plan is assigned as the threshold need amount for everyone (except those covered by Medicare). Resources include a net value of any health insurance benefits received, calculated for everyone (including those with employer-sponsored insurance) as the basic plan minus a capped premium payment.

The downside of using the FMR approach is that it fails to take into account within-market differences in the size and quality of homes owned by similarly sized households. Given that the CPS-ASEC has no information about the size or number of bedrooms in a home, there is no way to know whether a family of six owns a five-bedroom home or a two-bedroom home. Estimating rental equivalence with FMRs could overstate the value of lower-quality houses (with lower rental values) and could lead to misclassification of CUs as not experiencing poverty. Alternatively, using FMRs as a proxy will understate rental equivalence and overstate poverty for households that own higher-quality homes. But if the Census Bureau were to pursue one of the two options that do not directly use FMRs, the panel recommends that rental equivalences be capped at FMRs, since the difference between the FMR value and the rental equivalence of a home may not easily convert into disposable income.

---

[15] For discussion of the merits of a user cost/out-of-pocket approach versus rental equivalence, see Garner and Verbrugge (2009).

[16] Garner and Short (2009) consider the strengths and weaknesses of different methods for valuing net implicit rental income.

So, households with larger and more expensive homes would still be credited only with a rental equivalence equal to the FMR value.[17]

Another possibility involves capping the *net* implicit rental income (that is, rental equivalence amount minus user or operating costs) at the FMR value. This would allow homeowners with larger and more expensive homes to be credited with higher gross rents while ensuring that the *net* implicit rents estimates do not exceed the FMR value. For consistency with the treatment of medical care, the panel recommends capping the rental equivalence at the FMR value for household size while acknowledging that the Census Bureau should research the implications of each approach.

In the longer run, the Census Bureau should consider adding questions to the CPS-ASEC that more accurately capture rental equivalence. One simple approach would be adding a question about the number of bedrooms in the home, which would allow homeowners to be credited with the FMR value applicable to the size of their home. (As noted below, if rental equivalence varies by number of bedrooms, out-of-pocket housing cost estimates should also then vary by number of bedrooms.)

RECOMMENDATION 5.6: For estimating Principal Poverty Measure unit resources, implicit rental income should be included for households that own homes. In the short run, this implicit rental income could be the local Fair Market Rent (FMR) value for the particular family size, minus user costs—implying that implicit rental income will automatically be capped at the housing cost threshold. The Census Bureau should also analyze how the estimated implicit rent would differ under the FMR approach compared with alternative approaches of estimating rental equivalence based on self-reported home value or average American Community Survey rents for units of the same structure type in the local market. For these alternatives, the panel recommends that implicit rent be capped at the FMR value for the relevant consumer unit size, but the Census Bureau should research the alternative of capping net implicit rent at the FMR value.

Recommendation 5.6 is consistent with the report of the Interagency Technical Working Group on Evaluating Alternative Measures of Poverty (BLS, 2020). This report advises that further research be undertaken to evaluate alternative methods of estimating the net value of shelter service flows from owner-occupied housing in the income resource measure, including the possibility of imputing such values using statistical methods and data from the CE. The working group noted that such research should consider the availability of data from the CPS-ASEC and ACS. The report also provides a detailed discussion of the conceptual reasons to include implicit rent in the estimation of SPM resource unit resources.[18]

Netting Out Homeowner User Costs

Costs associated with home ownership are real outlays and should be reflected in the estimate of resources. For people experiencing periods of low income, the costs of homeownership, such as property taxes, insurance, and mortgage interest payments, can threaten their ability to keep their homes. These are real costs, not paid (directly) by renters, and must be covered with homeowners' available resources. These costs should thus be deducted from any estimate of implicit rent.[19]

RECOMMENDATION 5.7: Homeowners' user costs in the local area—including mortgage interest payments, property taxes, insurance, and other maintenance expenses—should be netted out of the implicit rental income when estimating Principal Poverty Measure (PPM) unit resources. The PPM should continue estimating user costs separately for homeowners with and without mortgages, as is

---

[17]This is a yet another example of a topic that could be revisited as research (and data) on measuring household assets progresses. See the discussion of alternative approaches to measuring resources in Chapter 2, section 2.5.

[18]See BLS (2020, pp. 31-32).

[19]The CE includes questions about homeowner costs such as mortgage payments, homeowner's insurance, property taxes, and maintenance and repairs. The CPS-ASEC does not ask about property-related expenditures.

currently done for the SPM. For consistency with FMRs, user costs could be estimated as the average of the 37th–43rd percentiles of costs for homeowners with and without mortgages. Also, if the Census Bureau accounts for within-market differences in the size and quality of homes in its estimates of rental equivalence, then it should similarly allow user costs to vary with home size and value. User costs should be capped at the value of the rental equivalence, so net implicit rental income cannot be negative.

Determining which user costs should be deducted and, in particular, whether to include the principal portion of mortgage payments when estimating homeowners' user costs is a key question. On the one hand, principal and interest payments occur simultaneously, and the principal component (while essentially an investment) is not available for use by the homeowner in the short or medium term. Also, existing SPM thresholds treat mortgage payments as inclusive of both interest and principal components. On the other hand, the interest-only portion of mortgage payments represents a more accurate depiction of user cost. Principal payments are effectively a long-term investment into the equity of an asset—in this case, a home. Principal payments are essentially transfers from one savings vehicle to another and do not represent a true user cost of homeownership. Further, homeowners can obtain interest-only mortgages that only require them to pay interest for the first several years. Finally, homeowners with more equity in their homes may pay lower interest payments, and thus user cost may differ significantly between new homeowners and longer-term homeowners. Therefore, including the principal component of mortgage payments as a user cost may mask significant heterogeneity across homeowners with differing lengths of ownership.

The report of the Interagency Technical Working Group on Evaluating Alternative Measures of Poverty (BLS, 2020) states that, in calculating homeowners' net implicit income, costs incurred should include only mortgage interest payments. While the majority of this panel's members agree with subtracting interest-only payments, it was not unanimous—a few panelists support inclusion of principal payments. The panel thus recommends the Census Bureau conduct additional research on the efficacy of treating interest only or principal and interest as part of the user cost of homeownership. Note that, in the panel's judgment, utility costs should not be included as part of homeowner user costs if benchmarking rental equivalence to FMRs, because FMRs are a measure of gross rents, or contract rents plus utility costs. In other words, the panel recommends that homeowners be credited with rents high enough to cover typical monthly utility costs.

In the short run, the Census Bureau could impute owner costs based on the costs reported by homeowners with and without mortgages in the CE. Given that the initial proceeds of home equity loans can be used for consumption, the Census Bureau may want to focus on first mortgages when calculating homeowners' user costs. In the longer run, the Census Bureau could consider introducing questions into the CPS-ASEC that more accurately capture homeowners' user costs and that would allow for separation of principal and interest payments.[20] Because of the often hybrid tenure (e.g., renting land, owning structure) of owning manufactured homes, the Census Bureau is advised to carefully differentiate costs across various types of living quarters (e.g., mobile homes).

RECOMMENDATION 5.8: The Census Bureau should consider adding new questions to the Current Population Survey Annual Social and Economic Supplement—for example, questions about number of bedrooms—to better capture housing unit size and quality information needed to accurately estimate rental equivalence. The Census Bureau should also consider adding questions to capture homeowners' user costs more accurately and with greater detail.

5.4.2. Housing Assistance

Current Practice

The housing subsidy valuation in the SPM is estimated as the difference between the "market rent" for the housing unit and the total tenant payment (Fox and Burns, 2021a). The CPS only asks respondents whether they

---

[20]The Census Bureau could ask homeowners to report on the amount of outstanding debt, the interest rate, and the year the mortgage was originated, to estimate principal and interest payments.

live in public housing or receive rental assistance from the government. No information about rent is collected, so market rent is estimated using a statistical match to HUD data. Specifically, for households reporting a subsidy, market rent reported by HUD is used for households of the same size receiving vouchers or living in public housing. The SPM-estimated subsidy equals this market rent minus the *expected* out-of-pocket housing cost which, as proxied in HUD payment rules, is the greater of 30 percent of adjusted income or 10 percent of gross income (Renwick, 2018). The subsidy is capped at the housing portion of the SPM threshold, minus the household's required rental payment.

The current practice is complicated and often delays the SPM because the Census Bureau must wait to receive data from HUD, which can take up to 2 years. Further, in practice, market rent is capped at the housing portion of the threshold for most (90%) of households; this means that, rather than market rent, the housing portion of the threshold is typically used.

Proposed Approach

In-kind housing assistance should continue to be accounted for in resource estimates for PPM units, but the approach should dovetail with the proposed approach of estimating shelter thresholds based on FMRs.

RECOMMENDATION 5.9: In assigning the value of in-kind housing assistance to Principal Poverty Measure unit resources, the calculation should be simplified by estimating the expected subsidy as Fair Market Rent value minus the greater of 30 percent of adjusted income or 10 percent of gross income.

This approach essentially mirrors that currently used by the Census Bureau, described by Renwick and Mitchel (2015), to calculate subsidies for the SPM. The only difference is that the PPM would use FMRs as opposed to estimated "market rents" from HUD (which are also anchored to FMRs). Using FMRs directly will be simpler and will streamline production of the PPM. While the Census Bureau could potentially perform a direct match to HUD data, this would be administratively difficult and would miss households receiving state and local subsidies.

Longer-Term Research

Beyond the PPM calculations proposed in this chapter, the issue of homelessness is an important future research topic. People experiencing homelessness are an important subset of the population living in poverty. Conceptually, in the panel's judgment, this population should be included in PPM estimates; however, there are many practical challenges in measuring the status of people experiencing homelessness. Research should focus on which data could be used (or created) to include this population. How accurately can the homeless population (at least those in shelters) be enumerated in the ACS? Single-contact censuses—typically undertaken by teams of field workers in clearly defined areas where preliminary studies suggest large populations of unhoused individuals can be found—have been used by cities to estimate the sizes of populations experiencing homelessness (Institute of Medicine, 1988).

Once counted, a method would need to be developed to estimate the basic PPM elements. Presumably, the shelter need would be calculated based on FMRs, the same way it is calculated for other PPM units. Housing resources could be approximated as zero, since there is no home ownership and no subsidies. The research should estimate the potential impact on the PPM—that is, what percentage of those living in poverty does the homeless population (which people flow into and out of) account for?

6

Data and Statistical Issues

For a poverty measure to be most useful for policy, research, and public understanding, relevant, accurate, and timely data with geographic and demographic detail are needed. This chapter considers the adequacy of available data—from surveys, administrative records, and other sources—to support the panel's recommended revisions to the Supplemental Poverty Measure (SPM). For reasons explained in Chapter 2, this report calls the updated SPM the Principal Poverty Measure (PPM). This chapter reviews the strengths and shortcomings of the current data infrastructure and the value of investing in that infrastructure; identifies additional data needs created by the new PPM specifications; examines opportunities for improving relevant data sources for the PPM; and discusses statistical issues in estimating the PPM thresholds and resources. Appendix 6A lists the data elements available for estimating thresholds for the current SPM and the new PPM from the Consumer Expenditure Survey (CE);[1] Appendix 6B similarly lists the availability of data elements for estimating resources from the Current Population Survey Annual Social and Economic Supplement (CPS-ASEC) and the American Community Survey (ACS).

6.1. THE NEED FOR AND BENEFITS OF IMPROVING THE DATA INFRASTRUCTURE

Data needs for estimating thresholds and resources for the current SPM are orders of magnitude greater than for the Official Poverty Measure (OPM). The OPM thresholds were set in the 1960s and last revised in 1978, and only require an annual inflation adjustment, based on the Consumer Price Index (CPI).[2] For resources, the OPM requires estimates of pretax money income, data that are not always easy to collect but have been readily available in surveys beginning with the income supplement to the CPS in 1948. The tradeoff for this relative simplicity is that the OPM does not appropriately capture the economic circumstances of many American households. For example, it does not account for the portion of earnings unavailable to workers' households because it is spent on taxes and various work expenses, and it does not include some essential resources available to households, such as in-kind transfers.

The recommendations in a 1995 National Academies of Sciences, Engineering, and Medicine report that led to the SPM (NRC, 1995) added substantially to the data requirements for estimating poverty thresholds and

---
[1] References to the CE are to the Interview Survey, unless otherwise noted.
[2] As documented in National Academies (2022), and in many other review articles, the CPI has its own complex and challenging issues.

resources, and the current panel's revisions recommend a few more. In response to the National Academies' 1995 report, the Census Bureau added content to the CPS-ASEC. Recently, to supplement CE data, the Bureau of Labor Statistics (BLS) began imputing in-kind benefits for use in the estimation of SPM thresholds. Yet the current data infrastructure is not ideal even for the OPM, let alone the current SPM and recommended PPM. Significant improvements are needed to advance the accuracy and detail of data underlying poverty measurement.

As the methodology underlying the SPM is periodically updated to keep pace with changes in economic conditions, social norms, and the policy environment, the data infrastructure must likewise be modified to respond to challenges and leverage opportunities. In recent decades, economic statistics, whether produced by government or private-sector organizations, are being constructed from an ever-widening range of data sources. This "modernization" of statistics has accelerated in response to both decreased sustainability of data collection rooted in the 20th-century survey paradigm and the rise of alternative data sources.[3]

The move toward a multiple-data-source approach in the reengineering of key economic statistics is already well under way among federal statistical agencies and elsewhere. Use of satellite imagery to improve crop estimates (National Academies, 2017), use of transactions data to create high-frequency and high-detail geographic measures of consumer spending (Aladangady et al., 2022), and use of payroll data to produce employment statistics (Cajner et al., 2019) are just a few examples. Perhaps the most prominent example of this trend is in price measurement—statistical offices around the world are modernizing CPIs through use of alternative data sources, including point-of-sale and household-based scanner data, credit card payment information, web-scraped prices, and insurance claims data.[4] Beyond government agencies, the Billion Prices Project, a joint initiative between Massachusetts Institute of Technology and Harvard University, has demonstrated the value of high-frequency price data collection to macroeconomic research—in this case, from hundreds of online retailers based in more than 70 countries.[5] The SPM is already a "multiple-data-source" statistic, as it draws from several surveys (the CPS-ASEC, CE, Survey of Income and Program Participation [SIPP], and ACS) and, if guidance from this report is followed, will also incorporate information on Fair Market Rents (housing), Affordable Care Act (ACA) health plans (medical care), and possibly childcare reimbursement rates.

The real potential of alternative data—whether obtained by new types of surveys, greater use of administrative records, or tapping into commercial sources—is the capacity to generate more accurate, timely, and disaggregated estimates. In poverty measurement, as discussed in Chapter 2, researchers and policy makers clearly need more granular information for assessing differential wellbeing at substate—e.g., county, rural/urban, community-level—geographic areas. As the major driver of cross-area cost-of-living differences, geographic detail is especially important for revealing the high variation in rental and home prices across and within regions (Guerrieri et al., 2013).[6] In the price-measurement context, a report by the National Academies (2022) describes how commercial data (e.g., from property management companies, which have access to rental data on millions of multifamily rental units) can be used to expand and increase the detail of BLS's information on rent changes. Similarly, for poverty measurement, such data sources could be used to estimate rental-price differentials within a state's nonmetropolitan areas, which are currently treated homogenously in the SPM.

The benefits of investing in the PPM data infrastructure extend well beyond improving the usefulness of the nation's key poverty statistics. More accurate measurement of income and other resources will improve research on the effectiveness of anti poverty assistance programs and a range of other policies (e.g., increases

---

[3]National Academies (2017) and Abraham (2022) are two of the many sources documenting fundamental changes that have occurred to the survey-centric foundation of federal statistics over the last decade or so. Paramount among these changes are the increasing costs of traditional modes of data collection and, relatedly, declining response rates. These trends have created a situation in which growing demands for more timely and detailed information (e.g., at state and local levels) cannot always be met.

[4]National Academies (2022) provides an in-depth assessment—along with a series of recommendations to BLS—for expanding use of multiple data sources in the CPI to keep up with rapidly changing market conditions and consumer behavior patterns.

[5]As documented in National Academies (2022), a number of statistical offices in the United States and elsewhere are collaborating with scholars from the Billion Prices Project (www.thebillionpricesproject.com/) and commercial data firms to advance price-measurement methods.

[6]Research by Diamond and Moretti (2021) and Howard and Liebersohn (2021) is indicative of the growing interest in geographic variation in the price of housing.

in the minimum wage). For many purposes, establishing the source—not just the amount—of income and other resources is important. Data on income, other household resources, and expenditures that factor into the PPM are also important in the broader production of economic statistics and analyses of income and consumption inequality in the population.

The data ecosystem has changed considerably over the past two decades—in terms of both the availability and relative importance of surveys, government administrative records, and commercial data sources; and the data infrastructure for the PPM and other economic statistics should leverage new data sources where appropriate. The panel's vision for the PPM data infrastructure, described in greater detail later in this chapter, includes:

- Enhanced content for the PPM, through added survey questions (as few as possible to minimize respondent burden) and imputations from other sources;
- Improved accuracy (reduced variance and bias) of income recipiency and amounts through combining survey and administrative records;
- Poverty estimates that are at least as timely as current estimates, achieved by developing models for projecting administrative records that lag in availability;
- Enhanced geographic detail of poverty estimates, made possible by utilizing the large sample size of the ACS;
- Quarterly or even monthly updates of selected PPM rates through use of ACS intra-year data, monthly CPS data, or both; and
- Comparable PPM estimates using other major surveys, such as the ACS and SIPP.

6.2. DATA NEEDS CREATED BY THE PROPOSED PRINCIPAL POVERTY MEASURE

For purposes of developing the PPM, the need for a flexible data-infrastructure approach is perhaps most evident for filling data gaps in the coverage of difficult-to-measure categories such as medical care, childcare, housing, and transportation, as discussed in previous chapters.[7] As emphasized throughout this report, the PPM is designed to be more conceptually consistent and accurate than the SPM. However, the new data needs required for estimating the PPM add an element of complexity. Given the panel's recommendation that the Census Bureau periodically update the conceptual approaches to estimating PPM needs and resources in the crucial measurement areas featured in Chapters 3–5, the Census Bureau should likewise take the opportunity to explore a range of accompanying data strategies.

6.2.1. Medical Care

In the current SPM methodology, the treatment of medical care is handled exclusively in the estimate of household resources, from which medical out-of-pocket (MOOP) spending—which includes insurance premiums, copayments, over-the-counter health-related products, deductibles, and other payments—is subtracted. These nondiscretionary expenses are, in effect, treated like taxes or work-related expenses. MOOP estimates are derived from self-reported amounts for the relevant categories in the CPS-ASEC (and from imputations, for those not reporting). The proposed PPM method of handling medical needs and resources requires additional information above and beyond that used in the current SPM (see Chapter 3). Most centrally, data are needed on insurance policies—specifically, ACA Marketplace premiums detailed by age, family type (size/composition), and geographic location—to account for medical care need on the threshold side of the PPM. For estimating needs thresholds, the panel recommends using the unsubsidized age- and region-specific cost of the ACA's benchmark Silver plan. For resource estimates, data will continue to be needed on the value of health insurance benefits and subsidies provided to households by government or employers, as will data on MOOP costs and health insurance premiums.

---

[7]See Appendix 6B for a summary of data needs generated by the panel's recommended SPM/PPM components.

The Census Bureau (Creamer, 2022) has already begun testing the feasibility of integrating a health-inclusive concept into the SPM, as developed by Korenman and Remler (2016); a major aspect of the Census Bureau research involves assessing data options. Relevant findings from this work can be summarized as follows:

- *Survey updating.* Information about MOOP spending is collected from CPS-ASEC respondents. The survey asks about: (1) premiums for comprehensive and supplemental health coverage (but not Medicare premiums); (2) expenditures on copays, prescriptions, and other medical care; and (3) expenditures for other over-the-counter spending. To capture information needed for a health-inclusive approach, the Census Bureau is researching the validity of new variables that may need to be added to the survey, testing updated questions and processing systems implemented in 2018, and assessing methods to account for sub-annual health insurance coverage (Creamer, 2022, p. 1). This testing does not address health insurance and medical care data needs for PPM estimates constructed from the ACS, which does not collect as much detail as the CPS-ASEC (see Appendix 6B).

  The PPM will use much of the same CPS-ASEC data found in annual Census Bureau reports on health insurance coverage. Internal CPS-ASEC data would, where possible, be linked to external medical insurance plan data sources at the county level, followed by core-based statistical area, and then by state, with the second-lowest-cost Silver plans being chosen at each level. Note that linkage at the county level is not possible for all counties—the CPS-ASEC sample currently includes 1,385 of 3,143 counties (BLS, 2014). Linkage for all rating area county geographic units would, however, be possible for the ACS.

  For data users to replicate the estimates within any data product, variables must be added to the CPS-ASEC or ACS data files. Specifically, information on health insurance units must be included if users are to understand the detailed relationships underlying the estimates; and, to set medical needs and benefits, a variable (or code to generate this variable) must be added to determine a "primary" insurance type. Together, these two pieces of information would allow data users to accurately recreate the medical benefits and needs added to PPM resources and thresholds.

- *Broadening data sources.* The Census Bureau is also exploring the potential use of other data sources identified in research by Korenman et al. (2019). Among the most important is cost-sharing information on the second-lowest-cost Silver plan from either Healthcare.gov or state-run health care exchanges. Collecting these data yearly from each state would be time intensive; however, as suggested by Creamer (2022), the Census Bureau could "follow the simplification in Hyson, Korenman et al. (2021) which sets caps for Medicaid premium and nonpremium expenditures to 5 percent of family income instead of gathering the state specific information" (p. 6).

- *Timeliness considerations.* Availability of data for valuing health insurance would need to conform with the annual production schedule of the PPM—essentially by September of each year. Fortunately, this is typically the case, as information on monthly plan premiums must be set before the open enrollment period. The same is true for the government's average Medicare contribution (Creamer, 2022).

- *Historical continuity.* While the panel values accuracy more highly, work can be done to extend the consistency of the proposed PPM back in time. Most of the key data elements have been collected for some time. HIX Compare,[8] a free service provided by the Robert Wood Johnson Foundation, collects and maintains data on the ACA Silver plan (proposed for benchmarking the basic medical care need in the PPM) and on households with private insurance or Medicaid, and includes out-of-pocket maximums for various plans. The data are available, albeit with some gaps, from 2014–2021 by rating area.

6.2.2. Childcare

Chapter 4 introduces the idea of incorporating childcare into the PPM in a way that improves consistency, by treating childcare as a basic need on the threshold side and accounting for childcare assistance on the resource side. The panel recommends initial implementation of these changes for families who use paid childcare, while also pursuing research to consider how childcare needs can be accounted for among *all* families with children,

---

[8] See www.hixcompare.org/.

regardless of whether paid childcare is used. The current recommendations on childcare will require new data to be incorporated into the PPM, and future research may suggest additional expansions.

Currently, the SPM accounts for childcare as a work expense that is subtracted from the estimate of resources available to a family to reach the FCSUti threshold. The CPS-ASEC asks parents whether they pay for childcare and, if so, how much they spend. The amounts paid for any type of childcare while parents are at work are summed over all children (Fox, 2020). The ACS does not include childcare questions. To implement Recommendation 4.2—to add childcare need as a PPM threshold category—the panel recommends drawing on childcare reimbursement guidelines under the Child Care and Development Fund policy. Developing a basic childcare need portion of the PPM threshold would thus require a new approach but can rely on existing sources of information. The panel leaves the details on preferred approaches to the Census Bureau, although a number of current efforts to estimate basic childcare costs are referenced in Chapter 4.[9]

Recommendation 4.3 balances the inclusion of childcare in the threshold by including childcare assistance in resources. As discussed in Chapter 4, new survey questions and imputation methods would be required to ascertain this information and to develop a complete picture of childcare assistance. New questions on the CPS-ASEC and ACS covering the types of childcare respondents used for each child under age 13, and whether a government (or other) agency helped pay for that care, are needed to fully implement the recommendation. If government support was received, respondents would ideally be asked whether that support covered the full cost of care or a part of the cost. Households are best equipped to report on out-of-pocket expenses, rather than (unobserved) subsidies paid directly to providers, so it would make sense for the Census Bureau to impute the value of subsidies based on reported type of care used.

6.2.3. Housing

Like other components of FCSUti, the current SPM housing threshold is calculated by BLS using information reported in the CE and geographically adjusted using the ACS. As detailed in Chapter 5, separate thresholds are calculated for homeowners with a mortgage, homeowners without a mortgage, and renters. CE estimates of outlays on shelter are similar to those based on alternative data sources. For example, data from the 2018 ACS indicates that the national median two-bedroom gross rent (which includes utilities) was around $1,050 per month (Joint Center for Housing Studies, 2020). The shelter-and-utilities portion of the 2018 SPM threshold for renters was about $1,170 per month. Geographic differences in housing costs are applied to the SPM based on ACS estimates of rental rates for 343 areas. These areas can often be defined at the county level which, in many cases, is the smallest geographic unit that can reliably match housing-cost and ACS data.

On the resource side of the SPM, estimates of housing subsidies are based on administrative data on market rents from the U.S. Department of Housing and Urban Development (HUD). Amounts paid are estimated using HUD program rules and income information from the CPS-ASEC.[10] The value of housing subsidies is estimated as the difference between the "market rent" for the housing unit and the total tenant payment; subsidies are capped at the housing portion of the threshold minus the household's required rental payment.

Recommendation 5.1 states that PPM housing thresholds should be set based on the rental cost of housing; this would apply to renters as well as homeowners (who implicitly rent their homes to themselves). This standardized treatment reduces the complexity in the existing SPM which currently creates three separate housing thresholds by housing tenure type. In calculating thresholds, the panel recommends that rent levels be based on HUD's annual Fair Market Rents (FMRs), which vary by location and number of bedrooms and include basic utilities except telephone and internet. Households would be matched to home size (number of bedrooms) based on the number and composition of household members, according to HUD guidelines. Thus, the data foundation for estimating shelter and utilities thresholds would shift from the CE to the ACS, on which FMRs are based.

HUD provides FMRs on an annual basis for metropolitan areas, which may comprise multiple counties; at the zip code level within metropolitan areas; and for all nonmetropolitan counties. An FMR-based approach to setting

---

[9]See footnote 7 in Chapter 4 for details.
[10]See Renwick and Mitchel (2015) for details about this estimation procedure.

needs thresholds would tend to yield slightly lower estimates than the current SPM method but, as explained in Chapter 5, this is not always the case. As noted above, HUD data are also used in determining housing assistance to families (e.g., standard payment amounts for the Housing Choice Voucher Program).

Recommendations 5.5 and 5.6 suggest accounting for differences in tenure and home ownership type on the resource side—specifically, by including implicit (or imputed) rental income for households that own homes. The implicit rental income estimate would subtract homeowners' user costs such as mortgage interest payments, property taxes, insurance, and maintenance expenses; the resulting amount would be the net flow of income for homeowners from this asset. This recommendation creates new data needs for the PPM. Most of the data needed to estimate owners' user costs and imputed rent are already captured in the ACS, including housing tenure, homeowners insurance, property taxes, mortgage payments (combined principal and interest), and the home's market value. However, the CPS-ASEC lacks most of these variables, meaning questions would need to be added or the information imputed from other sources (e.g., the CE, ACS, or American Housing Survey[11]).

The CE or American Housing Survey could be used to impute rental income (often referred to as rental equivalence) minus operating expenses. Alternatively, the ACS could be used to impute rents minus expenses, although this survey does not include maintenance and repairs payments and mortgage interest payments (see Appendix 6B). The ACS is used by the Bureau of Economic Analysis (BEA) to impute rental income of homeowners (Aten and Heston, 2020) and to measure operating expenses including property taxes, insurance, mortgage payments, and condo fees. Additionally, just as income measurement can be improved through use of administrative data, administrative and commercial data sources have been used, including by HUD, to improve the measures of housing costs in the ACS and thereby in the CPS-ASEC (e.g., property taxes, property values, and other housing characteristics).[12]

6.3. THE CURRENT SURVEY-BASED DATA INFRASTRUCTURE

6.3.1. Features of Relevant Surveys

Four surveys—the CE, ACS, SIPP, and CPS-ASEC—factor prominently in the regularly published SPM estimates. The CPS-ASEC is the primary data source for estimating the components of resources; however, work-related expenses (other than childcare) are based on the SIPP. The thresholds that are compared to resources to determine poverty status are estimated from the CE, with geographic adjustments made to the housing and utilities component by a median rent index based on the ACS. Table 6-1 provides information on key features of the CPS-ASEC, CE, ACS, and SIPP.

Recently, the Census Bureau has implemented a version of the SPM using the ACS as the basis for estimates (Fox et al., 2020); and the Census Bureau explicitly recommends using the ACS for state-based poverty estimates. The panel strongly supports efforts to add the ACS to the CPS-ASEC as a major platform for the PPM (see Recommendation 6.1). The most compelling advantage of the ACS is the capability to produce local-area PPM rates due to its sample size (2.1 million interviews per year compared with approximately 78,000 for the CPS-ASEC). The most obvious downside of using the ACS is that it offers fewer details about the sources of respondents' income and fewer details on program participation.

---

[11] The American Housing Survey conducted by the Census Bureau provides information on the size, composition, and quality of the nation's housing, and measures changes in housing stock over time. This longitudinal survey is conducted biennially in odd-numbered years and covers major U.S. metropolitan areas.

[12] An example of such proposed alternative data use by HUD arose for fiscal year 2023 FMR estimates, in response to issues created by the COVID-19 pandemic. As a work-around to the lack of available 2020 ACS 1-year data, the agency proposed using private-sector rental data, which were demonstrated to more accurately reflect changes in local market rent inflation in the wake of the pandemic. Among the data sources evaluated were RealPage average effective rent per unit; Moody's Analytics REIS average gross revenue per unit; CoStar Group average effective rent; CoreLogic, Inc. single-family combined three-bedroom rent index; ApartmentList rent estimates; and the Zillow Observed Rent Index (U.S. Housing and Urban Development Department, 2022).

TABLE 6-1 Survey Features: CPS-ASEC, ACS, SIPP, and CE

Feature	CPS-ASEC	ACS	SIPP	CE (Interview Survey)
Universe	Household population plus people in noninstitutional group quarters (includes college students in dormitories if reported at home and Armed Forces members if living in a household with at least one civilian adult); excludes individuals experiencing homelessness and people in nursing homes, prisons, other institutions, and Armed Forces barracks	Total household and group quarters population except for individuals experiencing homelessness and residents of domestic violence shelters—college students in dormitories sampled at college	Same as CPS-ASEC	Same as CPS-ASEC
Content (Topics)	Detailed questions per topic: family/household composition, person demographics, marital status, educational attainment, health insurance coverage and costs, nativity, previous year's income from all sources, work experience, receipt of noncash benefits, program participation, geographic mobility, childcare costs	1–2 questions per topic: family/household composition, person demographics, ancestry, citizenship, nativity, commuting, place of work, disability status, education, employment, fertility, grandparents as caregivers, health insurance, income and earnings (6 categories), Supplemental Nutrition Assistance Program status, industry, occupation, class of worker, language spoken at home, marital history, residence 1 year ago, period of military service, undergraduate field of degree, veteran status, work status last year, housing characteristics, housing costs/value, computer/internet use, vehicles available	Detailed questions per topic: family/household composition, person demographics, language at home, citizenship, nativity (self and parents), veteran status, residences, marital history, education, employment, unemployment, commuting, medical care utilization, insurance and costs, program participation, income, assets, vehicles, child and dependent care, disability, fertility, adult and child wellbeing	Family/household characteristics, person demographics, stock of vehicles (1st interview) employment and earnings (1st and 4th interviews), income and assets (4th interview); detailed questions on 60–70% of expenditures (month of purchase and quarterly expenses), global questions on 20–25% of expenditures (e.g., food, and apparel); diary survey has detailed expenditures collected over 2 weeks, but is not used for SPM threshold production
Sample Design	Supplement to the monthly CPS, which has a multistage, stratified, clustered, rotational design (addresses are in sample for 4 months, out for 8 months, and in again for 4 months); CPS-ASEC has 100% oversample of Hispanic households; oversample for estimates of states' children's health insurance program; potential to link addresses for part of sample to previous year	Nonclustered sample every month (addresses can be in sample only once every 5 years); small governmental units oversampled, large census tracts undersampled; 5-year sampling rates range from 0.5% to 15%; nonrespondents (after mail follow-up) subsampled for field follow-up (one-third subsample on average, rates vary inversely by response rates)	Multistage, stratified, clustered design; low-income areas oversampled; panel (longitudinal) design; new panel selected every year (as of 2018); each panel with 4 annual waves (2019 panel had one wave; 2020 panel had response problems due to COVID-19)*	Multistage, stratified, clustered, rotational design; addresses are in sample for 4 quarters (treated independently for estimating SPM thresholds); new sample introduced each quarter

continued

TABLE 6-1 Continued

Feature	CPS-ASEC	ACS	SIPP	CE (Interview Survey)
Sample Size	89,000 addresses in sample selected from 1,385 of nation's 3,143 counties; 78,000 interviewed households (73,000 interviewed in 2020 due to COVID-19)	295,000 addresses in sample every month; 3.54 million addresses per year; 2.1 million final interviews per year (due to COVID-19, the 2020 ACS had fewer sample addresses and fewer final interviews)**	45,000 Wave 1 eligible households, 2018 panel; 24,500 Wave 1 eligible households, 2019 panel; 22,000 Wave 1 eligible households, 2020 panel; household members followed for later waves	13,000 addresses contacted each quarter for interview and 18,000 addresses for Diary each year; 6,900 usable interviews obtained each quarter
Periodicity	Annual (ASEC interviews conducted in February–April)	Monthly (estimates are cumulated to calendar year)	Annual (interviews conducted in winter–spring of following year)	Monthly (each month, one-sixth of addresses are in 1st month, 2nd ... 6th month)
Reference Period for Income/ Expenditures	Prior calendar year	Prior 12 months	Month (most variables); year for some variables (e.g., income from assets)	For interview, prior 3 months for expenditures; prior 12 months from Interview for income; current value and value 12 months earlier for assets/liabilities
Unit(s) Available for Analysis	Household (all people at an address); family (related people at an address); unrelated individual (in group quarters or household); SPM resource unit (related people at an address plus cohabiting couples, foster children, and unrelated children under age 15)	Same as CPS-ASEC	Same as CPS-ASEC	Consumer unit (family members at an address, including foster children; unrelated people in a household who share major expenses; unrelated individuals who are financially independent)
Publications/ Data Products	*Income and Poverty* [OPM] *in the United States* released mid-September (5 months after end of data collection); *The Supplemental Poverty Measure* released concurrently; additional tables and microdata file released concurrently	1-year cumulative tables for areas with 65,000+ people in mid-September (7 months after end of data collection for December of publication year); reduced set of 1-year cumulative tables for areas with 20,000+ people and 1-year microdata file in mid-October; 5-year cumulative tables for all areas, tabulated down to block group, and 5-year microdata file in mid-December	Special national-level publications released sporadically; microdata files released by wave; latest waves available are Wave 1 of the 2020 Panel (income year 2019); Wave 1 (only wave) of the 2019 Panel (income year 2018); and Waves 1–3 of the 2018 Panel (income years 2017–2019)	Regular national-level publications on consumer expenditures (based on integration of the Interview and Diary Surveys) released every 6 months; integrated tables covering 12 months of data released twice a year (calendar 2020 tables released early September 2021; July 2019–June 2020 tables released late April 2021); microdata files available annually

SOURCE: Compiled by panel staff from BLS and Census Bureau websites.
NOTES: *Design has changed substantially several times since SIPP began in 1984.
**The public-use file, however, includes only about 2 million households; to protect privacy the Census Bureau's ACS SPM work uses the public-use microdata sample version of the data so that non-Census Bureau researchers can use the data.

6.3.2. Survey Strengths and Weaknesses

The survey-based infrastructure underlying the Census Bureau's poverty statistics—including the SPM and the proposed PPM—has key advantages mainly due to the breadth of questions included in the surveys. Key strengths include:

- The CPS-ASEC has questions on almost all items needed to calculate SPM resources as currently defined (see Appendix 6B), although some questions would need to be added for the PPM. The ACS lacks the detail on income and in-kind benefits of the CPS-ASEC but does capture major income categories and has questions that would facilitate measurement of housing as a component of resources. It, too, would require additional questions for the PPM.
- The CPS-ASEC and ACS include a wealth of demographic information (e.g., household type, employment, race/ethnicity) for calculating SPM/PPM poverty rates for population groups of interest. Much of this demographic information (e.g., race and ethnicity) is not available from other administrative records.
- The CE includes questions on almost all expenditures needed to calculate SPM thresholds as currently defined for consumer units (CUs) with children. It also includes all the questions needed to calculate the food, clothing, and internet category thresholds in the PPM for all CUs.

Key weaknesses of the survey-based infrastructure include:

- The surveys that provide input to the SPM suffer from impaired data quality created by nonresponse, coverage error, and reporting error. In particular, underreporting is significant and imputation rates are high for many sources of income. These defects skew poverty rates and other economic measures for households (Hokayem et al., 2015; Meyer et al., 2015; Bollinger et al., 2019). There is also underreporting of income for high-income households. Data-quality deficits also increase the uncertainty (variance) in estimates of poverty and other economic measures. The use of administrative records could remedy these problems to a significant extent.
- The CPS-ASEC sample size is not ideal for PPM estimates of subnational geographic areas. While representative at the state level, the Census Bureau recommends 3-year averages for more reliable state estimates. However, such smoothing of estimates is not as timely as desirable for poverty statistics, particularly when households' economic situations are in flux, as has been the case since the start of the COVID-19 pandemic. The ACS could provide the remedy for both drawbacks, although it lacks the detail on income components that the CPS-ASEC provides and requires imputation for receipt and amounts of in-kind benefits and other variables needed for poverty statistics. While the ACS provides additional geographic details, it is not clear how the Census Bureau's newly proposed changes for privacy protection would impact the level of geographic detail publicly available.
- The CPS-ASEC is an address-based sample, and hence, excludes the homeless population (and any other people not living in housing units). The lack of including people experiencing homelessness in the poverty calculation can yield an underestimate of poverty (Meyer et al., 2021). As stated in Chapter 5, research is recommended to examine the possibility of estimating the size and poverty status of the homeless population.

Ideally, all relevant surveys (including CPS-ASEC, ACS, and SIPP) would allow production of the PPM. Of course, expanding the ACS to provide the new data that would be required for PPM calculations needs to be weighed against potential costs and drawbacks of increasing the number of questions on the survey. At present, data-quality problems complicate comparisons of the SPM and OPM among surveys. As noted above, the Census Bureau is exploring how the SPM can be estimated from ACS data,[13] and demand for this exists among researchers and policy analysts as it allows for state and substate estimates using yearly data with high demographic detail. A number

---

[13] See Fox et al. (2020) and www.census.gov/content/dam/Census/library/working-papers/2020/demo/SEHSD-WP2020-09.pdf.

of states, including New York, California, Wisconsin, and Virginia, produce their own SPM using the ACS, as do several cities, including New York City, which pioneered an ACS-based SPM, and San Francisco (e.g., Smeeding and Thornton, 2020; Bohn et al., 2021). The Urban Institute's ATTIS microsimulation model also generates SPM estimates from the ACS, building on Census Bureau methods but with alternative methods for imputing benefits and calculating taxes.[14]

6.3.3. Survey Quality Concerns

Household surveys have been the flagship of federal statistics on income, poverty, expenditures, and many other topics for at least 75 years. Over the last 30 years, however, survey quality has deteriorated in many cases. Specifically, response rates (unit and item) have declined in recent decades and underreporting has increased, requiring a greater reliance on imputation and weighting adjustments. Other concerns include coverage error, reporting errors such as confusing Supplemental Security Income (SSI) with Social Security, and imputation bias. These concerns are well documented[15] and include the examples that follow.

Household (Unit) Response Rates

Household (unit) response rates have been declining in nearly all surveys, in the United States and abroad. The Census Bureau obtains higher response rates in its surveys than do other organizations, but even Census Bureau surveys have not been immune to the problem. Figure 6-1 shows the decline in response rates to the basic CPS, CPS-ASEC, and CE surveys from 1984 to 2019. Based on findings (of an earlier version of a paper) by Sabelhaus et al. (2015), in 2014, BLS began using zip-code-level income estimates from the Internal Revenue Service (IRS) for nonresponse weighting adjustments; such adjustments are needed to correct for underrepresentation of high-income households and overrepresentation of low-income households in the CE. BLS is currently conducting research on using IRS data on income at the household level for nonresponse weighting adjustments (Steinberg et al., 2020). The Census Bureau is also doing this type of research for the CPS-ASEC and ACS.[16]

Borgschulte et al. (2022) examine whether partisanship can help explain the trend in unit nonresponse in the CPS, noting that the sharp increase in nonresponse in the CPS main survey and the ASEC after 2010 coincided with the emergence of the Tea Party, which espoused strong anti–federal government sentiments. Their analysis found evidence of a partisan cycle in survey response, but partisanship, and notably the growth of the Tea Party, did not explain the observed trend increase. Improving survey response rates, or at least stemming the growth in nonresponse, is and should continue to be a high priority for the Census Bureau.

Item Nonresponse to Income Questions

In addition to unit nonresponse, survey item nonresponse to income questions has increased. The CPS-ASEC is, as noted above, the primary source for resource measures used in the OPM and the SPM. Of those resources, labor-market earnings make up the dominant source of income among nonretired households, comprising at least 80 percent of personal income. The substantial increase in earnings nonresponse is a complicating factor of the CPS-ASEC in recent decades (Hokayem et al. 2015; Bollinger et al., 2019). This nonresponse can occur either from refusal to answer earnings questions (item nonresponse), or from refusal to respond to most or all of the ASEC (supplement nonresponse). Publicly available data from the CPS for the population of individuals age 16–64 indicates that earnings item nonresponse more than doubled from 1990 to 2004, then trended down for the next decade, only to jump several percentage points over the last 5 years. Even more striking is the increase in ASEC

---

[14] See www.urban.org/research-methods/attis-microsimulation-model.
[15] See, for example, Hirsch and Schumacher (2004); Bollinger and Hirsch (2006); Meyer et al. (2009, 2015); Bee et al. (2015); Hokayem et al. (2015); Rothbaum (2015); Bee and Rothbaum (2019); Bollinger et al. (2019); and Borgschulte et al. (2022).
[16] See, for example, www.census.gov/library/working-papers/2020/demo/SEHSD-WP2020-10.html.

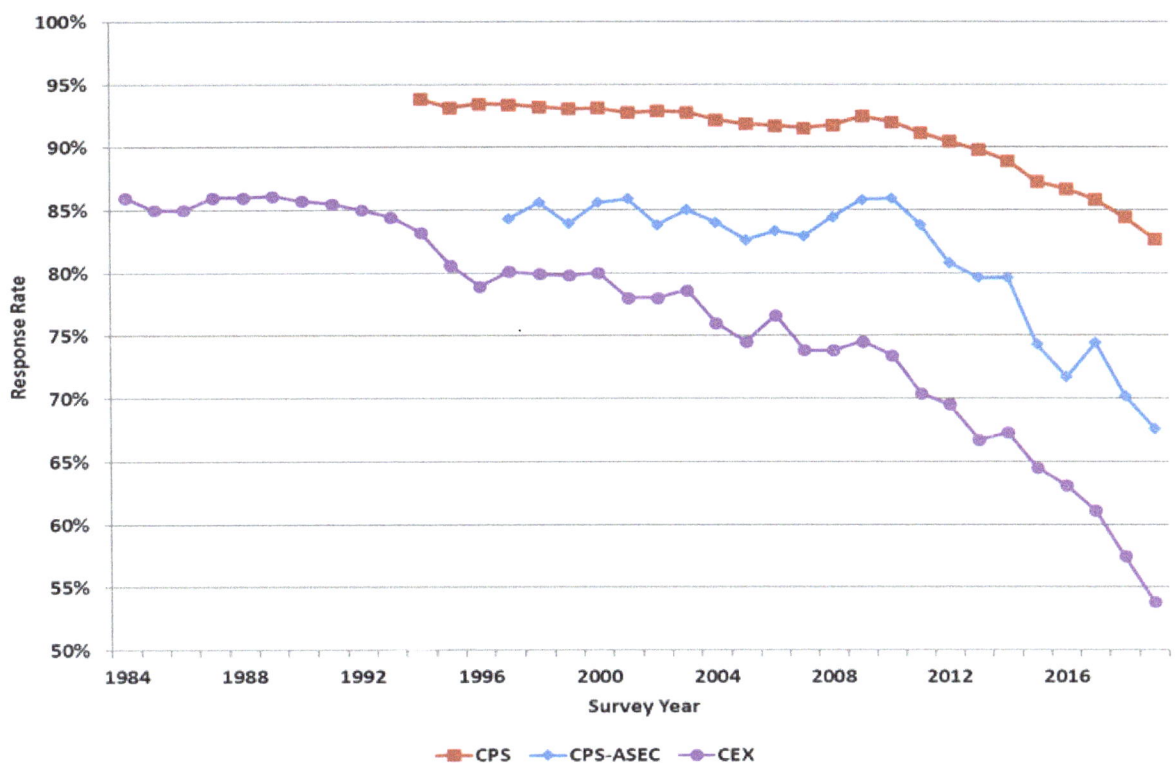

FIGURE 6-1 Unit response rates to selected household surveys conducted by the U.S. Census Bureau, 1984–2019.
SOURCE: Abraham (2022, Figure 1).
NOTES: CPS = monthly Current Population Survey. CPS-ASEC = CPS Annual Social and Economic Supplement. CEX = Consumer Expenditure Interview Survey. Annual or annual average response rates reported.

nonresponse, which jumped from 10 percent in 2010 to 23 percent in 2021. Combined, this means that earnings are missing for at least 40 percent of potential prime-aged workers.

The Census Bureau does not drop observations with missing earnings or a missing supplement, but instead retains these observations and imputes values for the missing data. Depending on the questions being addressed and the reasons for nonresponse, use of imputed values can either have little effect or can produce severe bias (Hirsch and Schumacher, 2004; Bollinger and Hirsch, 2006; Hokayem et al., 2015; Bollinger et al., 2019). If earnings data are "missing completely at random," then nonresponse is completely independent of earnings; if earnings are "missing at random" (MAR), then nonresponse is not dependent on earnings after conditioning on covariates; and if earnings are not MAR, then nonresponse depends on the value of missing earnings even after conditioning on covariates (Rubin, 1976; Little and Rubin, 2002). The last case is generally referred to as "nonresponse bias." Both Census Bureau imputation procedures and common methods to deal with nonresponse assume that nonresponse is MAR; that is, those not reporting earnings have earnings similar to those with equivalent measured attributes. If this MAR assumption holds, there will be no bias in measures of poverty from the hot deck; however, if earnings are not missing randomly, there can be bias. Indeed, Bollinger et al. (2019) present evidence that missing earnings are not MAR; and Hokayem et al. (2015) show that the OPM is biased downward by about 10 percent in a typical year during the period 1998–2009, which was prior to the large runup in supplement nonresponse.

While explicit recommendations for improving response rates in the CPS-ASEC are beyond the scope of this report, the panel notes that long-running household panels like the Panel Study of Income Dynamics (PSID) have item nonresponse rates on earnings that are about one-third the level found in the CPS-ASEC. The Census

Bureau could usefully explore best practices from surveys like the PSID for improving CPS-ASEC nonresponse. The next section focuses on innovations in linking surveys to administrative records and on imputations as a means of improving data quality in the presence of nonresponse.

Item Nonresponse Rates to Expenditure Questions

In the CE, item response rates are not easily calculated. Since many questions ask only for the dollar amount and not the incidence of purchase, standard item response rates are not available. However, BLS produces a data-quality report that includes edit, allocation, and imputation rates (Armstrong et al., 2022). Many of these rates have not changed during the past decade. Some research suggests that the frequency of reporting zero expenditures in a 3-month period could indicate that respondents are less willing to report expenditures. Bee et al. (2015; Appendix Table 7.6) show that the percentage of CUs in the CE Interview Survey reporting zero expenditures on women's and girls' clothing, for example, increased from 35 percent in 1986 to 53 percent in 2010. Similarly, reporting of zeroes went from 48 to 62 percent for men's and boys' clothing, and from 50 to 67 percent for shoes and other footwear. Percentage increases in zeroes were smaller for other items (e.g., from 57 to 67%for off-premises alcoholic beverages) or showed no change (e.g., only about 1% of CUs reported zero expenditures for off-premises food and nonalcoholic beverages in 1986 and 2010).

Substantial and Increased Underreporting of Transfer Income

When comparing survey aggregate amounts to administrative records, substantial and increased underreporting of transfer income is well documented for many sources (see, e.g., Meyer et al., 2009, 2015). This research highlights two main impacts on poverty measurement caused by underreporting—specifically, poverty could be overstated and the impacts of government programs in reducing poverty could be understated. The growing problem of transfer income nonresponse and underreporting of in-kind transfers is not unique to the CPS-ASEC, nor to surveys in the United States (Brewer et al., 2017). The reasons for these developments are not well understood.

Imputation can make up for missing income amounts for respondents who report receipt and can add income for respondents who do not answer a receipt-related question and are imputed to receive the income source. This leaves income unaccounted for in instances in which respondents received an income source but reported that they did not, and when they reported a lower amount than they in fact received.

In the CPS-ASEC, ACS, and CE, Meyer et al. (2015, Tables 2, 3, 4, 7) find net underreporting of income from many transfer programs (both cash and in-kind) to be high and increasing up through 2005, and it is likely that reporting has not improved since these comparisons were made. For example, less than 50 percent of Aid to Families with Dependent Children/Temporary Assistance for Needy Families (AFDC/TANF) benefits were reported in the CPS-ASEC and ACS in 2004 (and only 25% of such benefits were reported in the CE). Reporting of Supplemental Nutrition Assistance Program (SNAP) benefits was not much better. Even Social Security benefits are somewhat underreported (90, 81, and 90% of benefits were reported in the CPS-ASEC, ACS, and CE, respectively, in 2005), while SSI benefits are somewhat worse reported (78, 84, and 66% of benefits were reported in the CPS-ASEC, ACS, and CE, respectively, in 2005).

Using samples linked to New York State administrative records, Meyer et al. (2015, Table 4) estimate the extent of net underreporting—in SNAP estimates in the CPS-ASEC and AFDC/TANF estimates in the CPS-ASEC and ACS—due to the combination of unit nonresponse, coverage error, and weighting; due to item nonresponse; and due to measurement error. They found measurement error to be the largest source of the discrepancy. Meyer and Mittag (2019) estimated the effect of net underreporting on estimates of deep poverty, poverty, and near poverty, using matched CPS-ASEC and administrative records for New York State for 2008–2011 for SNAP, TANF, General Assistance, and housing assistance. Using the administrative records, they found a reduction of 0.9, 2.5, and 3.1 percentage points (for people in deep poverty, poverty, and near poverty, respectively) compared with the survey estimates, and even larger reductions for certain types of households, such as those headed by single mothers.

It is worth noting that other government surveys, specifically SIPP and the U.S. Department of Agriculture's (USDA's) National Household Food Acquisition and Purchase Survey (FoodAPS)[17]—perform considerably better than the CPS in terms of income reporting. Kang and Moffitt (2019) matched administrative data from most of the states in the FoodAPS Primary Sampling Units to self-reported SNAP participation from the survey, and they found that FoodAPS showed little error in SNAP reporting. They also found that the minimal misreporting that did occur had little impact on estimates of SNAP's influence on food security, food spending, or dietary quality of acquired foods. Similar results were found for National School Lunch/Breakfast Program reporting.[18]

Underreporting of Some Expenditures and Omissions of Others

In the CE Interview Survey, there is underreporting of some expenditures and omissions of others. The survey does not collect spending from in-kind benefits except for SNAP—in response, BLS recently decided to impute Special Supplemental Nutrition Program for Women, Infants, and Children (WIC), National School Lunch Program, Low Income Home Energy Assistance Program, and rental assistance into the CE data for developing SPM thresholds. Meyer et al. (2015, Table 7.1) find that, for comparable categories in 2010, CE aggregates generally fell short of Personal Consumption Expenditure (PCE) aggregates produced by BEA. The differences were modest for some items—the CE captured 86 percent of spending on food consumed at home and 80 percent of spending on communications. However, the CE captured much less of the PCE aggregate for food eaten away from home (53%) and clothing (32%). In contrast, the CE performed better compared to FoodAPS on total food spending and spending on food at home, and it was very close to FoodAPS on spending on food away from home (see Clay et al., 2016). For constructing SPM thresholds, it is likely that median expenditures on the SPM bundle are reasonably accurate, although means are underreported due to underreporting by CUs with high income and spending.

Coverage of Population Groups Varies

In household surveys, coverage of populations groups varies substantially. For example, even after weighting for nonresponse, surveys disproportionately miss such groups as African American men when compared with decennial Census counts. Use of census-based population estimates by age, sex, and race/ethnicity as a final stage in weighting rectifies the disparities on these basic demographic characteristics based on the MAR assumption. Yet, it is difficult to correct for disparities that may exist for socioeconomic groups (e.g., men experiencing periods of low income), which, in turn, may distort estimates of poverty, unemployment, and other measures of household wellbeing.[19]

6.4. ADMINISTRATIVE DATA FOR IMPROVING INCOME ESTIMATES

Administrative records have a long history of use within household survey methodology, to provide control totals for weighting adjustments. Specifically, to estimate internal migration, the Census Bureau uses birth, death, immigration, and IRS records to annually update population estimates by age, race and ethnicity, and sex. These estimates are used in the final weighting stage for the CPS-ASEC, ACS, CE, SIPP, and other household surveys, to correct for coverage errors and reduce variance in survey estimates. Elsewhere, BLS uses IRS zip-code-level income estimates to weight adjustments for unit nonresponse in the CE; and the Census Bureau uses administrative

---

[17] FoodAPS is a nationally representative survey of U.S. households that collects comprehensive data about food purchases and acquisitions made by households. See www.ers.usda.gov/data-products/foodaps-national-household-food-acquisition-and-purchase-survey/. FoodAPS showed little error in SNAP reporting—perhaps because food is a significant concern for respondents and they are thus primed to remember the program, or perhaps the FoodAPS used recent SNAP recipients as a frame for finding people on SNAP.

[18] A few caveats regarding FoodAPS should be noted. The data project acquired administrative records from only 23 of the 28 states in the survey. Also, respondents had to give consent to the match (only 122 of 4,826 did not give consent), so perhaps just knowing that survey responses would be matched to administrative records encouraged more accurate reporting. But it also seems clear that more could be done by surveys to improve reporting error, potentially with administrative record matches (see USDA, 2021, for some broad findings).

[19] Bollinger et al. (2019) use a model applying copula-based process to correct for missing earnings values. That model could be modified to also address undercoverage of people.

records (SNAP and IRS records, specifically) to annually update small-area income and poverty (OPM) estimates for use by counties and school districts in allocating funds to schools serving populations with low incomes.[20]

Perhaps most crucial in the context of the PPM, administrative records offer the opportunity to considerably improve the accuracy of income estimates. To help offset inaccuracies in measurement of earnings due to nonresponse and underreporting of transfers, researchers have pursued linkages to administrative records, facilitated thorough cooperation with various agencies, and accessed via secure research data centers. Substantial progress has been made over the past two decades linking Census Bureau survey data to administrative tax records and transfer program data from the Social Security Administration (SSA), IRS, USDA, and numerous state agencies. SSA has provided information to the Census Bureau on individual earnings via the Detailed Earnings Records, as well as on transfer benefits from Social Security Retirement, Social Security Disability, and SSI. The IRS has provided access to 1040 tax returns, along with associated forms such as the W-2 wage statement, 1099s for self-employment and retirement income, and the Earned Income Tax Credit (EITC) (and recently the Child Tax Credit) recipient file. The USDA, with the cooperation of state agencies, has provided access to SNAP and WIC records for cooperating states, with some states also providing access to data on other programs such as TANF. The Census Bureau also has access to limited data from records for U.S. Department of Veterans Affairs benefits and other disability and survivor benefits. Table 6-2, adapted from Bee and Rothbaum (2019), summarizes the records currently available to the Census Bureau.

In these applications, the administrative records are linked to Census Bureau surveys such as the CPS-ASEC using a unique Protected Identification Key (PIK) produced within the agency. The PIK is a confidentiality-protected version of the Social Security Number (SSN). Since the Census Bureau does not currently ask respondents for SSNs as part of the CPS-ASEC, it uses its own record linkage software system, the Person Validation System, to assign SSNs from the SSA Numident file.[21] This assignment relies on a probabilistic matching model based on name, address, date of birth, and gender. The SSN is then converted to a PIK to link data like the CPS-ASEC to "PIKed" SSNs in tax and other administrative records. On average, about 90 percent of respondents receive a PIK on the CPS-ASEC, but this rate drops considerably among the low-earning population. Bollinger et al. (2019) report that failure to PIK is highest among noncitizens of Hispanic ethnicity, and Jones and Ziliak (2022) report that the antipoverty effectiveness of programs like the EITC is attenuated because of missing PIKs among this population, which tends to be more disadvantaged. The authors also demonstrate the importance of using the tax data to measure the effectiveness of the EITC, which is currently computed in the SPM estimation. These linkages between tax data and the CPS are also important in evaluating the take-up rates for the EITC and other tax credits.

If administrative records were available on a timely basis, the replacement of survey values of transfer income with administrative records data would be a viable solution to the underreporting problem. Administrative data on transfer income capture the dollar amounts of transfers flowing through the economy. Missing earnings from surveys could also be replaced with SSA detailed earnings records and would likely be more timely for production of annual poverty estimates. In this case, however, it is not clear that administrative data on earnings should replace survey responses, in part because not all earnings are taxable, and some earnings go unreported to tax authorities. Indeed, Bollinger et al. (2019) show that earnings reported in the SSA detailed earnings records are too low in the left tail of the earnings distribution compared to earnings reported (not imputed) in the CPS-ASEC. Research (e.g., Hokayem et al., 2015) shows that, for estimating earnings, a mixed-data approach combining tax reports together with survey reports appears to be preferable to either source alone. One reason is that under-the-table earnings are reported, at least to some extent, in the CPS-ASEC but not in tax records.[22]

Despite some limitations, discussed below, administrative transfer records generally provide a much more complete portrait of the financial wellbeing of low-income families than do their survey counterparts (Meyer et al., 2015; Larrimore et al., 2017; Jones and Ziliak, 2022). For this reason, this panel concurs with Recommendation 22 of the recent Interagency Technical Working Group (ITWG) on Evaluating Alternative Measures of Poverty (BLS, 2020) that the Census Bureau should accelerate its examination of a variety of approaches for integrating administrative data into poverty measurement, including replacement, using both sources, and regression-based imputation.

---

[20] See www.census.gov/programs-surveys/saipe.html.

[21] The Numident file is a record of applications for Social Security cards and includes data elements for name, date and place of birth, parents' names, and date of death (see McNabb et al., 2009).

[22] See Hokayem et al. (2015) for an application of this mixed approach to the measurement of the OPM.

TABLE 6-2 Available or Potentially Available Administrative Data for Money Income, In-Kind Benefits, and Taxes

Income Item	Data Source and Administrative Item (available to Census Bureau unless otherwise noted)	Notes
Wages and Salaries	IRS: Limited W-2 Information SSA (via IRS): Detailed Earnings Record (DER) States: Unemployment insurance data in Longitudinal Employer-Household Dynamics data	Earnings net of employee deductions for health insurance, etc.; excludes unreported earnings (e.g., tips) The DER has W2 earnings as well as deferred wage contributions to 401(k), 403(b), 408(k), 457(b), and 501(c) plans
Self-Employment (Sole Proprietor/ Independent Contractor)	SSA: DER IRS: 1040 Schedule C, SE; 1099-MISC; 1099-K; K-1—not available	Underreported income not in tax data
Self-Employment (pass-through)	IRS: 1040, Schedules E, F; K-1—not available	Income from owners of C-corps not reported unless dividends taken
Unemployment Compensation	IRS: 1099-G; 1040—not available	
Workers' Compensation	Not available	Mostly administered by private insurance firms
Social Security	SSA: Payment History Update System IRS: SSA 1099—not available	CPS-ASEC and SIPP only
Supplemental Security Income (SSI)	SSA: Supplemental Security Record	CPS-ASEC and SIPP only; nontaxable, not on any IRS form
Public Assistance	States: DHHS: TANF	Not available for all states; not all cash assistance covered
Veterans' Benefits	Veterans Administration: Administrative data (limited)	Some benefit data available for limited uses
Disability	IRS: 1099-R, limited data	Excludes Social Security and VA
Survivor Income	IRS: 1099-R, limited data	Excludes Social Security and VA
Interest	IRS: 1040 IRS: 1099-INT—not available	Includes taxable and nontaxable; excludes tax-preferred
Dividends	IRS: 1040 IRS: 1099-DIV—not available	Excludes tax-preferred
Rent and Royalty Income	IRS: 1040 IRS: 1040 Schedule E, K-1—not available	Only gross rent Excludes depreciation
Educational Assistance	IRS: 1098-T, 1099-Q—not available	1098-T covers financial aid; 1099-Q covers spending from tax-preferred education accounts (529, Coverdell)
Other Income	IRS: Capital gains, 1040, 1099-B, K-1—not available IRS: Alimony, 1040—not available IRS: Gambling Income, 2-2G—not available IRS: Alaska Dividend, 1099-MISC—not available	
Noncash/Deferred Compensation from Employers	Firms: Retirement plan contributions, Form 550 public data IRS: Health insurance contributions, other benefits (e.g., moving expenses, etc.), W-2—not available	Only available at aggregate firm level

continued

TABLE 6-2 Continued

Income Item	Data Source and Administrative Item (available to Census Bureau unless otherwise noted)	Notes
Government Taxes, Credits	IRS: EITC, other credits (e.g., child tax, education expense, etc.), 1040—not available	Census Bureau models federal and state income taxes, including various credits
	IRS: Federal tax obligations, 1040—not available	
	IRS: State, local, property tax obligations (for itemizers up to cap), 1040—not available	
Near-Income Items	States: SNAP, WIC	Availability varies by year; not available for all states
	Centers for Medicare & Medicaid Services (CMS)/DHHS: Medicare	Does not cover all possible sources of housing assistance
	CMS/DHHS: Medicaid	Available for one state for some years
	States: School Lunch—not available	
	HUD: Housing Assistance	
	States: Low Income Home Energy Assistance Program	

SOURCE: Adapted from Bee and Rothbaum (2019, Table 1).

The ITWG report supports its recommendation with a careful discussion of the advantages and disadvantages of incorporating administrative data into poverty statistics.

Their potential notwithstanding, there are practical factors slowing the incorporation of administrative records into economic statistics. For many transfer programs, data ownership resides with the states, and memoranda of understanding (MOUs) must be executed for each state and program so that data can be shared with the Census Bureau for linkages. To date, in part due to the complex legal agreements needed to include administrative records in the microrecords, fewer than half of U.S. states allow such sharing, and those that do provide data with a considerable time lag and incomplete coverage across years. Moreover, the MOUs that govern access to many records are, by design, regularly at risk of expiring and not being renewed by the custodial federal or state agency. The Foundations for Evidence-Based Policymaking Act of 2018 (Section 303)[23] establishes a presumption that federal agency administrative records will be available to the Census Bureau and other federal statistical agencies, but implementation of the Act is a work in progress.

Drawing from their Census Bureau experience acquiring and linking administrative records to each other and to surveys, Bee and Rothbaum (2019, p. 4) identify additional challenges to using administrative records to improve income estimates. Among the challenges described are that populations (universes) intended to be represented in surveys do not necessarily match those contained in administrative records, and that administrative records can change for reasons unrelated to income changes. There are also practical considerations. The Census Bureau currently lacks access to some useful administrative records or is limited in how it may use certain records.

Even among the set of administrative records that the Census Bureau does access, not all are available nationwide on a recurring basis. Moreover, while the Census Bureau generally has greater latitude in using records for research and (indirectly) for the production of estimates (e.g., for improved imputations), use of records to substitute for responses to survey questions is generally less feasible due to lags in availability of records and restrictions on how some records may be used. As discussed by Bee and Rothbaum (2019), the Census Bureau only has access to states' programmatic administrative data; currently, the Census Bureau has 19 states with WIC data, 15 states with SNAP data alone, and 15 with both SNAP and TANF data. For the food assistance programs, the fact that states choose whether and when to share their administrative data is problematic and makes incorporating the administrative data more challenging than it is with programs run by SSA.[24]

---

[23] See https://www.govinfo.gov/app/details/PLAW-115publ435.

[24] See National Academies (2020) for a discussion of progress made toward, and challenges of, coordinating state-level program data in the nation's consumer food data sets.

6.5. DATA RECOMMENDATIONS FOR THE PRINCIPAL POVERTY MEASURE

The foundational data approach underlying the PPM can be improved by broadening the use of existing data sources. Specifically, the ACS offers data advantages—primarily a larger sample size, which enables smaller geographic and subgroup estimates, and proactive use of administrative records, which offers opportunities to improve income estimates in surveys. The panel notes the continued need for public-use microdata files that make it possible to recreate and evaluate the PPM, just as files are currently available for the SPM.

RECOMMENDATION 6.1: The Census Bureau should prioritize its work to improve poverty measurement using data from the American Community Survey (ACS) as a springboard to the development of an ACS-based Principal Poverty Measure (PPM) that is released, along with the 1-year ACS data, in September of each year. The Census Bureau should also develop guidance for comparing PPM measures in the Current Population Survey Annual Social and Economic Supplement and ACS.

RECOMMENDATION 6.2: The Census Bureau should expand the use of administrative data (income and program benefits) to improve estimates of resources in the Principal Poverty Measure (PPM). Methods should be developed to incorporate state-level administrative data to improve survey-based PPM estimates, and to extrapolate from currently available state data to other states. In particular, the Census Bureau should aggressively explore the strategy of using federal and state administrative records to improve models for imputation for item nonresponse, including nonreporting of receipt as well as amounts.

RECOMMENDATION 6.3: In developing a Principal Poverty Measure that integrates administrative data to the greatest extent possible, the Census Bureau should produce a historical series comparing an experimental Supplemental Poverty Measure (SPM) that aggressively links administrative data into estimates with the SPM produced using current methods. A key aspect of this research should be evaluating how lags associated with administrative data affect data quality. Work can begin immediately on state data for which agreements exist for Census Bureau use.

Several factors make it challenging to produce and release a public-use microdata file for researchers to use in evaluating the PPM. Challenges include the expanded use of administrative data, the depth of geographic adjustments for housing (see Chapter 5), and the utility of geographic and racial/ethnic detail. Currently, the Census Bureau releases all variables necessary to replicate SPM calculations on the CPS-ASEC. It is vitally important that the Census Bureau continue to release high-quality public-use data sets for the CPS-ASEC and the ACS, with all the variables necessary to replicate PPM calculations on the two data sets. Similar to the current public release data, it is essential that any new data sets include detailed thresholds for each household so that researchers can replicate the PPM. Although such thresholds are built on detailed geographic differences, the panel believes that, with the adjustments for medical care, shelter, and eventually childcare, identifying geographic areas using PPM thresholds will be more difficult and thus releasing them will be less risky. While some detailed information may need to be accessed within secure research data centers, the Census Bureau must assess the appropriate trade offs between new disclosure-avoidance methods and the usefulness of PPM data for researchers and other data users, such as mayors of small towns, minority advocates, and policy makers.

6.6. OPPORTUNITIES FOR IMPROVING ESTIMATION OF THRESHOLDS

6.6.1. Improving Reporting and Increasing Sample Size in the Consumer Expenditure Survey

As with income in the CPS, substantial underreporting of spending occurs in CE data. Bee et al. (2015) and Passero et al. (2015) document the spending components in the CE that are much lower than the comparable totals in the PCE series produced by BEA. While food at home is well reported, clothing is underreported in the CE. Issues with underreporting in spending data have been discussed in previous National Academies reports

(National Academies, 2022; NRC, 2013). Both reports recommended alternatives for estimating household spending, including using a household-based scanner recording program and commercial data—e.g., financial records, budgeting software, store loyalty card information—although the proprietary sources are not created to be nationally representative. This panel supports these previous recommendations and any research BLS can conduct to improve estimates of spending in the CE, especially for the components of the SPM basic needs bundle.

It is also critical to use the largest sample feasible for calculating the medians used in the thresholds, but there is a trade off between accuracy (sample size) and timeliness. Current SPM thresholds represent a sample of all CUs with children, which is an improvement on the previous method—which sampled only units with exactly two children—in that it yields a larger CE sample size. The data are equivalized to a common family of two adults and two children using a three-parameter equivalence scale. That is, BLS adjusts each CU's threshold such that FCSUti is equivalized to two adults and two children. In this process, BLS uses 5 years of data (the panel recommends 3 years for the PPM), adjusting each year to the most recent year using an appropriate CPI for the threshold bundle, and then calculates the median (actually the mean of the 47th–53rd percentiles) spending level. This value is then used to determine the threshold for the two-adult, two-child CU (multiplied by 0.83 and increased by a multiplier of 1.2), which is adjusted by the equivalence scale to obtain the thresholds for the other CU sizes.

For the PPM, the food, clothing, telephone, and internet component of the basic bundle (FCti) could be calculated the same way using the pooled sample over a 3-year moving average and calculating the median and multiplying by 0.83. The motivation for using multiple years is that spending can fluctuate, as was illustrated in atypically dramatic fashion by the spending responses to the COVID-19 pandemic. However, 5 years may be too long a period to smooth spending, since recent fluctuations generally need to be accounted for in a timely manner. It is important to know, for example, the extent to which spiking used car and food prices have impacted family budgets. For these reasons, and because the National Academies' 1995 report suggested using 3 years of data, this panel believes that the 3-year time frame strikes a reasonable balance between accuracy and timeliness.

RECOMMENDATION 6.4: For estimating the basic needs categories (FCti) in the Principal Poverty Measure (PPM), the Bureau of Labor Statistics should use 3 years of Consumer Expenditure Survey data instead of the current 5 years of data. Expenditures would continue to be inflation adjusted to threshold year dollars using a component-specific Consumer Price Index for All Urban Consumers (for FCti). The inflation adjustment should be consistent with the adjustments made to the other components of the PPM thresholds—housing, medical care, and (eventually) childcare.

6.6.2. Technical Issues—Consumer Unit Universe, Equivalence Scale, Multiplier

The broadest and most representative group of CUs for estimating thresholds for the PPM would include single persons, couples, and all other CU types in the common threshold calculation.[25]

RECOMMENDATION 6.5: For calculating Principal Poverty Measure thresholds, the Bureau of Labor Statistics should use all consumer units captured in the Consumer Expenditure Survey (CE) (not just those with children) to determine the median values for basic needs categories (e.g., food, clothing, internet). Equivalence scales should then be used to adjust each CE unit to the two-adult, two-child reference (as is done currently for consumer units with children).

Since the basic bundle proposed for the PPM only includes FCti, the economies of scale by family size will differ from those of the SPM. The SPM's FCSUti bundle includes housing (shelter), which has larger economies of

---

[25]Based on 5 years of CE Interview Data pooled from 2012 Q2–2017 Q1, Renwick and Garner (2020) presents the following figures indicating the large impact of expanding the types of households sampled:
Total Estimation Sample (percentage of all CUs)
CUs with 2 children   n = 14,668 (11.3%)
CUs with 1+ children   n = 40,623 (31.3%)
All CUs   n = 129,604 (100%)

scale than the other basic bundle categories. While it is unclear how large the economies of scale are for food and clothing (see Renwick and Garner, 2020), estimates suggest that the equivalence scale elasticity for food should be close to 1.0, suggesting the presence of little to no economies of scale.

In the short run, the equivalence scale for FCti can be selected such that the overall scale, including the average FMR housing need, yields a parameter equal to the current three-parameter scale for FCSUti. Alternatively, the FCti scale can be determined following the methods in Renwick and Garner (2020). In the long run, the appropriate equivalence scale will need to be determined individually for the new components of the PPM threshold—that is, for FCti, FMR housing, the basic health plan, and any childcare adjustment. In addition, these component-specific scale adjustments may interact with each other. For example, aggregating the individual adjustments for a single parent with two children who is renting, receives Medicaid, and uses childcare may yield an overall adjustment that suggests fewer economies of scale than would be estimated by considering the economies of scale for the entire spending bundle.

Comments from the call for public input to the panel (see Appendix B), along with other research (Bishop et al., 2018), suggest that the adjustments for adults and children in the current three-parameter scale should be reexamined. Renwick and Garner (2020) estimate alternative equivalence scales based on the idea that scale parameters should possibly differ depending on the ages of children in the household. The adjustments for the basic health plan will depend on the ages of children, and the eventual threshold component for childcare will also depend on the children's ages. For example, the Child and Dependent Care Tax Credit expansion for 2021 provided a higher benefit to families with children under the age of 6, recognizing the higher cost of care, and USDA's estimates differ for various age groupings. Additionally, a number of Australian studies have shown that the (nonchildcare) costs of children increase with the age of the child.[26] Furthermore, USDA's *Cost of Raising a Child* approach (Lino et al., 2017) shows the costs of food increasing with the ages of children. For the derivation of the Thrifty Food Plan (TFP), which is the basis for SNAP benefits, it is assumed that teenage males have a higher calorie requirement than male adults, and hence, households with teenage males have a higher TFP cost.

RECOMMENDATION 6.6: The Census Bureau and Bureau of Labor Statistics should reexamine the use of the three-parameter scale to respecify the basic needs bundle for the Principal Poverty Measure (PPM). This evaluation should include:

- **Comparing an overall equivalence scale to component-specific scales for medical care, childcare, and housing, including the impact of using the household as the PPM unit;**
- **Evaluating whether interactions exist between the component-specific scales;**
- **Estimating scales for the basic needs bundle of FCti; and**
- **Evaluating spending patterns to determine whether the scales should reflect children's ages and other special needs, such as children with disabilities.**

This recommendation is very much consistent with one issued by the 2020 Interagency Technical Working Group (BLS, 2020, p. 65) suggesting that an expert panel reexamine the way equivalence scales are applied to income and resource estimates in the SPM.

---

[26]See, for example, Lee (1989), Tran Nam and Whiteford (1990), Saunders et al. (1998), and Percival and Harding (2005).

Appendix 6A

SPM/PPM Threshold Components—Availability in the CE Interview Survey/Taken from Other Sources

Component	Source
	REQUIRED FOR CURRENT SPM
CONSUMER UNIT (CU) COMPOSITION	Required to obtain estimation sample
Presence of adults and children	CE estimation sample includes all CUs with children
BASIC BUNDLE (FCSUti)	FCSUti estimated at 83% of the 47th–53rd percentiles of expenditures for basic bundle for reference CU, then S + U estimated separately by housing tenure (rent, own without a mortgage, own with a mortgage); replaces the SU component in FCSUti
Food purchased with money income	CE includes food at home and away from home
Food obtained with in-kind benefits	CE used for SNAP; BLS imputes WIC and the National School Lunch Program
Clothing	CE
Shelter (including obtained with subsidies)	CE used for housing tenure, rent, mortgage payment, property taxes, property insurance, maintenance; BLS imputes rental assistance
Utilities (including obtained with subsidies)	CE, BLS imputes Low Income Home Energy Assistance Program [LIHEAP]
Telephone	CE
Internet	CE
MULTIPLIER	1.2 times basic bundle to account for other necessary expenditures (e.g., nonwork-related transportation, personal care, household supplies)
ADJUSTMENTS	Equivalence scale applied based on number of adults and children; housing component (by tenure) adjusted geographically by the ratio of 5-year ACS tabulations of median rent and utilities for 2-bedroom units with complete kitchen and plumbing facilities in a state or metropolitan area to the U.S. median.
FINAL THRESHOLDS	Basic bundle + multiplier, adjusted for family composition and geographic shelter cost differences (see "Adjustments")

Component	Source
REQUIRED FOR PANEL'S RECOMMENDED PPM	
CONSUMER UNIT COMPOSITION	See above
REVISED BASIC BUNDLE (FCti)	FCti estimated at 83% of 47th–53rd percentiles of expenditures for revised basic bundle for reference consumer unit
Food	CE used (see above re: imputation of in-kind food benefits)
Clothing	CE
Telephone	CE
Internet	CE
MULTIPLIER	The current 1.2 multiplier will need to be updated to reflect the revised basic bundle accounting for other necessary expenditures
ADJUSTMENT	Equivalence scale applied based on number of adults and children
NEW/REVISED THRESHOLD COMPONENTS	Taken from other sources (see below) and added to revised basic bundle threshold
HEALTH INSURANCE	Sum of health insurance needs for health insurance units in CU (e.g., parents and children one unit, grandparent a second unit): for people under 65 and over 64 but not on Medicare, need is benchmark ACA plan—second-lowest-cost Silver plan in the health insurance Marketplace in an individual's geographic area; for Medicare recipients, need is full cost of least expensive Medicare Advantage plan with prescription drugs (premium subsidies added to resources; premium and other MOOP costs subtracted up to MOOP cap in benchmark plan)
HOUSING (including utilities)	HUD FMRs (includes utilities) for applicable number of adults and children (based on number of bedrooms) for applicable metropolitan area/nonmetropolitan county (housing subsidies added to resources for renters; implicit rent net of expenses added to resources for owners)
FINAL THRESHOLDS	For applicable CU composition/location, revised basic bundle + multiplier + health insurance + housing/utilities
FUTURE ADDITION—CHILDCARE	The PPM extends childcare out-of-pocket costs that are subtracted from resources to parents who are in school or disabled; in a future revision, the panel recommends that childcare needs be added to the thresholds in a similar manner to health insurance and childcare subsidies be added to resources

SOURCE: For current SPM methodology, see www.bls.gov/pir/spmhome.htm.

Appendix 6B

SPM/PPM Resource Components— Availability in the CPS-ASEC and ACS

Component	CPS-ASEC	ACS
REQUIRED FOR CURRENT SPM AND RECOMMENDED PPM		
HOUSEHOLD/FAMILY COMPOSITION	Required to determine poverty unit for resource estimation/ applicable poverty threshold	Required to determine poverty unit for resource estimation/applicable poverty threshold
Family type, number of adults and children, etc.	YES (detailed information on family relationships)	YES (but limited information, which makes it more difficult to establish SPM units; see Fox et al. (2020)
HOUSING TENURE	Current SPM: Required to determine applicable poverty threshold and subsidies (renters); PPM: Required to impute implicit rent (owners)	Current SPM: required to determine applicable poverty threshold and subsidies (renters); PPM: Required to impute implicit rent (owners)
Tenure	YES (owned without mortgage; owned with mortgage [including home equity loan]; rented; no cash rent)	YES (owned without mortgage; owned with mortgage [including home equity loan]; rented; no cash rent)
MONEY INCOME	Reference period—prior calendar year (except where noted)	Reference period—prior 12 months (except where noted)
Earnings (gross)	YES	YES
Self-employment (net)	YES	YES
Unemployment compensation	YES (federal/state; supplemental; union)	Included in All Other income category
Worker's compensation	YES	All Other
Social Security	YES	YES
SSI	YES	YES
Disability	YES	All Other
Veterans' payments	YES	All Other
Survivor benefits	YES	All Other
Public assistance (cash)	YES	YES

Component	CPS-ASEC	ACS
Pensions	YES	All Other
Annuities	YES	All Other
Retirement withdrawals	YES	All Other
Other income earning assets	YES (interest, dividends)	Property Income
Property income	YES (net rent + royalties)	Property Income
Educational assistance	YES (Pell grants; other assistance)	All Other
Child support	YES	All Other
Financial assistance from friends/relatives	YES	All Other
Other income	YES (Alaska dividend; all other)	All Other
IN-KIND BENEFITS	Generally requires amount imputation; could also add questions	Generally requires receipt and amounts imputation; could also add questions[a]
SNAP	YES (receipt and amounts)	Receipt only; requires amount imputation
School lunch	Receipt only; requires amount imputation (Census Bureau uses program information from USDA to estimate amounts)	NO; requires imputation (receipt and amount)
Public and subsidized housing	Receipt only; requires amount imputation (Census Bureau sets value of housing subsidy by subtracting estimated amount paid by the tenant from the HUD market rent value for the housing unit)	NO; requires imputation (receipt and amount)
WIC	Receipt only; requires amount imputation (Census Bureau uses program information from USDA to estimate amounts)	NO; requires imputation (receipt and amount)
Energy assistance (LIHEAP)	YES (receipt and amounts)	NO; requires imputation (receipt and amount)
TAXES/TAX CREDITS	Calculated by Census Bureau tax model	Calculated by National Bureau of Economic Research's TAXSIM model
Stimulus payments	Receipt only; requires amount imputation (relevant for 2020–2021 only)	NO; requires imputation (receipt and amount; relevant for 2020–2021 only)
Federal/state taxes	NO; simulated	NO; simulated
FICA taxes	NO; simulated	NO; simulated
EITC; other tax credits	NO; simulated	NO; simulated
NONDISCRETIONARY EXPENSES	Subtracted from resources	Subtracted from resources
Childcare expenses (work-related)	Whether paid for childcare while working; which children needed care; childcare payment; total paid prior year	NO; requires imputation
Other work-related expenses (transportation, uniforms, etc.)	NO (currently imputed from SIPP)	NO (currently imputed from SIPP)
Child support paid	YES	NO; requires imputation (whether owe and amount)
MOOP	Annual MOOP spending for premiums, copays, nonprescription medical care products	NO (ascertains whether pays premium, receives premium subsidy); requires imputation (amount)

Component	CPS-ASEC	ACS
REQUIRED FOR RECOMMENDED PPM		
EXPANDED CHILDCARE EXPENSE DEDUCTION	Extended to parent(s) in school, disabled	Extended to parent(s) in school, disabled
Education/disability status; childcare costs	Education and disability status ascertained; requires expanded childcare cost questions	Education and disability ascertained; requires childcare cost questions
HEALTH INSURANCE COVERAGE	Required to determine applicable poverty threshold; caps for MOOP costs/subsidies	Required to determine applicable poverty threshold; caps for MOOP costs/subsidies
Type of health Insurance	YES; current coverage by: Medicare; Medicaid; state Medicaid; VA; job (private employer, government, military); privately purchased; parent or spouse; Medicare supplements; exchange; group; school; months of coverage	YES; current coverage by: current/former employer/union; privately purchased; Medicare; Medicaid; TRICARE; VA; Indian Health Service; other plan
Health insurance premium subsidized by government/ employers (capped at health insurance need in threshold)	Asks whether premium subsidized; requires imputation (amount)	Asks whether premium subsidized; requires imputation (amount)
IMPLICIT NET RENT (owners) (capped at housing need in threshold)	Implicit rent (including utilities) net of ownership expenses added to owner resources	Implicit rent (including utilities) net of ownership expenses added to owner resources
What unit would rent for (owners)	NO; but home value available for imputation	NO; but home value available for imputation
Property taxes/insurance/ condo fees/mobile home fees (subtracted for owners)	NO; requires added questions or imputation	YES; annual real estate taxes; annual fire, flood insurance; monthly condo fee; annual mobile home fees
Maintenance (subtracted for owners)	NO; requires added questions or imputation	NO; requires added questions or imputation
Mortgage payment (interest and principal on 1st mortgage) (subtracted for owners)	Whether mortgage (no amount, no indication of whether mortgage payment includes taxes/insurance); whether 2nd mortgage/home equity loan (no amount); requires added questions or imputation (also may require ascertaining principal separately from interest)	YES; whether 1st mortgage; monthly mortgage payment; does mortgage payment include taxes/insurance; whether 2nd mortgage/home equity loan, monthly payment on all such; may require ascertaining principal separately from interest

SOURCE: CPS-ASEC Questionnaire, www2.census.gov/programs-surveys/cps/techdocs/cpsmar21.pdf; ACS Questionnaire, www.census.gov/programs-surveys/acs/methodology/questionnaires/2021/quest21.pdf?msclkid=20e8cd0cc00511ec9b0fd8cd62e6a9ae.
[a]See Fox et al. (2022) for imputation methods used for SNAP and other resource components to produce SPM measures for 2014–2017 from the ACS Public Use Microdata Files.

References

Abraham, K.G. (2022). Big data and official statistics. *Review of Income and Wealth, 68*(4), 835-861. https://doi.org/10.1111/roiw.12617

Aladangady, A., Aron-Dine, S., Dunn, W., Feiveson, L., Lengermann, P., and Sahm, C. (2022). From transaction data to economic statistics: Constructing real-time, high-frequency, geographic measures of consumer spending. *Big Data for Twenty-First-Century Economic Statistics*, 115-145. University of Chicago Press.

Albright, K.A., and Asiala, M.E. (2015). *Investigating methods to support subannual state-level estimates*. Memorandum Series #ACS15-RER-09, United States Census Bureau.

Andrews, D., and Caldera Sánchez, A. (2011). *Drivers of homeownership rates in selected OECD countries*. OECD Economics Department Working Papers 849, OECD.

Armstrong, G., Jones, G., Miller, T., and Pham, S. (2022). *CE data quality profile reference guide*. Program Report Series, the Consumer Expenditure Surveys. Bureau of Labor Statistics.

Aten, B.H., and Heston, A. (2020). *The Owner-Premium Adjustment in Housing Imputations*. Bureau of Economic Analysis Working Paper Series WP2020-7. https://www.bea.gov/system/files/papers/BEA-WP2020-7_0.pdf

Atkinson, A.B. (2019). *Measuring poverty around the world*. Princeton University Press.

Bateman, N., and Ross, M. (2021). The pandemic hurt low-wage workers the most—and so far, the recovery has helped them the least. Brookings Institution.

Bauman, K.J. (1999). Shifting family definitions: The effect of cohabitation and other nonfamily household relationships on measures of poverty. *Demography, 36*(3), 315–325.

Bavier, R. (2000). *Medical out-of-pocket spending in poverty thresholds*. United States Census Bureau Supplemental Poverty Measure Working Papers. https://www.census.gov/library/working-papers/2000/demo/bavier-01.html

_____. (2006). Misclassification in an experimental poverty measure. *Monthly Labor Review, 129*, 46.

Bee, C.A., Gathright, G.M.R., and Meyer, B.D. (2015). *Bias from unit non-response in the measure of income in household surveys*. Working Paper, University of Chicago.

Bee, A., and Rothbaum, J. (2019). *The Administrative Income Statistics (AIS) project: Research on the use of administrative records to improve income and resource estimates*. United States Census Bureau SEHDS Working Paper No. 2019-36. https://www.census.gov/content/dam/Census/library/working-papers/2019/demo/sehsd-wp2019-36.pdf

Betson, D. (1996). Is everything relative? The role of equivalence scales in poverty measurement. Unpublished manuscript, University of Notre Dame.

Biemer, P.B., and Amaya, A. (2018). A total error framework for hybrid estimation. Paper presented at the BigSurv18 Conference, October 26. Barcelona, Spain.

Binh, T.N., and Whiteford, P. (1990). Household equivalence scales: New Australian estimates from the 1984 Household Expenditure Survey. *Economic Record, 66*(3), 221-234. https://doi.org/10.1111/j.1475-4932.1990.tb01724.x

Bishop, J.A., Lee, J., and Zeager, L.A. (2018). Adjusting for family size in the supplemental poverty measure. *Applied Economics Letters, 25*(8), 553-556.

Blank, R. (2011). *The supplemental poverty measure: A new tool for understanding US poverty*. Stanford Center on Poverty and Inequality. https://inequality.stanford.edu/sites/default/files/media/_media/pdf/pathways/fall_2011/PathwaysFall11_Blank.pdf

Bohn, S., Danielson, C., and Malagon, P. (2021). Poverty in California: Fact sheet. Public Policy Institute of California. https://www.ppic.org/publication/poverty-in-california/

_____. (2019). Trouble in the tails? What we know about earnings nonresponse thirty years after Lillard, Smith, and Welch. *Journal of Political Economy, 127*(5), 2143-2185.

Bollinger, C.R., and Hirsch, B.T. (2006). Match bias from earnings imputation in the Current Population Survey: The case of imperfect matching. *Journal of Labor Economics, 24*, 483-519.

Borgschulte, M., Cho, H., and Lubotsky, D. (2022). Partisanship and survey refusal. *Journal of Economic Behavior and Organization, 200*, 332–357.

Borowsky, J., Brown, J.H., Davis, E.E., Gibbs, C., Herbst, C.M., Sojourner, A., Tekin, E., and Wiswall, M.J. (2022). *An equilibrium model of the impact of increased public investment in early childhood education*. National Bureau of Economic Research Working Paper No. 30140. https://www.nber.org/system/files/working_papers/w30140/w30140.pdf

Brewer, M., Etheridge, B., and O'Dea, C. (2017). Why are households that report the lowest incomes so well-off? *The Economic Journal, 127*(605), F24–F49.

Bureau of Labor Statistics. (2014). *Redesign of the sample of the Current Population Survey*. Current Population Survey, Technical Documentation, April 2014. https://www.bls.gov/cps/sample_redesign_2014.pdf

_____. (2020). *Final report of the interagency technical working group on evaluating alternative measures of poverty*. https://www.bls.gov/evaluation/final-report-of-the-interagency-technical-working-group-on-evaluating-alternative-measures-of-poverty.pdf

Burkhauser, R.V., Corinth, K., Elwell, J., and Larrimore, J. (2020). *Evaluating the success of President Johnson's war on poverty: Revisiting the historical record using a full income poverty measure*. National Bureau of Economic Research Working Paper No. 26532. https://www.nber.org/system/files/working_papers/w26532/w26532.pdf

Burrows, M. (2022). Reconsidering commuting costs in the Supplemental Poverty Measure. Presentation to the Panel of Evaluation and Improvements to the Supplemental Poverty Measure for National Academies of Sciences, Engineering, and Medicine, Washington, DC: January 14.

Cajner, T., Crane, L.D., Decker, R.A., Hamins-Puertolas, A., and Kurz, C. (2019). Improving the accuracy of economic measurement with multiple data sources: The case of payroll employment data. *Big Data for Twenty-First-Century Economic Statistics*, 147-170. University of Chicago Press.

Carlson, M., and Danziger, S. (1999). Cohabitation and the measurement of child poverty. *Review of Income and Wealth, 45*(2), 179-191.

Case, A., and Deaton, A. (2020). *Deaths of despair and the future of capitalism*. Princeton University Press.

Casselman, B., and Smialek, J. (2021). U.S. poverty fell last year as government aid made up for lost jobs. The New York Times, September 14. https://www.nytimes.com/2021/09/14/business/economy/census-income-poverty-health-insurance.html

Caswell, K.J., and O'Hara, B. (2010). *Medical out-of-pocket expenses, poverty, and the uninsured*. SEHSD Working Paper 2010-17. United States Census Bureau, Social, Economic, and Housing Division. www.census.gov/hhes/povmeas/methodology/supplemental/research/Caswell-OHara-SGE2011.pdf

Catlin, A.C., and Cowan, C.A. (2015). *History of health spending in the United States, 1960–2013*. Centers for Medicare and Medicaid Services. https://www.cms.gov/Research-Statistics-Data-and-Systems/Statistics-Trends-and-Reports/NationalHealthExpendData/Downloads/HistoricalNHEPaper.pdf

Clay, D.M., Ver Ploeg, M., Coleman-Jensen, A., Elitzak, H., Gregory, C.A., Levin, D., Newman, C., and Rabbitt, M.P. (2016). *Comparing National Household Food Acquisition and Purchase Survey (FoodAPS) data with other national food surveys' data*. Economic Information Bulletin No. EIB-157. United States Department of Agriculture, Economic Research Service. https://www.ers.usda.gov/publications/pub-details/?pubid=79892

Congressional Budget Office. (2021). *Estimated budgetary effects of Tittle II, Committee on Education and Labor, H.R. 5376, the Build Better Act*. http://www.cbo.gov/publication/57622

Congressional Research Service. (2021). *Child and dependent care tax benefits: How they work and who receives them*. CRS Report No. R44993. https://sgp.fas.org/crs/misc/R44993.pdf

_____. (2015). *Need-tested benefits: Estimated eligibility and benefit receipt by families and individuals*. CRS Report No. R44327. https://crsreports.congress.gov/product/pdf/R/R44327

Council of Economic Advisors. (2019). *Economic report of the President*. The Executive Office of the President and the Council of Economic Advisers. https://www.whitehouse.gov/wp-content/uploads/2021/07/2019-ERP.pdf

REFERENCES

Creamer, J. (2022) Examining the impact of medical expenses on supplemental poverty rates. United States Census Bureau. 2021 APPAM Fall Research Conference. https://www.census.gov/content/dam/Census/library/working-papers/2022/demo/sehsd-wp2022-13.pdf

Creamer, J., Shrider, E.A., Burns, K., and Chen, F. (2022). *Poverty in the United States: 2021*. United States Census Bureau, Current Population Reports No. P60-277.

Cubanski, J., Neuman, T., and Freed, M. (2022). Explaining the prescription drug professions in the Inflation Reduction Act. Kaiser Family Foundation. https://www.kff.org/medicare/issue-brief/explaining-the-prescription-drug-provisions-in-the-inflation-reduction-act/

Danielson, C., and Thorman, T. (2019). *The Impact of Expanding Public Preschool on Child Poverty in California*. Public Policy Institute of California. https://www.ppic.org/wp-content/uploads/the-impact-of-expanding-public-preschool-on-child-poverty-in-california.pdf

Diamond, R., and McQuade, T. (2019). Who wants affordable housing in their backyard? An equilibrium analysis of low-income property development. *Journal of Political Economy, 127*(3), 1063-1117.

Diamond, R., and Moretti, E. (2021). *Where is standard of living the highest? Local prices and the geography of consumption*. National Bureau of Economic Research Working Paper No. 29533.

Fisher, G.M. (1992). The development and history of poverty thresholds. *Social Security Bulletin, 55*(4), 3-14. https://www.census.gov/content/dam/Census/library/working-papers/1997/demo/orshansky.pdf

Fitzgerald, J., and Moffit, R. (2022). The supplemental expenditure poverty measure: A new method for measuring poverty. Brookings Papers on Economic Activity Conference Draft. https://www.brookings.edu/wp-content/uploads/2022/03/SP22_BPEA_FitzgeraldMoffitt_conf-draft.pdf

Fox, L. (2020). *The supplemental poverty measure: 2019*. United States Department of Commerce, United States. United States Census Bureau, Current Population Reports No. P60-272. https://www.census.gov/content/dam/Census/library/publications/2020/demo/p60-272.pdf

Fox, L., and Burns, K. (2021a). *The supplemental poverty measure: 2020*. United States Census Bureau Report No. P60-275. https://www.census.gov/library/publications/2021/demo/p60-275.html

_____. (2021b). What's the difference between the supplemental and official poverty measures? United States Census Bureau. https://www.census.gov/newsroom/blogs/random-samplings/2021/09/difference-between-supplemental-and-official-poverty-measures.html#:~:text=At%20the%20U.S.%20Census%20Bureau,as%20taxes%20and%20medical%20expenses)

Fox, L., Glassman, B., and Pacas, J. (2020). *The supplemental poverty measure using the American Community Survey*. United States Census Bureau Working Paper No. 2020-09. https://www.census.gov/library/working-papers/2020/demo/SEHSD-WP2020-09.html

Fox, L.E., and Garner, T.I. (2018). *Moving to the median and expanding the estimation sample: The case for changing the expenditures underlying SPM thresholds*. SEHSD Working Paper No. 2018-02. https://www.census.gov/content/dam/Census/library/working-papers/2018/demo/SEHSD-WP2018-02.pdf

Fox, L., Rothbaum, J., and Shantz, K. (2022). Fixing errors in a SNAP: Addressing SNAP underreporting to evaluate poverty. *AEA Papers and Proceedings, 112*, 330-334.

Fox, L., Wimer, C., Garfinkle, I., Kaushal, N., and Waldfogel, J. (2015). Waging war on poverty: Poverty trends using a historical Supplemental Poverty Measure. *Journal of Policy Analysis and Management, 34*, 567-592.

Garner, T.I. (2006) Developing Poverty Thresholds: 1993–2003. 2005 Proceedings of the American Statistical Association, Social Statistics Section. American Statistical Association. https://www.bls.gov/osmr/research-papers/2005/pdf/st050180.pdf

Garner, T.I., and Munoz, J. (2021). Choices in defining and estimating poverty thresholds: Focus on the U.S. supplemental poverty measure. United States Bureau of Labor Statistics, United States Department of Labor. https://www.bls.gov/pir/spm/garner_spm_choices_03_15_21.pdf

Garner, T.I., and Short, K. (2009). Accounting for owner-occupied dwelling services: Aggregates and distributions. *Journal of Housing Economics, 18*(3), 233-248.

Garner, T.I., Short, K., and Gudrais, M. (2014). The supplemental poverty measure under alternate treatments of out-of-pocket medical expenditures. United States Bureau of Labor Statistics, United States Department of Labor. https://www.bls.gov/pir/spm/assa-2014-spmmit.pdf

Garner, T.I., and Verbrugge, R. (2009). Reconciling user costs and rental equivalence: Evidence from the US Consumer Expenditure Survey. *Journal of Housing Economics, 18*(3), 172-192.

Gould, E., Mokhiber, Z., and Bryant, K. (2018). The economic policy institute's family budget calculator: Technical documentation. Economic Policy Institute https://www.epi.org/publication/family-budget-calculator-documentation/

Gruber, J. (2022). *Public finance and public policy*. (7th ed.). Worth Publishers.

Guerrieri, V., Hartley, D., and Hurst, E. (2013). Endogenous gentrification and housing price dynamics. *Journal of Public Economics, 100*(C), 45-60.

Han, J., Meyer, B.D., and Sullivan, J.X. (2020). *Income and poverty in the COVID-19 pandemic*. Brookings Papers on Economic Activity, Working Paper No. 27729, 85-118. https://www.nber.org/papers/w27729

Hartman, M., Martin, A.B., Washington, B., Catlin, A., and the National Health Expenditure Accounts Team. (2022). National health care spending in 2020: Growth driven by federal spending in response to the COVID-19 pandemic: National health expenditures study examines US health care spending in 2020. *Health Affairs. 41*(1), 13-25.

Heisz, A. (2019). An update on the Market Basket Measure comprehensive review. *Income Research Paper Series*. https://www150.statcan.gc.ca/n1/pub/75f0002m/75f0002m2019009-eng.htm

Henman, P. (2005). *Updated costs of children using Australian budget standards*. Report to the Ministerial Task force on Child Support.

Hirsch, B.T., and Schumacher, E.J. (2004). Match bias in wage gap estimates due to earnings imputation. *Journal of Labor Economics, 22*, 689-722.

Hokayem, C., Bollinger, C., and Ziliak, J.P. (2015). The role of CPS nonresponse in the measurement of poverty. *Journal of the American Statistical Association, 110*(511), 935-945.

Hokayem, C., and Heggeness, M.L. (2014). *Living in near poverty in the United States: 1966–2012*. U.S. Government Printing Office.

U.S. Housing and Urban Development Department. (2020). *Fair market rents for the Housing Choice Voucher Program, moderate rehabilitation single room occupancy program and other programs fiscal year 2021*. Office of the Assistant Secretary for Policy Development and Research. https://www.federalregister.gov/documents/2020/08/14/2020-17717/fair-market-rents-for-the-housing-choice-voucher-program-moderate-rehabilitation-single-room

Howard, G., and Liebersohn, J. (2021). Why is rent so darn high? The role of growing demand to live in housing-supply-inelastic cities. *Journal of Urban Economics, 124*, 103369.

Iceland, J. (2000). *The 'family/couple/household' unit of analysis in poverty measurement*. Poverty Measurement Working Paper. United States Census Bureau. http://www.census.gov/hhes/poverty/povmeas/papers/famhh3.html

Institute of Medicine. (1988). *Homelessness, heather, and human needs*. National Academies Press.

Interagency Technical Working Group. (2010). *Observations from the interagency technical working group on developing a supplemental poverty measure*. United States Census Bureau. https://www.census.gov/content/dam/Census/library/working-papers/2010/demo/SPM_Wkg-Grp.pdf

Joint Center for Housing Studies of Harvard University. (2020). *America's rental housing 2020*. Harvard Graduate School of Design, Harvard Kennedy School. https://www.jchs.harvard.edu/sites/default/files/reports/files/Harvard_JCHS_Americas_Rental_Housing_2020.pdf

Jones, M.R., and Ziliak, J.P. (2022). The antipoverty impact of the EITC: New estimates from survey and administrative tax records. *National Tax Journal, 75*(3), 451-479.

Joyce, R. (2022). Assets and liabilities: Reflections from the work of the UK Social Metrics Commission. Presentation to the Panel on Evaluation and Improvements to the Supplemental Poverty Measure for National Academies of Sciences, Engineering, and Medicine, January 14, Washington, DC.

Kang, K.M., and Moffitt, R.A. (2019). The effect of SNAP and school food programs on food security, diet quality, and food spending: Sensitivity to program reporting error. *Southern Economic Journal, 86*(1), 156-201.

Korenman, S., and Remler, D.K. (2016). Including health insurance in poverty measurement: The impact of Massachusetts health reform on poverty. *Journal of Health Economics, 50*, 27-35.

Korenman, S., Remler, D.K., and Hyson, R.T. (2018). *The impact of health insurance and other social benefits on poverty in New York state*. Howard J. Samuels State and City Policy Center. http://www.cuny.edu/wp-content/uploads/sites/4/page-assets/about/centers-and-institutes/demographic-research/New-York-HIPM_2018-08-06.pdf

_____. (2019). *Accounting for the impact of Medicaid on child poverty*. National Bureau of Economic Research Working Paper No. 25973. https://www.nber.org/papers/w25973

_____. (2021). Health insurance and poverty of the older population in the United States: The importance of a health inclusive poverty measure. *Journal of the Economics of Ageing, 18*.

Larrimore, J., Mortenson, J., and Splinter, D. (2017). *Household incomes in tax data: Using addresses to move from tax unit to household income distributions*. Finance and Economics Discussion Working Paper No. 2017-002. https://papers.ssrn.com/sol3/papers.cfm?abstract_id=2895315

Lee, D. (1989). *Calculations of the direct costs of children based on the 1984 ABS Household Expenditure Survey*. Australian Institute of Family Studies.

Lin, Y., Monnette, A., and Shi, L. (2021). Effects of Medicaid expansion on poverty disparities in health insurance coverage. *International Journal of Equities in Health, 20*(171). https://doi.org/10.1186/s12939-021-01486-3

Lino, M., Kuczynski, K., Rodriguez, N., and Schap, T. (2017). *Expenditures on children by families, 2015*. United States Department of Agriculture, Center for Nutrition Policy and Promotion, Miscellaneous Report No. 1528-2015. https://cdn2.hubspot.net/hubfs/10700/blog-files/USDA_Expenditures%20on%20children%20by%20family.pdf?t=1520090048492

Little, R.J.A., and Rubin, D.B. (2002). *Statistical analysis with missing data*. (2nd ed.). John Wiley & Sons, Inc.

Lloro, A., Merry, E., Brevoort, K., Jones, K., Larrimore, J., Lockwood, J., Tranfaglia, A., Troland, E., Webber, D., and Zabek, M. (2022). *Economic well-being of US households in 2021*. Working Paper No. 4724. Board of Governors of the Federal Reserve System. https://www.federalreserve.gov/publications/2022-economic-well-being-of-us-householdsin-2021-executive-summary.htm

Mattingly, M.J., and Wimer, C.T. (2017). *Child care expenses push many families into poverty*. University of New Hampshire, Carsey School of Public Health, National Fact Sheet No. 36. https://scholars.unh.edu/cgi/viewcontent.cgi?referer=&httpsredir=1&article=1303&context=carsey

McNabb, J. Timmons, D., Song, J., and Puckett, C. (2009). Use of administrative data at the Social Security Administration. *Social Security Bulletin*, 69(1).

Meyer, B.D., Wyse, A., Grunwaldt, A., Medalia C., and Wu, D. (2021). *Learning about Homelessness Using Linked Survey and Administrative Data*. National Bureau of Economic Research Working Paper Series, No. 28861. National Bureau of Economic Research, Cambridge, MA. https://www.nber.org/papers/w28861

Meyer, B.D., and Mittag, N. (2018). *Errors in survey reporting and imputation and their effects on estimates of Food Stamp program participation*. National Bureau of Economic Research Working Paper No. 25143.

_____. (2019). Using linked survey and administrative data to better measure income: Implications for poverty, program effectiveness, and holes in the safety net. *American Economic Journal: Applied Economics, 11*(2), 176-204.

_____. (2021). An empirical total survey error decomposition using data combination, *Journal of Econometrics, 224*(2), 286–305.

Meyer, B.D., and Sullivan, J.X. (2012). Winning the war: Poverty from the Great Society to the Great Recession. Brookings Papers on Economic Activity. https://www.brookings.edu/wp-content/uploads/2012/09/2012b_meyer.pdf

Meyer, B.D., Mok, W.K.C., and Sullivan, J.X. (2009). *The under-reporting of transfers in household surveys: Its nature and consequences*. National Bureau of Economic Research Working Paper No. 15181. https://ideas.repec.org/p/nbr/nberwo/15181.html

_____. (2015). Household surveys in crisis. *Journal of Economic Perspectives, 29*(4), 199-226.

Mills, C.K., Landau, R., Rodriguez, B., and Scally, J. (2022). *The state of low-income America: Credit access & debt payment*. Federal Reserve Bank of New York. https://tinyurl.com/3ecaxcnf

Mittag, N. (2019). Correcting for misreporting of government benefits. *American Economic Journal: Economic Policy, 11*(2), 142-164.

Mueller, T., Brooks, M., and Pacas, J. (2021). Cost of living variation, non-metropolitan America, and implications for the supplemental poverty measure. *SocArXiv Papers*. https://doi.org/10.31235/osf.io/6rax9

Murphy, A.K., McDonald-Lopez, K., Pilkauskas, N., and Gould-Werth, A. (2022). Transportation insecurity in the United States: A descriptive portrait. *Socius, 8*. https://journals.sagepub.com/doi/epub/10.1177/23780231221121060

Mykyta, L., and Macartner, S. (2012). *Sharing a household: Household composition and economic well-being: 2007–2010*. Current Population Report. United States Census Bureau.

National Academies of Sciences, Engineering, and Medicine. (2022). *Modernizing the consumer price index for the 21st Century*. The National Academies Press. https://doi.org/10.17226/26485

_____. (2020). *A consumer food data system for 2030 and beyond*. The National Academies Press. https://doi.org/10.17226/25657

_____. (2019). *A roadmap to reducing child poverty*. The National Academies Press. https://doi.org/10.17226/25246

_____. (2017). *Improving crop estimates by integrating multiple data sources*. The National Academies Press. https://doi.org/10.17226/24892

_____. (2012a). *Medical care economic risk: Measuring financial vulnerability from spending on medical care*, 51-66. The National Academies Press.

_____. (2012b). Implementing measures of medical care, economic burden, and risk. *Medical Care Economic Risk: Measuring Financial Vulnerability from Spending on Medical Care*, 101-296. The National Academies Press.

National Research Council (NRC). (1995). *Measuring poverty: A new approach*. The National Academies Press. https://doi.org/10.17226/4759

_____. (2005). *Beyond the market: Designing nonmarket accounts for the United States*. Panel to Study the Design of Nonmarket Accounts. The National Academies Press.

_____. (2013). *Measuring what we spend: Toward a new consumer expenditure survey*. The National Academies Press. https://doi.org/10.17226/13520

National Research Council and Institute of Medicine. (2012). *Medical care economic risk: Measuring financial vulnerability from spending on medical care*. The National Academies Press. https://doi.org/10.17226/13525

Norris, L. (2021). How to beef up your health coverage if your employer offers 'skinny' or unaffordable benefits. HealthInsurance.org. https://www.healthinsurance.org/obamacare/how-to-beef-up-your-health-coverage-if-your-employer-offers-skinny-or-unaffordable-benefits/

O'Hara, A. (2006). *Tax variable imputation in the current population survey*. United States Census Bureau. http://www.irs.gov/pub/irs-soi/06ohara.pdf

Orshansky, M. (1969). How poverty is measured. *Monthly Labor Review, 92*(2), 37-41.

Pac, J., Nam, J., Waldfogel, J., and Wimer, C. (2017). Young child poverty in the United States: Analyzing trends in poverty and the role of anti-poverty programs using the Supplemental Poverty Measure. *Children and Youth Services Review, 74*(C), 35-49.

Pacas, J.D., and Rothwell, D.W. (2020). Why is poverty lower in rural American according to the Supplemental Poverty Measure? An investigation of the geographic adjustment. *Population Research and Policy Review, 39*(977).

Parolina, Z., Curran, M., Matsudaira, J., Waldfogel, J., and Wimer, C. (2022). Estimating monthly poverty rates in the United States. *Journal of Policy Analysis and Management, 41*(4), 1177-1203.

Passero, W., Garner, T.I., and McCully, C. (2015). Understanding the relationship: CE survey and PCP. *Improving the Measurement of Consumer Expenditures*, 181-203.

Percival, R., and Harding, A. (2005). *The estimated costs of children in Australian families in 2005–06*. Report to the Ministerial Task Force on Child Support, NATSEM, and University of Canberra.

Provencher, A. (2011). *Unit of analysis for poverty measurement: A comparison of the Supplemental Poverty Measure and the official poverty Measure*. SEHSD Working Paper No. 2010-14. United States Census Bureau.

Ravallion, M. (2015). *Toward Better Global Poverty Measures*. CGD Working Paper No. 417. Center for Global Development. https://www.cgdev.org/publication/toward-better-global-poverty-measures-working-paper-417

Remler, D.K., and Korenman, S. (2022). Incorporating cost-sharing needs and benefits in a health-inclusive poverty measure: Tradeoffs, limitations, and a new approach. Paper presented to the 2022 Meetings of the American Society of Health Economics, Austin TX, June.

_____. (2023). Health Insurance and Poverty Measurement. *Research Handbook on Measuring Poverty and Deprivation*. Elsevier.

Renwick, T. (2011). *Geographic adjustments of Supplemental Poverty Measure thresholds: Use the American Community survey five-year data on housing costs*. SEHSD Working Paper. http://www.census.gov/hhes/povmeas/methodology/supplemental/research/Renwick_SGE2011.pdf

_____. (2018). *Incorporating amenities into geographic adjustments of the supplemental poverty measure*. United States Census Bureau Working Paper No. SEHSD-WP2018-32. https://www.census.gov/library/working-papers/2018/demo/SEHSD-WP2018-32.html

Renwick, T., and Garner, T.I. (2020). *Changing the housing share of poverty thresholds for the Supplemental Poverty Measure and Equivalence Scales: Does consumer unit size matter?* Economic Working Paper No. 527. United States Bureau of Labor Statistics. https://www.bls.gov/osmr/research-papers/2020/ec200090.htm

_____ (2018). *Changing the housing share of poverty thresholds for the supplemental poverty measure: Does consumer unit size matter?* United States Census Bureau Working Paper No. SEHSD-WP2018-06. https://www.census.gov/library/working-papers/2018/demo/SEHSD-WP2018-06.html

Renwick, T., and Mitchell, J. (2015). *Estimating the value of federal housing assistance for the supplemental poverty measure*. United States Census Bureau Working Paper No. SEHSD-WP2016-01. https://www.census.gov/library/working-papers/2016/demo/SEHSD-WP2016-01.html

Renwick, T., Figueroa, E., and Aten, B. (2017). *Supplemental poverty measure: A comparison of geographic adjustments with regional price parities vs. median rents from the american community survey: An update*. United States Census Bureau Working Paper No. SEHSD-2017-36. https://www.census.gov/library/working-papers/2017/demo/SEHSD-WP2017-36.html

Rothbaum, J. (2015). *Bridging a survey design using multiple imputation: An application to the 2014 CPS ASEC*. United States Census Bureau SEHDS Working Paper No. 2015-15. https://www.census.gov/content/dam/Census/library/working-papers/2015/demo/SEHSD-WP2015-15.pdf

Rothbaum, J., and Bee, A. (2021). *Coronavirus infects surveys, too: Nonresponse bias during the pandemic in the CPS ASEC*. Social, Economic, and Housing Statistic Division Working Paper No. 2020-10. https://www.census.gov/library/working-papers/2020/demo/ SEHSD-WP2020-10.html

Rubin, D.B. (1976). Inference and missing data. *Biometrika, 63*(3), 581-592.

REFERENCES

Ruggles, P. (1990). *Drawing the Line: Alternative Poverty Measures and Their Implications for Public Policy.* Urban Institute Press.

Sabelhaus, J., Johnson, D., Ash, S., Garner, T.I., Greenlees, J., and Henderson, S. (2015). Is the Consumer Expenditure Survey representative by income? *Improving the Measurement of Consumer Expenditures*, 241-262.

Saksena, M.J., Okrent, A.M., Anekwe, T.D., Cho, C., Dicken, C., Effland, A., Elitzak, H., Guthrie, J., Hamrick, K.S., Hyman, J., Jo, Y., Lin, B.-H., Mancino, L., McLaughlin, P.W., Rahkovsky, I., Ralston, K., Smith, T.A., Stewart, H., Todd, J., and Tuttle, C. (2018). *America's eating habits: Food away from home.* Economic Information Bulletin No., EIB-196. United States Department of Agriculture, Economic Research Service. https://www.ers.usda.gov/publications/pub-details/?pubid=90227

Saunders, P., Chalmers, J., McHugh, M., Murray, C., Bittman, M., and Bradbury, B. (1998). *Development of indicative budget standards for Australia.* Policy Research Paper No. 74, Department of Social Security Canberra.

Schanzenbach, D., and Pitts, A. (2020). *How much food has insecurity risen? Evidence from the Census Household Pulse Survey.* Northwestern Institute for Policy Research. https://www.ipr.northwestern.edu/documents/reports/ipr-rapid-research-reports-pulse-hh-data-10-june-2020.pdf

Sen, A.K. (1997). From income inequality to economic inequality. *Southern Economic Association, 64*(2), 384-401.

Shaefer, H.L., and Rivera, J. (2018). *Comparing trends in poverty and material hardship over the past two decades.* Working Paper No. 5-17. University of Michigan Poverty Solutions.

Shantz, K. (2019). *Using administrative records to evaluate child care expense reporting among child care subsidy recipients.* United States Census Bureau Working Paper No. SEHSD-WP2019-11. https://www.census.gov/library/working-papers/2019/demo/SEHSD-WP2019-11.html

Shantz, K., and Fox, L.E. (2018). *Precision in measurement: Using state-level Supplemental Nutrition Assistance Program and Temporary Assistance for Needy Families administrative records and the Transfer Income Model (TRIM3) to evaluate poverty measurement.* United States Census Bureau Working Paper No. 2018-30. https://www.census.gov/content/dam/Census/library/working-papers/2018/demo/SEHSD-WP2018-30.pdf

Short, K. (2011). *The research supplemental poverty measure: 2010.* United States Census Bureau Current Population Reports No. P60-241. https://cps.ipums.org/cps/resources/spm/p60-241.pdf

_____. (2009). Cohabitation and Child Care in a Poverty Measure. Proceedings of the American Statistical Association, Social Statistics Section. Presented at the annual conference of the American Statistical Association, Washington, DC, August 2009.

Short, K., and Garner, T.I. (2002). Experimental poverty measures: Accounting for medical expenditures. *Monthly Labor Review, 125*(8), 3-13.

Short, K., and Smeeding, T.M. (2005). *Consumer units, households, and sharing: A view from the survey of income and program participation SIPP.* Working Paper, United States Bureau of the Census. https://www.census.gov/content/dam/Census/library/working-papers/2005/demo/consumerunits.pdf

Smeeding, T.M., and Thornton, K.A. (2020). *Wisconsin poverty report 2018: Still in the doldrums.* Institute for Research on Poverty, University of Wisconsin-Madison. https://www.irp.wisc.edu/resource/wisconsin-poverty-report-2018/

Social Metrics Commission. (2020). *Measuring Poverty 2020.* Report on Poverty in the UK. https://socialmetricscommission.org.uk/wp-content/uploads/2020/06/Measuring-Poverty-2020-Web.pdf

Steinberg, B., Voorheis, J., Reyes-Morales, S., and McBride, B. (2020). Using administrative data to improve nonresponsive weighting procedures in the Consumer Expenditure Survey. https://www.bls.gov/osmr/research-papers/2020/pdf/st200050.pdf

Suh, J., and Folbre, N. (2015). Value unpaid child care in the US: A prototype satellite account using the American Time Use Survey. *Review of Income and Wealth.* https://doi.org/10.1111/roiw.12193

Törmälehto, V.-M. (2017). *High income and affluence: Evidence from the European Union statistics on income and living conditions (EU-SILC).* Publications Office of the European Union. https://ec.europa.eu/eurostat/web/products-statistical-working-papers/-/ks-tc-16-027

Townsend, P. (1979). *Poverty in the United Kingdom.* Allen Lane, Penguin Books.

United Nations Economic Commission for Europe. (2011), *The Canberra Group Handbook on Household Income Statistics.* (2nd ed.). ECE/CES/11. Geneva.

United States Census Bureau. (2021a). *March 2021 current population survey Annual Social and Economic (ASEC) supplement technical documentation.* United States Census Bureau. https://www2.census.gov/programs-surveys/cps/techdocs/cpsmar21.pdf

_____. (2021b). *U.S. Census Bureau's Budget: Fiscal Year 2022.* https://www.commerce.gov/sites/default/files/2021-06/fy2022_census_congressional_budget_justification.pdf

_____. (2011). Who's minding the kids? Child care arrangements: 2011—Detailed Tables. Table 6: Average weekly child care expenditures of families with employed mothers that make payments by age groups and selected characteristics. https://www.census.gov/data/tables/2008/demo/2011-tables.html

United States Department of Agriculture. (2021). *Thrifty food plan, 2021*. FNS-916. https://FNS.usda.gov/TFP

Wheaton, L., and Stevens, K. (2016). *The effect of different tax calculators on the supplemental poverty measure*. United States Census Bureau Supplemental Poverty Measure Working Papers. https://www.census.gov/library/working-papers/2016/demo/wheaton-stevens-2016.html

Wheaton, L., Wemmerus, N., and Godfrey, T. (2021). *Factors contributing to high estimated SNAP participation rates: Insights from microsimulation model comparisons and analysis of CPS-linked SNAP administrative records data*. The Urban Institute Final Report. https://copafs.org/wp-content/uploads/2021/11/H2Wheaton.pdf

Wimer, C., Fox, L., Garfinkel, I., Kaushal, N., and Waldfogel, J. (2016). Progress on poverty? New estimates of historical trends using an anchored supplemental poverty measure. *Demography, 53*(4), 1207-1218.

Ziliak, J.P. (2011). *Cost of living and the supplemental poverty measure*. Center for Poverty Research, University of Kentucky. https://ukcpr.org/sites/ukcpr/files/research-pdfs/cost%20of%20living%20and%20SPM_ziliak.pdf

_____. (2016). *Modernizing SNAP benefits*. Brookings Institution, Hamilton Project. https://www.hamiltonproject.org/assets/files/ziliak_modernizing_snap_benefits.pdf

Appendix A

Background and Specification of the OPM and the SPM

The intent of these two tables, prepared by panel staff, is to provide a reference document with specifications for the Official Poverty Measure (OPM) and the Supplemental Poverty Measure (SPM) through the changes made in 2021, including commentary and selected references.

- Table A-1 provides specifications for the OPM, with observations from the panel staff and document changes (virtually none) since the measure was officially adopted in 1969.
- Table A-2 provides specifications for the SPM, notes differences from the OPM and from the recommendations of the National Academies of Sciences, Engineering, and Medicine panel that produced the 1995 report *Measuring Poverty: A New Approach*, which laid the foundation for the SPM. The table documents the changes that were made since the first SPM poverty rates were released in 2011, which were implemented for estimates released beginning in 2021.

TABLE A-1 Official Poverty Measure (OPM) Specifications[a]

Type of Measure/Updating Approach	*Economic*: The lack of sufficient economic resources to obtain minimum levels of necessary economic goods and services, measured by comparing a monetary poverty threshold for a unit of measurement to the unit's available resources over a period of time (typically a year, but OPM measures have been constructed for longer and shorter periods) *Absolute*: Updated for price changes only (although see Threshold Updating below) References: Fisher (1992); Fisher (1992); Interagency Technical Working Group (2021); National Academies of Sciences, Engineering, and Medicine (2019, especially App. D); NRC (1995)	
When Adopted	Developed by Mollie Orshansky for 1963; used by Office of Economic Opportunity; adopted by Bureau of the Budget in 1969 as official measure in Statistical Policy Directive 14 References: U.S. Census Bureau (annually): Consumer Income P-60 Publication Series and Poverty Thresholds	

Component	Current Definition	Commentary	Changes Since Inception
Unit for which Poverty Measured	*Family*: Two or more people related by blood, marriage, or adoption living in same household *Unrelated Individual*: Person living alone or with other(s) not related to the individual in same household (includes cohabitors) *Excluded*: Residents of institutions (nursing homes, prisons, etc.); unrelated individuals under age 15 (including foster children) living in a household; homeless	Does not recognize increase in cohabitation or sharing of household costs among unrelated people.	None
Poverty Threshold Concept	*Food Times 3*: Three times the cost of minimum food diet in 1963, derived from ratio of all (after-tax) spending to food spending for families of 3+ persons in 1955 survey (a so-called "expert" budget method of establishing poverty thresholds)	Threshold concept is outdated: today, families spend 8 times the cost of food consumed at home or eaten outside the home	None
Threshold Adjustments	*Number*: 48 thresholds varying by family size up to 9+ persons; number of children < age 18 up to 8+; and, for 1- and 2-person units, age of head </> 65 *Derivation*: Thresholds for families of 3+ persons based on USDA Economy Food Plan costs for adults, children, and various size families (assuming economies of scale), with assumptions about ages of children in each family size, times 3; thresholds for 2-person families use a multiplier of 3.7; thresholds for 1-person units set at 80% of corresponding 2-person thresholds; thresholds for people age 65+ set at about 90% of thresholds for younger people	Method to determine family size/composition threshold adjustments produced hard-to-justify variations; no adjustment for geographic variations in costs of living or for variations in housing benefits and costs associated with ownership status (owner/renter)	*1963*: 124 thresholds, including farm-nonfarm status of family (farm thresholds set at 70% of nonfarm) and gender of family head (male head thresholds higher than female head thresholds) *1969*: Farm thresholds raised to 85% of nonfarm thresholds *1981*: Nonfarm thresholds used for all families; thresholds by gender of head averaged; thresholds for family size increased from 7+ to 9+ persons (and number of children from 6+ to 8+)

Threshold Updating	CPI-U (flagship index published by the Bureau of Labor Statistics)	OPM is an absolute poverty measure conceptually, using an inflation index to adjust thresholds. Because the CPI-U (the inflation index used since 1969) overestimated inflation during the late 1970s–early 1980s, OPM thresholds increased ~13% from 1969 to 2019 in real terms vs. thresholds adjusted with a corrected CPI-U-RS	1963: Updated by Economy Food Plan costs 1969: Updated by CPI-U

Resource Measure (to compare to thresholds)	*Gross Before-Tax Regular Money Income*
	Market Income:
	  Wages and Salaries
	  Self-Employment Income (net)
	  Farm Income (net)
	  Returns from Assets (e.g., dividends, interest)
	  Child Support and Alimony (for custodial parent)
	  Private Disability and Retirement
	Cash Transfers:
	  AFDC/TANF
	  Social Security Retirement/Disability
	  SSI
	  Unemployment Insurance
	  Veterans Payments, Workers Compensation
		Gross money income concept relevant in the 1960s before expansion of government assistance through in-kind programs and tax credits but outdated today; captures effects of economic cycles but not of important programs or nondiscretionary expenses	None

Treatment of Medical Care Costs/Benefits	Thresholds implicitly include small amount for medical out-of-pocket spending; resources ignore medical care benefits/costs	OPM ignores expansion of medical care benefits/costs since the 1960s	None
Treatment of Taxes	Thresholds are after taxes (except for property and sales taxes implicitly included in the multiplier); resources are gross money income (inconsistent)	OPM ignores major changes in tax programs (e.g., EITC) that benefit low-income families	None
Treatment of Work Expenses	Thresholds implicitly include amounts for work-related transportation/dependent care spread across all families, working or not; resources ignore them	OPM ignores increased need/spending by workers for dependent care, commuting	None

continued

TABLE A-1 Continued

Component	Current Definition	Commentary	Changes Since Inception
Data Source	*CPS-ASEC*—sample of 100,000 households (includes noninstitutionalized group quarters and Armed Forces members living off base or with families on base; college students included in parental households; 100% oversample of Hispanic households beginning in 1976) interviewed in February–April following income reference year Known as the *March Income Supplement* prior to 2002 when the sample was expanded to improve state estimates of children's health insurance coverage; in addition to increasing the March sample in states with high sampling errors for uninsured children, the expansion involved asking the supplement questions of one quarter of the February and April CPS samples (not including households also interviewed in March) and interviewing selected sample households from the preceding November CPS sample during the February–April period	OPM measures have been constructed with many data sets—e.g., ACS for small-area estimates and SIPP for part-year estimates	See Data Source entry in Table A-2
Data Quality	CPS-ASEC obtains high unit response rates but much lower rates for income items (40% of income imputed); exhibits underreporting of many income types, even after imputation (which itself can create error) of amounts for respondents reporting receipt. Negative or very low incomes can also be misleading—e.g., for self-employed people who may have experienced a business loss but have an income flow from their businesses; college students supported by their families; and possibly others. Household and person response rates, although high, are declining, and coverage ratios compared with the Census are decreasing (post-stratification to population controls only partly corrects)	Concerns about income data quality are major drawback of OPM (and any poverty measure based on CPS-ASEC); ACS and SIPP have similar quality problems References: Meyer et al. (2009, 2015); Meyer and Mittag (2018); Bee et al. (2015); Hokayem et al. (2015); Scherpf et al. (2015); Fox and Burns (2021a); Shantz and Fox (2018); Bollinger et al. (2019); Meyer and Mittag (2019); Mittag (2019); Rothbaum and Bee (2021); Wheaton et al. (2021)	Percent income imputed and net underreporting have increased over time for many income sources, particularly transfers

a Abbreviations used in table: ACS, American Community Survey; AFDC/TANF, Aid to Families with Dependent Children/Temporary Assistance for Needy Families; CPI-U, Consumer Price Index for All Urban Consumers; CPI-U-RS, CPI-U Research Series; CPS-ASEC, Current Population Survey Annual Social and Economic Supplement; EITC, Earned Income Tax Credit; SIPP, Survey of Income and Program Participation; SSI, Supplemental Security Income; USDA, U.S. Department of Agriculture.

TABLE A-2 Supplemental Poverty Measure (SPM) Specifications[a]

Type of Measure/ Updating Approach	*Economic*: The lack of sufficient economic resources to obtain minimum levels of necessary economic goods and services, measured by comparing a monetary poverty threshold for a unit of measurement to the unit's available resources over a period of time (typically a year) *Quasi-relative*: Updated for real changes in consumption of basic bundle of goods—originally FCSU estimated from the CE; currently FCSUti References: Meyer and Sullivan (2012); Winmer et al. (2016); Shaefer and Rivera (2018)
When Adopted	Proposed by 2010 report of Interagency Technical Working Group, based on recommendations of 1995 National Academies' report *Measuring Poverty: A New Approach* (MP); implemented by Census Bureau and BLS; first SPM measures published in 2011 (income year 2010) References: U.S. Census Bureau (annual), Supplemental Poverty Measure; Bureau of Labor Statistics website, Experimental Poverty Measures
Original Differences from National Academies (1995)	*Thresholds/Threshold Adjustments*: Originally, expenditures for all families with 2 children instead of 2 adults and 2 children (although latter still the reference unit); revised 3-parameter (instead of 2-parameter) equivalence scale for family characteristics/economies of scale; separate thresholds for renters with rent >$0, homeowners with a mortgage, and homeowners without a mortgage *Updating*: Originally 33rd percentile of FCSU instead of % of median; average of 5 instead of 3 years of CE quarterly data Reference: National Academies (2019)

Component	Definition (2011–2020)	Commentary vis-à-vis OPM and *Measuring Poverty* (MP)	Changes Since 2011/Adopted in 2021
Unit for which Poverty Measured (Unit of Analysis)	*Family (expanded definition)*: Two or more people related by blood, marriage, or adoption or by cohabitation and living in same household; includes foster children under age 22 and other unrelated children under age 15 living with a family *Unrelated Individual*: Person living alone or with other(s) not related to the individual in same household *Excluded*: Residents of institutions (nursing homes, prisons, etc.); homeless	Re *OPM*: SPM recognizes increase in cohabitation; in 2010 the SPM estimated 124,199 units of analysis compared with 131,946 for the OPM (while the CE estimated 121,107 consumer units for 2010). Most of the decrease for the SPM compared to the OPM was due to treating cohabiting partners as parts of family units instead of as unrelated individuals. (At the same time, the SPM added about 1 million children under 15 to the poverty universe) References: Provencher (2011); Hokayem and Heggeness (2014)	None

continued

TABLE A-2 Continued

Component	Definition (2011–2020)	Commentary vis-à-vis OPM and Measuring Poverty (MP)	Changes Since 2011/Adopted in 2021
Poverty Threshold Concept	*Basic necessities*: FCSU plus a little more; FCSU set at 30th–36th percentile of spending for families (consumer units, CUs) with 2 children from CE; "a little more" set at 20% of FCSU; 5 preceding years (20 quarters) of CE data used for estimation (each quarter updated to last quarter using CPI-U) (percentile range implemented to allow for 3 thresholds by housing tenure) *CUs* comprise: (1) all members of a household related by blood, marriage, adoption, or other legal arrangement; (2) financially independent persons, including people living alone, sharing a household with others, rooming in a private home or lodging house or in permanent quarters in a hotel or motel; or (3) 2+ people living together who use their income to make joint expenditure decisions. To be considered financially independent, the respondent must provide entirely or in part at least 2 of the 3 major expense categories of food, housing, and all other; 97% of CUs include the entire household; the CU definition for estimating thresholds is similar to the SPM definition for assessing poverty status	Re *OPM*: SPM recognizes larger bundle of necessities; derives thresholds from actual spending instead of expert judgments Re *MP*: SPM uses 5 instead of 3 years of CE data to reduce sampling error and adjust thresholds with a lag; uses families with 2 children because they are a larger fraction of CE sample than families of 2 adults/2 children Re *OPM*: The initial 2010 SPM threshold (ignoring tenure status) for 2-adult/2-children families of $24,343 was 10% above the OPM threshold of $22,113, but this is a misleading comparison. Assuming the OPM threshold was $18,650 when converted to the SPM concept (which subtracts some budget items from resources), then the increase for the SPM threshold was 31%—near the top end of the 9–33% range suggested by *Measuring Poverty* (see pp. 53-56), but in the middle of the range of other budgets the 1995 panel examined. For 2019, the SPM threshold was only 24% greater than the converted OPM threshold References: Heisz (2019); Garner and Munoz (2021)	2021 (implemented beginning with revised 2019 thresholds—see spm_threshold_200520. xlsx (live.com)): • Move base-year thresholds from 30th–36th percentiles of FCSU to 83% of 47th–52nd percentiles of FCSUti (expectation of greater stability and less constrained spending around the median) • Expand threshold estimation sample from CUs with 2 children to all CUs with children (represents larger share of population—31% vs. 11%—and retains focus on children as primary beneficiaries of poverty programs) • Lag CE data for the thresholds by one year (permits adding imputed in-kind benefits) • Add imputed in-kind benefits to the thresholds (consistent with resources): rental assistance, LIHEAP, NSLP, WIC (SNAP implicitly included in food expenditures) • Move telephone expenditures out of utilities (no longer geographically adjusted—with increased cell phone use, geographic variation not as important)—basic bundle is FCSUti • Add home internet to the thresholds as a separate item (not geographically adjusted)—becoming a necessity—basic bundle is FCSUti

Threshold Adjustments	*Family composition*: 3-parameter equivalence scale used to adjust 2-adult/2-child threshold for differing numbers of adults and children, economies of scale: • One and two adults: scale = $(\text{adults})^{0.5}$ • Single parents: scale = $(\text{adults} + 0.8 * \text{first child} + 0.5 * \text{other children})^{0.7}$ • All other families: scale = $(\text{adults} + 0.5 * \text{children})^{0.7}$ *Housing tenure*: Separate thresholds developed for homeowners without a mortgage, homeowners with a mortgage, and renters paying rent, using average of 30th–36th percentile expenditures for each group *Geographic price differences*: ACS used to adjust thresholds for housing costs across geographic areas—specifically, 5-year ACS median gross rent for 2-bedroom units with complete kitchen and plumbing facilities estimated for 260 large MSAs, all nonmetropolitan areas within state (47), and combinations of smaller metropolitan areas within state (35); 342 adjustment factors applied to housing and utilities components of thresholds and results added to the other components	Re *OPM*: SPM's method for equivalizing family needs is an improvement on the original idiosyncratic method (although no equivalence scale can be said to be "truth"); recognizes differences in cost of housing across geographic areas (biggest item) Re *MP*: Subsequent research determined SPM 3-parameter scale gave more intuitive results than MP 2-parameter scale = $(\text{adults} + 0.7 * \text{kids})^{0.65-0.75}$; need became apparent for method to account for lower housing expenses of homeowners without a mortgage References: Family composition: Betson (1996); Social Metrics Commission (2020) Geographic price differences: Renwick (2011); Pacas and Rothwell (2020)	*2021*: See Poverty Threshold Concept above
Threshold Updating	30th–36th percentiles of spending on FCSU reestimated each year from previous 5 years (20 quarters) of CE, updated to latest quarter with CPI-U	Re *OPM*: SPM is a quasi-relative measure on assumption that increases in FCSU spending lag all spending but exceed price inflation; intended to achieve gradual increase of thresholds in real terms in contrast to stasis of OPM thresholds Re *MP*: SPM felt to be more transparent by recalculating each year at 30th–36th percentiles instead of percent change in median FCSU	*2001*: • Change from reestimating 30th–36th percentiles of FCSU each year to 83 percent of 47th–52nd percentiles of FSCUti each year • Change from using CPI-U (all items for urban consumers) to update CE data to threshold year, to using composite FCSUti-CPI-U (reflective of price change in threshold components)

continued

TABLE A-2 Continued

Component	Definition (2011–2020)	Commentary vis-à-vis OPM and Measuring Poverty (MP)	Changes Since 2011/Adopted in 2021

Resource Measure (to compare to thresholds)	After-Tax Disposable Income:
	Plus:
	Wages and Salaries
	Self-Employment Income (net)
	Farm Income (net)
	Returns from Assets (e.g., dividends, interest)
	Child Support and Alimony (for custodial parent)
	Private Disability and Retirement
	Cash Transfers:
	  AFDC/TANF
	  Social Security Ret./SSDI
	  SSI
	  Unemployment Insurance
	  Veterans Payments, Workers Comp
	In-kind Transfers:
	  SNAP, WIC, LIHEAP, NSLP, housing subsidies
	Minus:
	Net federal and state income taxes, FICA taxes
	MOOP expenses, including health insurance premiums
	Childcare expenses
	Other work-related expenses (e.g., commuting, uniforms)
	Child support paid by noncustodial parent
		Re *OPM*: SPM recognizes that tax and in-kind transfer programs are major sources of income support in the U.S.; recognizes that workers incur nondiscretionary costs; recognizes child support as nondiscretionary expense of the noncustodial parent; recognizes MOOP costs as nondiscretionary for the low-income population	*2021*: Change from national average value for WIC benefits to state-varying values

Treatment of Medical Care Costs/Benefits	Consistent Treatment: *Thresholds* do not include medical care expenditures *Resources* subtract health insurance premiums and other MOOP costs (copays, deductibles, other); MOOP costs estimated	Re *OPM*: SPM captures effects of medical care policy changes that reduce (increase) MOOP spending, but does not explicitly value medical care or health insurance; medical care not included in thresholds because of difficulties of determining need for differently situated families References: Fox et al. (2015); Korenman and Remler (2016); Burkhauser et al. (2020); Korenman et al. (2019); Remler and Korenman (2021)	None
Treatment/Valuation of In-Kind Transfers	Partially Consistent Treatment: *Thresholds* include food expenditures with SNAP benefits but no other in-kind benefits *Resources* subtract SNAP, NSLP, WIC, LIHEAP, housing subsidies		*2021*: Add imputed in-kind benefits to thresholds (consistent with resources): rental assistance, LIHEAP, NSLP, WIC (SNAP implicitly included in food expenditures)

Treatment of Taxes	Consistent Treatment: *Thresholds* are after taxes (except for property and sales taxes included in FCSU spending and multiplier) *Resources* subtract federal and state income taxes and FICA taxes, using Census Bureau tax simulator	None
Treatment of Work-Related Expenses	Consistent Treatment: *Thresholds* include nonwork transportation *Resources* subtract childcare expenses and other work-related expenses (e.g., work-related transportation, uniforms), capped by earnings of single parent or lower earner of two parents Other work-related expenses calculated as: weeks worked for each earner 18+ from CPS-ASEC * 85% median per earner weekly work-related expenses from most recent SIPP	Re *OPM*: SPM recognizes increased need/spending by workers for childcare, commuting. For 2010 and 2019, *not* subtracting work expenses (childcare and other) from resources would have decreased the overall poverty rate by 1.5 and 1.5 percentage points, respectively (2.0 and 2.0 for kids <18, 1.5 and 1.6 for ages 18–64 and 0.3 and 0.45 for ages 65+)	None
Data Source	*Thresholds*: (CE), four quarters (annualized) for 5 years *Resources*: CPS-ASEC—sample of 100,000 households interviewed in February–April following income reference year (see Data Source Entry in Table A-1)	Like *OPM*, SPM measures have been constructed with many data sets—e.g., ACS for small-area estimates and SIPP for part-year estimates; SPM measures have also been constructed by states and cities (e.g., California, NYC, Wisconsin) using ACS and state/city administrative records	Income questions: *1948*: Wages and salaries; all other sources *1949*: Self-employment asked separately *1950*: Farm and nonfarm self-employment asked separately *1967*: Social Security, interest, dividends, and rent asked separately *1968*: Interest, dividends, rents, royalties combined; public assistance, unemployment/workers' compensation asked separately *1975*: SSI, AFDC, general assistance, private/government pension income asked separately *1980*: 51 sources of income separately identified as to receipt including numerous noncash benefits (e.g., food stamps, housing assistance); up to 27 amounts could be recorded *2000*: Whether paid for work-related childcare added *2010*: MOOP costs added (premiums, other OOP) *2014*: Retirement account withdrawals added; health insurance/MOOP spending questions improved (ACA Marketplace insurance added)

continued

121

TABLE A-2 Continued

Component	Definition (2011–2020)	Commentary vis-à-vis OPM and Measuring Poverty (MP)	Changes Since 2011/Adopted in 2021
Data Quality	CPS-ASEC obtains high unit response rates but lower rates for income items (40% of income imputed); exhibits underreporting of many income types, even after imputation (which itself can create error) of amounts for respondents reporting receipt; problem of misleadingly low or negative incomes; CE data also problematic	Like OPM, concerns about income data quality are major drawback of SPM (and any poverty measure based on CPS-ASEC); ACS and SIPP have similar quality problems	See Data Quality entry in Table A-1

[a] Abbreviations used in table: ACA, Affordable Care Act; ACS, American Community Survey; AFDC/TANF, Aid to Families with Dependent Children/Temporary Assistance for Needy Families; BLS, Bureau of Labor Statistics; CE, Consumer Expenditure Survey; CPI-U, Consumer Price Index for All Urban Consumers; CU, consumer unit; FCSU, food, clothing, shelter, utilities; FCSUti, food, clothing, shelter, utilities, telephone, internet; LIHEAP, Low Income Home Energy Assistance Program; MOOP, medical out-of-pocket; MSA, Metropolitan Statistical Area; NSLP, National School Lunch Program; OPM, Official Poverty Measure; SSDI, Social Security Disability Insurance; SSI, Supplemental Security Income; SNAP, Supplemental Nutrition Assistance Program; WIC, Special Supplemental Nutrition Program for Women, Infants, and Children.

Appendix B

Summary of Public Comments

As part of the process to ensure the final report is objective, balanced, informed, and inclusive, the National Academies of Sciences, Engineering, and Medicine's Committee on National Statistics *Panel on Evaluation and Improvements to the Supplemental Poverty Measure* invited public comments to gain the input of poverty-measurement stakeholders. Researchers, policy makers, and antipoverty advocacy groups were among the stakeholders that responded. Those submitting comments were asked to outline their perceived strengths of the supplemental poverty measure (SPM) and to identify aspects in need of improvement. The public comment period was open from May 10, 2021, until July 2, 2021. This Appendix highlights several (although not all) of the prominent themes that emerged. Full text of the public comments can be acquired upon request. Those submitting comments were

- The Federation of Protestant Welfare Agencies (FPWA), an antipoverty, policy, and advocacy nonprofit with a membership network of nearly 170 human service and faith-based organizations working across New York City;
- The Contra Costa County Family Economic Security Partnership (FESP), a coalition of over 50 agencies providing a range of services to help families become financially self-sufficient;
- Children's HealthWatch, a nonpartisan network of pediatricians, public health researchers, and children's health and policy experts committed to improving children's health in America;
- Richard V. Burkhauser (Cornell University), Kevin Corinth (University of Chicago), Bruce D. Meyer (University of Chicago), Angela Rachidi (American Enterprise Institute), Matt Weidinger (American Enterprise Institute), and Scott Winship (American Enterprise Institute);
- The New York City Mayor's Office for Economic Opportunity (NYCO);
- Shawn Fremstad (Center for Economic and Policy Research), Nancy Folbre (University of Massachusetts Amherst), Pilar Goñalons-Pons (University of Pennsylvania), and Jeff Madrick (The Century Foundation). This group's comments draw in part on recommendations made in *Defining Deprivation Down: Why We Need to Reset the Poverty Line*, a joint report published by the Center for Economic and Policy Research and The Century Foundation in 2020;
- The National Women's Law Center (NWLC), which fights for gender justice—in the courts, in public policy, and in society—working across the issues that are central to the lives of women and girls;
- The Mayor's Policy Office, City of Philadelphia;

- Robert Moffitt (Johns Hopkins University);
- Zachary Morris (Stony Brook University), Nanette Goodman (Burton Blatt Institute), Debra Brucker (University of New Hampshire), and Stephen McGarity (University of Tennessee);
- J. Tom Mueller (University of Oklahoma);
- Arloc Sherman (Vice President for Data Analysis and Research Center on Budget and Policy Priorities);
- Laura Wheaton (The Urban Institute); and
- Christopher Wimer (Columbia University), Megan Curran (Columbia University), Zachary Parolin (Columbia University), Elizabeth Ananat (Barnard College).

Theme: The SPM Should Explicitly Include More Categories of Basic Needs

Several public commenters suggested that the SPM's food, clothing, shelter, and utilities (FCSU) basic needs categories should be modernized. Zarin Ahmed, Senior Policy Analyst at FPWA, argued that the current SPM methodology results in thresholds that are only slightly higher than the official poverty measure (OPM), in part due to omission of the expenditures required for households to attain some basic needs. Along these same lines, New York City's Center of Economic Opportunity (CEO) reported that their alternative poverty threshold—which is grounded in analyses of the Self Sufficiency Standard and income adequacy developed by the Center for Women's Welfare at the University of Washington—was about 127 percent greater than that of the SPM in 2018.

Sherman echoed the view that the SPM should explicitly recognize a broader set of basic needs categories and that the threshold should be higher to reflect current needs. In addition to FCSU, Sherman suggested that the SPM threshold should account for medical care needs (as in the Health Inclusive Poverty Measure)—a sentiment expressed by other commenters. Fremstad et al. added that, if operationally feasible, the developmental needs of children should likewise be included. The group articulated a preference that the SPM take needs such as health insurance and other goods and services necessary for social participation into account, in a parallel manner to FCSU.

Fremstat et al. argued for factoring in childcare and transportation expenditures beyond those related to work. Wimer et al. agree, noting that the Center on Poverty and Social Policy has advocated for inclusion of medical and childcare needs—currently addressed only through the subtraction of out-of-pocket expenses—in the threshold.

The NWLC representatives added that childcare and child development are basic needs and, as such, factors that SPM thresholds should reflect. NWLC acknowledged that establishing what is needed to account for diverse caregiving arrangements—e.g., those who pay for child and/or adult dependent care, those who receive childcare assistance, those who have care provided by a family member—requires consulting with experts.

Fremstad et al. addressed this point as well, noting that the National Academies' panel and Interagency Technical Working Group on Developing a Supplemental Poverty Measure did not explicitly address children's developmental needs beyond food, clothing, and shelter, or the related social- and cultural-participation needs. Given changing norms of what constitutes a basic standard of living and an evolved understanding of child development and wellbeing over the past half century, the group argued that such needs should be an explicit part of a contemporary poverty measure. Fremstad et al. pointed out that subtracting out-of-pocket spending on childcare needed for a parent to be employed is better than nothing, but not enough, because families who need childcare, but who are not able to pay for it out of pocket (and do not receive free or subsidized public care), are treated as having no need for childcare.

Fremstad's group bolstered their position by citing how the SPM thresholds fall below the public's understanding of the income needed to "not be poor." In the mid-2010s, two surveys, one sponsored by the Center for American Progress and the other sponsored by the American Enterprise Institute, found that Americans guessed the poverty line to be 16–22 percent higher than that estimated by the SPM. Similar conclusions, they noted, have emerged from budget studies and expert plans. The group proposed that establishing more "reasonable" SPM thresholds could be done by increasing the multiplier to better account for additional goods and services that are part of the subsistence norm; by directly adding in the cost of basic needs such as transportation and child development services; or by tying the threshold to a percentage of median consumption.

Several commenters raised a subtheme of the component-expansion argument: that additional basic needs exist for the full scope of expenses incurred by people with disabilities. This point, most comprehensively articulated in the memo by Morris et al., implies that the failure to accurately capture the extent of nondiscretionary expenses experienced by people with disabilities leads the SPM to understate the extent of poverty among households that include members with disabilities (only some would be captured by the SPM subtracting medical out-of-pocket expenses). The group cited research estimating that, on average, a household at the national median income including a working-age adult with a disability incurs approximately $22,000 a year in disability-related expenses, a figure far greater that what can be accounted for by the subtracted medical out-of-pocket expenses used in SPM income calculations.

Theme: Basic Needs Are Changing in Response to Broader Societal, Economic, and Environmental Developments

Another subtheme, raised by the Children's HealthWatch group, is how the needs of families, households, or consumer units have been changing over time. Among the broader exogenous shifts identified by HealthWatch as being especially relevant and urgent are

1. systemic racial and ethnic inequities;
2. escalating shifts in employment within the U.S. economy away from manufacturing and toward services (financial services but even more into lower-paying services such as hospitality services and the so-called "gig economy," which pay relatively low wages, do not provide benefits, and lack stability of work schedules); and
3. the rapidly intensifying effects of climate change.

Climate change, they noted, is exposing people in the United States and throughout the world to unanticipated adverse consequences that are requiring extraordinary adaptations, and thus additional expenses in the form of insurance, home modifications, disaster recovery, medical care expenditures, and more. The group believes these needs and others related to changing realities should be incorporated into our understanding of poverty as represented in the SPM.

In his comments, Sherman suggested that future expert panels should reassess the SPM approximately every 10 years or so, to account for evolving household needs.

Theme: Resource Measurement—Treatment of Credits and Debts

Several commenters raised questions about the role of tax credits in estimating consumer unit resources. The FPWA group noted that, while tax credits are important financial resources for households with low incomes, not every household eligible for the Earned Income Tax Credit claims the credit (in tax year 2017, for example, almost 19 percent of eligible filers did not claim the credit in New York). Several commenters, including NWLC and Fremstad et al., identified the importance of proper timing of tax credits in the SPM. Specifically, the income from refundable tax credits should ideally be counted in the year families receive them, rather than the tax year during which they are earned (as is currently done for the SPM). The bulk of specific refundable tax benefits, they point out, is not actually received by families until after mid-February of the calendar year after the tax year in which the credits are earned. Commenters pointed out that administrative data could help resolve this timing inaccuracy as well as other aspects of the SPM resource calculation.

On the other side of the ledger, the burden of debt to families was raised. FPWA took the position that repayment of student loan debts should be considered as a deduction from income. Fremstad et al. concurred, stating that, like other mandatory expenses, repayments of student debt reduce the income available for housing, food, and other necessities. Moffitt made a pitch for broader research on resource timing—i.e., whether low-income families transfer resources from other periods into the current one. He noted that information on how families spend down assets to finance current expenditures and borrow against future resources to do the same would ideally be incorporated. In the latter category, credit cards, payday loans, and other near-cash alternatives all come into play.

Burkhauser et al. also expressed concern about the accuracy of SPM resource accounting, emphasizing the substantial resources provided to Americans through health insurance plans provided by their employers or the government. This, they argued, makes the omission of the value of health insurance from the SPM problematic. Similarly, the SPM caps the value of rental housing assistance at the housing portion of the SPM threshold minus the tenant-paid portion of the rent. In their view, this practice ignores the full value of housing—including access to amenities—reflected in its price. For homeowners with or without mortgages, Burkhauser et al. pointed out that the substantial consumption value received from living in their homes is not fully reflected in SPM estimates of resources.

Theme: Appropriate Measurement Unit—Household, Consumer Unit, Other?

Comments by Children's HealthWatch supported the idea of changing the unit of analysis for the SPM from the consumer unit (as currently defined) to the household. They argued that the household unit is more consistent with other measures of resource adequacy, including the OPM and various food security measures.

Wimer et al. also commented on the specifications of the unit of analysis. They suggested that the SPM would be more valuable if the Current Population Survey (CPS) contained more information on the presence of, and obligations toward, children outside of the co-resident household. Currently, they noted, the CPS has valuable information on child support payments made to other households, but—absent those payments—it cannot be ascertained which respondents have biological children living elsewhere. Adding this capability may become even more important as refundable tax credits continue to grow as an antipoverty tool, given that tax-filing rules and behaviors often depend on custodial arrangements. More data on obligations toward children outside the household would also inform initiatives to better allocation credit values and other needs/resources across households.

Theme: Setting and Updating of Thresholds

A number of public comments recommended revisiting the basic approach to setting thresholds. NWLC was critical that the SPM threshold is set at "the thirty-third percentile of spending on shelter, certain utilities, food, and clothing," rather than the 1995 National Academies' recommendation to set and update thresholds "equal to a percentage of median annual spending on food, clothing, shelter, and utilities multiplied by 1.2" (NRC, 1995). Their rationale was that rent for a modest two-bedroom apartment in many areas plus the cost of food alone consumes most of the poverty threshold for a two-adult family.

Questions were also raised about the SPM data approach. Sherman observed that updating the threshold annually based on 5 years of consumer expenditure data has proven to be an awkward compromise. Five years is neither short enough to reflect current conditions nor long enough to ensure a stable threshold across business cycles. The result, he argued, is that in any given year, changes in the SPM rate may perversely reflect changes in consumption 6 years ago as much as they reflect changes in family resources in the past year. He proposed that the simplest solution to this temporal problem would be for the Census Bureau to release a separate, limited set of "anchored SPM" trend tables each year, based on a recent threshold adjusted for inflation.

Burkhauser et al. were of the view that the baseline threshold calculation is overly complex and difficult to understand. This, they wrote, makes interpretation of poverty changes over time almost impossible. They would prefer to see adoption of a simple baseline concept, such as pegging the SPM threshold to the percentile given by the official poverty rate in the initial year. An absolute standard—and potentially a purely relative standard—for adjusting poverty thresholds could then be updated based on the Chained Consumer Price Index for All Urban Consumers; the relative measure could update thresholds by the same percentage at which the median income changes each year.

Burkhauser et al. were also critical of the current method of adjusting thresholds for families based on housing tenure. They argued that basing SPM thresholds on the same expenditure percentiles for renters, homeowners with a mortgage, and homeowners without a mortgage fails to recognize differences between these groups and difference in housing equity within groups. Their proposed solution was to include the value of home ownership in SPM resources.

Theme: Appropriate Geographic Adjustment

Several of the public comments supported the idea of more granular geographic adjustment of poverty thresholds, while recognizing data constraints. Biderman (Contra Costa County FESP) outlined her organization's perspective that federal poverty measures do not adequately adjust for the San Francisco Bay area's (and other areas') high costs of living and therefore underestimate their true poverty rates. She cited figures from the Bay Area Equity Atlas indicating that 52 percent of renters in Contra Costa County are housing burdened (i.e., those households that pay more than 30% of their income to housing), which creates a "large gap in the system of support for young children and families." Based on an alternative measure developed by FESP, the high cost of housing in the county means that acquiring the basic needs for a family of four with an infant and a toddler requires a household annual income of $141,641; meanwhile, the median household income for a family with children in Contra Costa is $103,685. The FESP memo concluded that a better measure of poverty, especially at the county level, is "essential to helping understand the range of needs facing families and is critical to helping policy makers and providers target services more effectively."

Hinckley (Director of Policy Mayor's Policy Office, City of Philadelphia) agreed that for organizations like hers, poverty measurement must be local to be useful. She argued that current CPS measurements obscure substate variation in household resources, especially for regions and jurisdictions that are deeply disadvantaged. In part, this involves near-cash transfers that are administered locally (including things like school lunch programs) and vary significantly at substate levels, and local tax structures that have statistically significant effects on poverty rates. These impacts are particularly relevant for cities like Philadelphia, where a local wage tax is assessed, or New York City, where there is a local Earned Income Tax Credit.

At the same time, Hinckley congratulated the Census Bureau on making "impressive strides in supporting local policymakers" with the release of a working version of the SPM built from American Community Survey (ACS) data. Hinckley would like to see the Census Bureau formalize this product by: (1) committing to an annual schedule of releasing the ACS SPM; and (2) including the questions about near-cash transfers and necessary expenses in the ACS questionnaire.

The NYCO Office for Economic Opportunity took a stance similar to those of commenters from the other locally based organizations—that national, or even statewide, measures cannot adequately capture local environments. While acknowledging that the ACS is a valuable tool that allows poverty measurement at the public use microdata area (PUMA) level, the NYCO comment made the case for data at a sub-PUMA level to capture differences across neighborhoods. Given their specific information demands, the NYCO implemented an alternative measure of poverty for New York City in 2008, while continuing to produce an annual measure similar in methodology to the SPM. However, the NYCO measure employs ACS microdata to represent the base population and an adaptation of the SPM poverty threshold that accounts for the high cost of local housing.

Mueller et al. argued for rural/urban cost-of-living adjustments and more refined threshold adjustments for nonmetropolitan counties—an explicit criticism of the current SPM practice of assigning all nonmetropolitan areas within the same state the same adjustment which, in his view, may be severely biasing our understanding of rural poverty. To remedy the situation, he suggested that the most desirable outcome would be a county-specific adjustment. However, he acknowledged limitations of publicly available Census Bureau data to support this solution. For example, neither the CPS nor ACS microdata provide reliable information about county of residence for rural places. He pointed out that the SPM's failure to reflect substate geographic levels limits its policy value such that many researchers and policy-focused practitioners use the OPM even when they would rather not.

Wimer et al. pointed out that an increased CPS sample size would allow for greater precision in the estimation of poverty rates and policy effects for smaller geographic areas and smaller demographic subgroups. He noted, for example, with current sample sizes it is difficult to precisely measure poverty for Native Americans, residents of major cities, or those who identify with finer-grained racial and ethnic subgroups as opposed to broad classifications like "Hispanic/Latino/a" or "Asian American/Pacific Islander." While some progress can be made on this front by augmenting the CPS with ACS data (which have a much larger sample size) the amount of imputation involved in generating accurate SPM poverty rates in the ACS is daunting and often prohibitive.

Taking a somewhat opposing view, Burkhauser et al. suggested that adjusting thresholds across geographic areas may not be justified, since higher home prices can reflect access to greater amenities. His group advocated for removing geographic adjustments from the SPM thresholds.

Wimer et al. added that the value of the SPM could be greater if the underlying data (the CPS) were also collected in the U.S. territories, such as Puerto Rico, Guam, etc. Without such data, researchers and policy makers cannot compare poverty levels between these areas and U.S. states or subpopulations using the SPM, and therefore cannot understand the ways that policies affect poverty in the territories. In Wimer's view, such analyses would be enormously useful for understanding policy gaps in the territories, including how policies could be made more equitable.

Theme: Concerns About Use of Expenditure Data to Establish Basic Needs

Several commenters expressed concerns about the underlying data, and particularly the expenditure data, used to construct the SPM. The FPWA group was one of these, explaining that a critical difference between the SPM and the Self Sufficiency Standard used by NYC's CEO is that the latter is based on data on the cost of housing, childcare, food, medical care, transportation, and miscellaneous costs, while the SPM uses expenditure data to deduce the costs of these items. It is a long-held argument in the literature that many families and individuals go without basic needs because they do not have the funds to purchase these services in the first place; thus, relying on expenditure data undermines the critical issue of unmet need. Additionally, the FWPA group pointed out that the existence of benefits programs does not necessarily guarantee that those benefits are accessible. For example, while a childcare subsidy exists in the United States it is grossly underfunded and families who are unable to access the benefit due to eligibility, coverage, and hardship gaps must make difficult choices in managing childcare, including forgoing paid help and employment opportunities.

NYCO also argued for improved information on parental expenditures on childcare. The NYCO poverty measure (described above) imputes childcare spending from the SIPP and, like the SPM, deducts this work-related cost from resource estimates. The SIPP sample is relatively small and inadequate for local imputation; thus, in their view, a detailed national survey on childcare is needed and would have benefits beyond poverty measurement. A well-designed survey, they suggested, could provide information on how much childcare is needed, as opposed to what parents can afford. This is key to understanding resources needed for parents to spend more time in school or the workplace—both factors that can move families out of poverty. The survey could occur on a less-than-annual basis and may be most usefully conducted as a supplement to the ACS, to capture the relation between family structure, work, income, and childcare.

Theme: Transparency of SPM Methodology

Several commenters called for simplification of the SPM methodology. The FPWA memo stated that the complex nature of the measure prevents it from being accessible, and people with low incomes have little opportunity to provide feedback on what they view as their basic needs. To improve the SPM, the FPWA urged the panel to consider the views of individuals and families with lived experiences of poverty.

Children's HealthWatch expressed difficulty parsing equivalence scale adjustments, pointing out that explanation of the role of equivalence scales is not made adequately clear in documentation published on the Census Bureau's website. Consequently, they felt there was a degree of arbitrariness in the use of those adjustments. However, based on published information and results from their own research, Children's HealthWatch "supports equivalence scale Option 1: Use 0.7 for all." In the same vein, to facilitate examination and interpretation of potential changes to the SPM in future reviews, the Children's HealthWatch recommended listing working papers and related materials—especially status indications of which potential changes are under consideration and which have been discarded or postponed—on the Census Bureau SPM website, in chronological order.

Theme: Data Improvement

Public commenters identified a number of weaknesses with the SPM data infrastructure, some of which overlap with themes outlined above. Burkhauser et al. argued that the SPM is overly reliant on survey data. Their take on the literature is that survey response inaccuracies distort what individuals report as earned income and government benefits; and the accuracy of imputed items such as taxes are affected as well. If true, such inaccuracies would cause the SPM to misidentify the most economically deprived populations and underestimate the poverty-reducing effects of safety net programs. For these reasons, Burkauser et al. support an increased role for use of administrative data on earnings, government program benefits, and other income sources, to more accurately measure SPM resources.

The NYCO public comment also indicated support for greater incorporation of administrative data into the SPM. By way of example, to address underreporting and other survey problems, NYCO uses New York State and New York City enrollment data to supplement benefit receipt information reported in the ACS. The Supplemental Nutrition Assistance Program (SNAP) and local administrative data are used to more accurately portray the number of recipients and the dollar value of benefit allotments, both of which are highly sensitive to local program rules. Replacing surveyed SNAP benefits data with state-level administrative data also helps remove statistical error introduced in the imputation process.

In her comment, Wheaton pointed out that the Census Bureau and others are actively working on approaches that use linked administrative data and survey data to address the problem of underreporting of program benefits in survey responses. The hope is that such linkages will result in a better measure of resources and improved poverty estimates. When considering the use of linked administrative data and survey records (or imputations based on such linkages) to measure resources, Wheaton identified three key issues requiring additional attention and research:

1. The role of imputed income in the survey data in any such approach.
2. The extent of inconsistencies in household membership and family relationships according to survey data and administrative data records. For example, the group's recent study of linked SNAP administrative data and CPS data in three states found many cases in which a single parent with children appeared as some other family type in the CPS. This could occur because the children were not in the household, the adult was missing from the household, or the family appeared as a married-parent family in the CPS.
3. The underrepresentation of some types of families in the survey data.

The NYCO comment cautioned that administrative data are not always available. The absence of reliable medical expenditure data is a notable example. Medical expenditures (premiums and out-of-pocket costs) are imputed into the ACS from the U.S. Department of Health and Human Services Medical Expenditure Panel Survey. Although this relatively small national sample is not well suited to local imputation models, local administrative data are difficult to obtain and do not provide precise costs paid by individuals.

The frequency and timeliness of data was another subtheme that emerged from public comments. Hinckley pointed out that, while statistical agencies have had some success in measuring the effects and responses to the COVID-19 pandemic with the Household Pulse Survey, for example, large emergency relief programs created as a response to the pandemic, like the Emergency Rental Assistance Program (ERAP), were not included in nationally representative household surveys. ERAP, which provided money to renters or landlords, neatly fit the definition of a near-cash transfer that should, she argued, be included in the SPM. The SPM does not capture this important variation across state, county, territorial, and tribal government jurisdictions. Hinckley also offered support for use of administrative data to improve the quality of the SPM, but only if inclusion of those data maintains or reduces the current delay in data releases.

Hinckley also wondered if monthly poverty estimates from the CPS, which were useful for policy makers in assessing quickly changing economic need during the pandemic, should be formalized by the Census Bureau as part of the SPM program. The memo from Wimer et al. raised the same issue. His group noted that monthly poverty statistics would also allow exploration of the extent to which the SPM—which, like the OPM, is reported for the calendar year—is affected by assumptions about income smoothing across the year. More generally, policy makers, the media, and the public would benefit from more real-time measures of poverty, as are available with other major statistics such as the unemployment rate. The Wimer group argued, further, that calculating a monthly poverty measure would be useful in capturing intra-year income volatility—more common in times of economic upheaval, but also a constant reality for some segments of the population. They noted that their team at Columbia

University has recently explored and produced variants of a monthly poverty measure, as has a group at the University of Notre Dame and the University of Chicago (though this group produces annual poverty measures on a monthly basis). More frequent estimates would, in the Wimer group's view, carry greater weight and would continue to be produced consistently over time if the federal government established a regular reporting system for poverty calculated on a monthly basis.

Moffitt offered a broad observation about the SPM data infrastructure: "Everyone recognizes the disadvantage of drawing thresholds and resources from different data sets with different sampling frames, different definitions of the family/consumer unit, different definitions of the variables, etc. Ideally, a survey would be designed for purpose with a sampling frame identical to that of the [Annual Social and Economic Supplement] ASEC but which asks the relevant CE income and expenditure questions. This would allow a direct ASEC-CE correspondence." It is, he argued, important to have information on whether ASEC income data actually map into the expenditure items in the SPM threshold.

Appendix C

Biographical Sketches of Panel Members

James P. Ziliak (*Chair*) is professor and Carol Martin Gatton endowed chair in microeconomics in the Department of Economics, chair of the Economics Department and university research professor at the University of Kentucky, and founding director of the Center for Poverty Research, and founding executive director of the Kentucky Federal Statistical Research Data Center. He is also an elected member of the National Academy of Social Insurance, on the advisory board of the Economic and Social Research Council Centre for the Microeconomic Analysis of Public Policy, and is a research fellow of the Institute for Fiscal Studies. Ziliak has served on several National Academies' committees, including as chair of the Workshop on an Agenda for Child Hunger and Food Insecurity Research and as a member of the Committee on the Examination of the Adequacy of Food Resources and SNAP Allotments. His research interests focus on tax and welfare policy, poverty, and food insecurity. Ziliak is co-editor of *Fiscal Studies*, a member of the American Economic Association, the Econometric Society, and the Society of Labor Economists. He has a Ph.D. in economics from Indiana University.

Randall K.Q. Akee is associate professor of public policy in the Department of Public Policy and American Indian Studies at the University of California, Los Angeles (UCLA), chair of the American Indian Studies Interdepartmental Program at UCLA, Luskin School of Public Affairs, and nonresident fellow in the economic studies program at The Brookings Institution. He also serves as faculty research fellow at the National Bureau of Economic Research, research fellow at the Harvard Project on American Indian Economic Development and at the Institute for the Study of Labor, faculty affiliate at the UCLA California Center for Population Research, and faculty affiliate at UC Berkeley Center for Effective Global Action. Akee's main research interests are labor economics, economic development, and migration. His current research focuses on income inequality and immobility by race and ethnicity in the United States. Akee has worked on several American Indian reservations, Canadian First Nations, and Pacific Island nations in addition to working in various Native Hawaiian communities. He has a Ph.D. in political economy from Harvard University.

Sarah E. Bohn is vice president of research and senior fellow at the Public Policy Institute of California (PPIC), where she also holds the John and Louise Bryson chair in policy research and is a member of the PPIC Higher Education Center. As vice president of research, Bohn works with PPIC staff to bring high-quality, nonpartisan research to important policy issues in California. Her own research focuses on the role of social safety net policy and education policy in alleviating poverty and enhancing economic mobility, and also on immigration policy, labor economics, workforce skills gap, and California's economy, as well as inequality and mobility. Bohn's work has been published in major academic journals, including the *American Economic Review, Demography, American Economic Journal: Economic Policy,* and *The Review of Economics and Statistics.* She has a Ph.D. in economics from the University of Maryland, College Park.

Indivar Dutta-Gupta is president and executive director of the Center for Law and Social Policy (CLASP), where he leads the 50+-year-old national nonprofit that develops and implements federal, state, and local policies (in legislation, regulation, and on the ground) that reduce poverty, improve the lives of people with low incomes, and create pathways to racial justice and economic security. Prior to joining CLASP in June 2022, he was co-executive director of Georgetown Center on Poverty and Inequality (GCPI). There, he led a portfolio of the work that also developed and advanced policy recommendations to alleviate poverty and inequality, and he was an adjunct professor of law. Dutta-Gupta is a board member on several advisory groups, including Indivisible Civics, the National Academy of Social Insurance, the Aspen Institute's Benefits 21 Leadership Advisory Group, and the Liberation in a Generation's Advisory Group. Prior to joining GCPI, he was senior policy advisor at the Center on Budget and Policy Priorities and served as professional staff in the U.S. House of Representatives for the Subcommittee on Income Security and Family Support. Dutta-Gupta has served as the Bill Emerson national hunger fellow, consultant to the Poverty Task Force at the Center for American Progress, and as a food stamp outreach specialist at DC Hunger Solutions. He was named a Champion for Children by the First Focus Campaign for Children and was awarded the Congressional Hunger Center Alumni Leadership Award. He has a B.A. in law, letters, and society from the University of Chicago.

Ingrid Gould Ellen is Paulette Goddard professor of urban policy and planning and faculty director at the Furman Center for Real Estate and Urban Policy at New York University. She teaches courses in microeconomics, urban economics, and urban policy research. Ellen's research interests center on housing and urban policy. She has written numerous peer-reviewed journal articles and book chapters relating to housing policy, community development, and school and neighborhood segregation. Ellen has held visiting positions at the Department of Urban Studies and Planning at MIT, the U.S. Department of Housing and Urban Development, the Urban Institute, and the Brookings Institution. She serves on the editorial boards of numerous journals in public policy, economics, and urban planning, and she will serve as the president of the American Real Estate and Urban Economics Association in 2023. She has a Ph.D. in public policy from Harvard University.

Bradley L. Hardy is associate professor in the McCourt School of Public Policy at Georgetown University. Prior to this, he was associate professor in the Department of Public Administration and Policy at American University, where he also served as department chair. Hardy is a nonresident senior fellow in economic studies at the Brookings Institution, a research fellow in the Center for Household Financial Stability at the Federal Reserve Bank of St. Louis, and a research affiliate of both the University of Wisconsin Institute for Research on Poverty and the University of Kentucky Center for Poverty Research. His research interests focus on labor economics (with an emphasis on economic instability), intergenerational mobility, poverty policy, racial economic inequality, and socioeconomic outcomes. Hardy is on the executive board of the Association for Public Policy Analysis and Management, is an elected member of the National Academy of Social Insurance, and is a member of the American Economic Association, National Economic Association, Association for Public Policy Analysis and Management, and Society of Government Economists. He has a Ph.D. in economics from the University of Kentucky.

David S. Johnson is a senior program officer at the Committee on National Statistics at the National Academies of Sciences, Engineering, and Medicine. For most of the panel's deliberations, he was a research professor in the Survey Research Center of the Institute for Social Research and the Gerald R. Ford School of Public Policy at the University of Michigan, and director of the Panel Study of Income Dynamics. Johnson's research interests include the measurement of inequality and mobility (using income, consumption, and wealth), the effects of tax rebates, equivalence scale estimation, poverty measurement, and price indexes, and his research focuses primarily on inequality and poverty measurement, equivalence scale estimation, and consumption. He is a member of numerous organizations, including the Association of Public Policy Analysis and Management, American Economic Association, Population Association of America, and the Conference on Research in Income and Wealth, National Bureau of Economic Research. He has a Ph.D. in economics from the University of Minnesota.

Sanders Korenman is professor in the Austin W. Marxe School of Public and International Affairs, Baruch College, City University of New York (CUNY). At CUNY, he also holds appointments on the doctoral faculty in the CUNY Graduate Center and as faculty associate in the CUNY Institute for Demographic Research. Prior to joining CUNY, he held positions at the University of Minnesota and Princeton University. Korenman was senior economist to the Council of Economic Advisers. His research interests focus on public policy, public finance, and heath economics. With support from the Russell Sage Foundation and Robert Wood Johnson Foundation, Korenman and Dahlia Remler have developed a poverty measure that includes a basic need for health care and incorporates health insurance benefits. He has been a member of the National Academies Committee on Promoting Child and Family Well-being through Family Work Policies and a member of the Board on Children, Youth, and Families. Korenman has a Ph.D. in economics from Harvard University.

Helen G. Levy is research professor in the Department of Health Management and Policy at the University of Michigan, the Institute for Social Research, and the Ford School of Public Policy. She also serves as research associate at the National Bureau of Economic Research and was senior economist to the President's Council of Economic Advisers in Washington, DC. Currently, Levy is the associate director on the Health and Retirement Study, a long-running longitudinal study of health and economic dynamics at older ages. She is a member of the American Economic Association and the American Society of Health Economists. Levy's research interests include the causes and consequences of lacking health insurance, evaluation of public health insurance programs, and the role of health literacy in explaining disparities in health outcomes. She has a Ph.D. in economics from Princeton University.

Jordan D. Matsudaira is deputy undersecretary of education at the Department of Education, associate professor of economics and education policy at Teachers College, Columbia University, visiting associate professor at the Woodrow Wilson School of Public Policy at Princeton University, senior research scholar at the Community College Research Center, nonresident fellow in the Income and Benefits Policy Center at the Urban Institute in Washington, DC, and fellow at the Rockefeller Institute of Government in Albany, New York. He was previously an assistant professor of public policy and economics at Cornell University and a Robert Wood Johnson post-doctoral fellow in health policy research at the University of California, Berkeley. Matsudaira's research focuses on using government administrative data to understand the causal impact of education and labor market policies and institutions on the economic outcomes of low-income Americans. He served on President Obama's Council of Economic Advisers as Chief Economist and he also worked on labor, education, and safety net policies, including gainful employment regulations of for-profit colleges and an expansion of the federal overtime protections in the Fair Labor Standards Act. He has a Ph.D. in economics and public policy from the University of Michigan.

José D. Pacas is the chief of data science and research at Kids First Chicago (K1C), a nonprofit focused on dramatically improving education for Chicago's children. Prior to joining K1C, Dr. Pacas was a research scientist for the Minnesota Population Center (MPC) at the University of Minnesota. Before joining the MPC, he served as an economist in the Poverty Statistics Branch at the U.S. Census Bureau. His research focuses on the factors influencing poverty transitions, methodological improvements to urban and rural poverty measurement in public-use data, as well as estimating the supplemental poverty measure in the American Community Survey. Dr. Pacas has a Ph.D. in applied economics from the University of Minnesota.

Michele Ver Ploeg is the chief of the Food Assistance Branch of the Economic Research Service of the U.S. Department of Agriculture, where she leads a team of economists and social scientists charged with producing data and research on food security, food assistance programs, and food store access. She was previously director of the Food and Health Policy Institute and associate professor of exercise and nutrition sciences in the Milken

Institute School of Public Health at the George Washington University. Ver Ploeg was also a study director of the Committee on National Statistics at the National Academies of Sciences, Engineering, and Medicine, where she led studies on data and methods for evaluating welfare reform and estimating eligibility and participation in the Special Supplemental Nutrition Program for Women, Infants, and Children. Ver Ploeg has a Ph.D. in policy analysis and management from Cornell University.

Jane Waldfogel is Compton Foundation Centennial professor for the Prevention of Children's and Youth Problems at the Columbia University School of Social Work, and co-director of the Columbia Population Research Center. She is also visiting professor at the Centre for Analysis of Social Exclusion at the London School of Economics and Political Science. Waldfogel's current research includes studies of poverty and social policy, the impact of public policies on child and family wellbeing, and cross-national differences in inequalities in child health and development. She is a research fellow of the Institute for the Study of Labor, research affiliate at the Center for Research on Child Wellbeing, and a senior research affiliate at the National Poverty Center. She is a member of several professional organizations, including the American Economic Association, Association for Public Policy Analysis and Management, and the Population Association of America. Waldfogel has a Ph.D. in public policy from the Kennedy School of Government at Harvard University.

Barbara L. Wolfe is Richard A. Easterlin professor emerita of economics, population health sciences, and public affairs, and faculty affiliate at the Institute for Research on Poverty at the University of Wisconsin–Madison. Her research focuses broadly on poverty, education, and health issues. Wolfe's current projects examine whether housing subsidies lead to less risk-taking among adolescents, and better school performance of children in the household. She is a member of the National Academy of Medicine, having served on numerous committees including the Board on Children, Youth, and Families; the Roundtable on the Communication and Use of Social and Behavioral Sciences; and the Committee to Evaluate the Supplemental Security Income Disability Program for Children with Mental Disorders. Her recent articles have appeared in numerous journals including the *Journal of Public Economics*, *Journal of Human Resources*, *Demography,* and the *Journal of Policy Analysis and Management*. Wolfe has a Ph.D. in economics from the University of Pennsylvania.

COMMITTEE ON NATIONAL STATISTICS

The Committee on National Statistics was established in 1972 at the National Academies of Sciences, Engineering, and Medicine to improve the statistical methods and information on which public policy decisions are based. The committee carries out studies, workshops, and other activities to foster better measures and fuller understanding of the economy, the environment, public health, crime, education, immigration, poverty, welfare, and other public policy issues. It also evaluates ongoing statistical programs and tracks the statistical policy and coordinating activities of the federal government, serving a unique role at the intersection of statistics and public policy. The committee's work is supported by a consortium of federal agencies through a National Science Foundation grant, a National Agricultural Statistics Service cooperative agreement, and several individual contracts.